This is a brilliant commentary t[...]
is lucid, sane, helpful and well a[...]
standard of exposition we have [...]
Revelation is a book of enorm[...]
finding it hard to live for Christ, and it needs deliverance from the
way it has been misused by many. Dr. Gardner's are a safe pair of
hands to guide you through. I warmly and highly recommend
this commentary.

The Right Reverend Wallace Benn
Bishop of Lewes

This perceptive book pulsates with the conviction that Revelation
is an urgent message for the contemporary church. It provides a
thorough and totally accessible guide through what has so often
seemed a maze of conflicting ideas and interpretations.
Theologically robust, this interpretation is both Biblically
consistent and eminently practical.

Here is a detailed explanation, verse by verse, of what the text
actually means, exploring its Old Testament roots, unpacking its
potent symbolism, but above all applying its message, personally
and pastorally to life today. The result is a heart-warming, faith-
building exposition of the great convictions of the gospel, which
will both invigorate and challenge.

David Jackman
Proclamation Trust, London

It is my sincere hope that every evangelical will read this
commentary on Revelation. Paul Gardner has given us an in-depth,
but clear, approach to this important part of the Bible. His outlooks
are thoroughly orthodox and practical. He avoids the host of radical
interpretations that are available today. His insights into the
meaning of this book will touch every dimension of the Christian
life.

Richard L Pratt
Reformed Theological Seminary, Orlando

Revelation

Paul Gardner

Christian Focus

ISBN 1 85792 329 4

Published in 2001
by
Christian Focus Publications,
Geanies House, Fearn, Ross-shire
IV20 1TW, Great Britain

Cover design by Owen Daily

Printed and bound in Great Britain by
The Guernsey Press Co. Ltd., Guernsey, Channel Islands

CONTENTS

INTRODUCTION

Undoubtedly it is strange that the one book in the Bible that claims to be an 'apocalypse' ('unveiling' or 'revelation') remains, for us in the twenty-first century, probably the most obscure of all the books in the Bible. Many Christians have hardly bothered to look beyond the first three chapters and others, who have spent much study in its intricacies, have occasionally ended up splitting churches over issues to do with the 'last things'! Hopefully this commentary will at least begin to open up a most wonderful book for any who, as yet, have found it too hard to fathom. For those who already love the book of Revelation, I hope this commentary will take you a little deeper and stimulate thinking about how the teaching should be applied to the modern church. While you may wish to go straight to the commentary, some introductory comments may prove useful.

Authorship and Dating

The Apocalypse (Revelation) was a revelation given to one called John (1:1), by God, through an angel. Traditionally from earliest times it has been assumed that this was the apostle John. In fact, John does not say that he was 'the apostle'. Some scholars have argued that the Greek used is very poor compared with other Johannine writings. Nevertheless, the use the author makes of the Old Testament and even the Targums (Aramaic versions of the Old Testament) suggests strongly that he was a Palestinian Jew who knew well what went on in the synagogue. Such a description would fit the apostle well. Elsewhere he says that what he writes is a 'prophecy' (1:3; 22:6-7, 18-19) and throughout he assumes a level of authority that was typical of the apostles. Also, much of the way the author discusses theology is reminiscent of the way ideas are presented in the

9

Gospel of John and John's epistles.

To some extent the dating of the book affects the authorship question. If it was written after the mid nineties AD, then it is most unlikely that the apostle John was still alive. Some have suggested that it was written shortly after Nero's time of persecution. Nero reigned from AD 54 to 68. In 64 Rome was burned and Nero, who was probably responsible for the fire himself, blamed the Christians for it. Many, including Peter and Paul, were tortured and killed in ways which horrified even the Romans. References to persecution in this book could fit such horror (see chapters 11, 13, 17:6). The reference to 'Babylon' (Rome) being burned (17:16) would further support this dating. It is also said that the idea of the 'beast' returning (13:3, 12; 17:8, 11-12) indicates a period shortly after Nero's suicide when the fable spread that Nero would return.

However, most people believe the book was written during Domitian's rule (81–96). Although there is little evidence of widespread persecution at this time, Domitian did assume to himself the title 'Lord and God', which might explain some of John's deep concerns. The early theologian, Irenaeus, talked of John seeing his vision 'not a long time ago ... at the end of Domitian's reign'. There is no need to assume a date *later* than the early to mid nineties, in which case John the apostle could still have been the author in his old age.

Prophecy and apocalypse

Even a cursory glance at the book from chapter 4 onwards reveals a different style or type of literature from much else to be found in the Bible. This means that we must be careful how we read the letter, and that we try to do justice to a form of literature which seems alien to us in the twenty-first century.

Firstly, it should be noted how very indebted John is to the Old Testament, particularly in those sections where symbolism is important. In fact, much of the symbolism of Revelation is an extension of that already found in Old Testament prophetic writings like Daniel and Ezekiel. We should also keep in mind that this book was written as a letter to a particular group of churches. As a prophet, John is determined to proclaim God's word specifically to these people. He brings them encouragement at a time of difficulty, for Christians were either suffering at that time or needed to be warned that what had happened (under Nero) was likely to happen again. John assures his people of God's sovereign rule right now in the *present*, while bringing consolation with promises of the second coming of Jesus. In this sense we are dealing with a prophecy similar to those found in the Old Testament: proclamations of God's present and future workings with his people, comfort to those who are oppressed, and warnings to those turning back from the truth to the evil of the world. John, working under the Spirit's inspiration, like the prophets, brings a message that is always relevant. It is no doubt for all these reasons that John sees himself as writing prophecy.

Secondly, this work is an 'apocalypse' ('revelation', 1:1), which is a word primarily applied to a type of Jewish writing which often had its roots in Old Testament prophecy, but which concentrated on two or three major themes. These would be, for instance, 'the day of the Lord', and the complete sovereignty of God even in the most severe times of distress for his people. History was seen as leading to a climax, when God would come and separate good from evil, 'this age' from the next, light from darkness. Normally these writings were written in the names of heroes of ancient Israelite history, e.g., the books of Enoch, or the Assumption of Moses. Another of the characteristics of this literature was that it was pessimistic and even deterministic about this world. The only hope was the future in another world.

Revelation shares some apocalyptic elements with these Jewish works especially, of course, its great use of symbolism and visions. John, for instance, also sees history in two ages and looks for the coming day of judgment and a new life in a new heaven and earth where evil will be banished.

However, there are also substantial differences between John's Revelation and apocalyptic literature. For example, the work is not attributed to a great person of the past but a living person called 'John'. It is not just what happens in the future which is held out as comfort to suffering Christians, but the comfort and compassion and protection of Christ offered to his people in the *present* is also offered to the readers. The book is clearly not just some wonderful literary masterpiece but is designed as a letter to be read to the churches among which it was circulated. John is primarily a pastor for the present. The victory of Christ must be worked out in the present life of a church experiencing or starting to experience real persecution. Thus it is best to view the book as a pastoral letter full of the characteristics of Old Testament prophecy, and incorporating some of the style of apocalyptic literature – but not necessarily its theology.

Interpretation

Recognising the prophetic and apocalyptic traits of this letter is an important starting point as we seek to understand John's message for us today. Even so, we must recognise that there are different 'schools' of thought on how best to interpret Revelation.

1. Some say that the book simply describes in vivid symbolism *the ongoing struggle between good and evil* in which, eventually, Christianity triumphs. The tendency here is that everything is 'spiritualised'. Revelation is seen not as real prophecy or prediction of future events but simply as a description of the continuing battle. There is, of course, considerable truth in this position, for part of the appeal and relevance of the book lies in the fact that each successive generation of Christians can identify with so much that it relates. However, it underestimates the immediate relevance to those to whom John was writing and eliminates the possibility of the direct identification of some of the symbols with events either in the future or in the history of the church.

2. Others interpret Revelation exclusively as *a tract for John's own age*. This view stresses the contemporary nature of the events described. All the events referred to and disclosed in symbolic language would have been understood clearly by the recipients as pertaining to their situation. Some then go on to say that the prophecies related to Christ's second coming and the destruction of the Roman Empire turned out to be mistaken. The usefulness of this understanding is that it draws attention to the fact that John did write for a specific audience at a specific time. Many of his symbols probably were understood by his readers in a way which we can no longer comprehend. On occasion John seems to have Rome and the Roman Empire at least at the back of his mind. However, the book claims more than contemporary significance and this view does not do justice to the predictive element of the work.

3. Another method of interpretation, which was followed by the Reformers such as Calvin and Luther, sees the book as *a symbolic description of the history of the church*. Once the symbols are deciphered then church history can be understood. 'Babylon' is seen as Rome, but not the Rome of John's day. For Luther it became papal Rome as well. This position certainly takes prophecy seriously and tries to fit John's symbols and prophecies into the history of the church, or vice versa. The real problem faced by such a view is the lack of consensus as to what is actually being described in different sections of the book.

4. Fourthly, there is a method of interpretation that is sometimes called *'futurist'*. From chapter 4 onwards, it is said, Revelation deals with what will happen in the future, just before and at the time of Christ's second coming. The symbolism and descriptions largely concern themselves with a future time of troubles and sufferings for Christians, called 'the tribulation', after which Christ will return and judge the

world, and eternal life with Christ will begin for the righteous.

People who adopt this position are usually *pre-millennialists* (see the discussion about the Millennium in comments on Revelation 20). Some in this camp believe that Christians will be taken from the earth before this time of tribulation occurs, that is, before the events related from chapter 6 onwards ('pre-tribulationism'). If this particular form of pre-millennialism should seem to make much of the book irrelevant, some draw together their futurist views with that given in 1 above, that each generation continues to see the ongoing struggle between Christ and his followers and Satan.

Committed Christians take a variety of different views on how to interpret Revelation. This alone is perhaps an indication that while we should search the Scriptures under the Spirit's guidance and come to understand as much as possible, it may be wise to refrain from being over-dogmatic in our views on some points.

Here, as we work through the commentary, we take seriously the fact that this book was written for specific people in a specific historical situation in Asia Minor, but we also take the challenge that the Spirit speaks to all the churches throughout the ages. Certainly parts of the book look to the future and the return of Christ, but much of the rest helps answer questions that we ask ourselves today just as, no doubt, those Christians in the original seven churches were also asking. For example, it offers help to understand the context in which we live and why there is suffering and pain even for those who follow Christ. It helps us understand that God is just and he will one day deal with sinful people who put to death the people of God. It also reminds us that this world is not the end but that one day, for those who follow Christ, there will be the most glorious resurrection and we shall 'see God' and be in his presence for ever in a new heavens and a new earth.

If this introduction has simply made things sound even more complicated than you thought they were going to be, let me suggest you sit back, read the book of Revelation and, using the commentary, enjoy and be comforted and challenged by one of the most wonderful books in Scripture!

Revelation 1

John's Commission to Write

The revelation of Jesus Christ, which God gave him to show his servants what must soon take place. He made it known by sending his angel to his servant John, who testifies to everything he saw – that is, the word of God and the testimony of Jesus Christ. Blessed is the one who reads the words of this prophecy, and blessed are those who hear it and take to heart what is written in it, because the time is near (1:1-3).

1. An Introduction

The opening verses form an introduction to this book and recount for us the process by which John received this **revelation**[1] and the purpose of the revelation. It is a revelation that has come from God through Jesus and then to John through the angel that has been sent to him. It is first and foremost a revelation that belongs to Jesus who will now **show [it to] his servants** but it is also a revelation *about* Jesus and about **what must soon take place.** As the book progresses, it becomes clear that John's eye on these events is a prophet's eye. Time often seems to be conflated, and events that may be far in the future seem to be near, while other aspects of what he recounts are already happening around him.

John writes as a witness testifying to the testimony of Jesus Christ, and what he writes is regarded as utterly true, for it is the **word of God** and a **prophecy**. As with all Scripture, readers must not only hear the word of God but also **take to heart** what they read. In other words, they must take note and adjust their attitudes, their conversation, their worship and their way of life in the light of God's word. Those who are willing to do this will be **blessed**. They will receive the fullness of God's blessings for them and inherit all that he has in store for those who trust and believe in him. The urgent need to take all this to heart is clear: **because the time is near.** That time, as the book will later show, is the Day of the Lord, the time when Christ will return to judge and to save.

i) John greets his readers on behalf of the sovereign God

John, To the seven churches in the province of Asia: Grace and peace to you from him who is, and who was, and who is to come, and from the seven spirits before his throne, and from Jesus Christ, who is the faithful witness, the firstborn from the dead, and the ruler of the kings of the earth (1:4-5a).

Initially, at least, this revelation is addressed to seven specific churches in Asia. 'Asia' was the name of a Roman province occupying an area which is now part of modern Turkey. Since the book is full of symbolism and numbers are often symbolic, it may be right to say that seven churches were chosen because the number seven is a sign of wholeness and completion. Nevertheless, the book almost certainly travelled round these churches in a circular direction from Ephesus, north to Smyrna and Pergamum, before moving south-east to Thyatira and south to Sardis, then Philadelphia and finally Laodicea (see chapters 2–3). No doubt the whole book went with the letters to those specific churches. But there is also good reason to believe that those specific letters of chapters 2–3, as well as the whole book, were intended for all churches of all time. This view is supported by the statement at the end of each of the seven letters: 'He who has an ear, let him hear what the Spirit says to the churches.'[2]

The greeting from the Triune God to this church is typical of early Christianity, **Grace and peace to you.** The words are a wonderful reminder of what it is to be *blessed* as a Christian. We receive the grace of God, his undeserved mercy and love and forgiveness and his sustaining power, to live the Christian life. We also know the peace with God that comes from our reconciliation with the Father brought about by Christ's death and resurrection.[3]

God is always present. As he has been in the past and is in

the present, so he will be in the future. This eternal character of God is vital for Christians to grasp. As they go through persecution for their faith in Christ, and as they cope with the continual changes of life and its difficulties, so they need to grasp the unchanging and eternal nature of the God in whom they trust. The **seven spirits** refer to the Holy Spirit in all his perfection as the one who now speaks to the churches and who enables the church to fulfil its calling. Now we see that the greeting also comes from Jesus Christ who is given three titles:

a) the faithful witness.[4]
Jesus faithfully proclaimed God to this world, persevering through suffering and even to his death on the cross. His testimony was true and perfect. He thus becomes the example for Christians to follow as they too are called upon to suffer and perhaps even face death as his witnesses. These Christians will need all God's grace in order to come through what awaits them in these last days before the return of Christ. As we read in the letter to Pergamum in 2:13, Antipas had already died for the truth. Jesus calls him 'my faithful witness'. Later other Christians will be called to give their lives, bearing testimony to the faithful witness, Jesus Christ (11:7; 17:6).

b) the firstborn from the dead.[5]
This reminds us of Christ's exalted position as the one who conquered death and was raised to life by the Father. He can thus be called the 'Living One' in verse 18, for he is alive forever. This too is significant for suffering Christians who, through faith in Christ, will themselves be raised from the dead. Where Jesus has gone before, his people will follow.

c) the ruler of the kings of the earth
The sovereignty of Christ over all that is going on in this world is again a vital teaching about the nature of Christ and his kingly rule, which is not just theoretical but deeply practical and pastoral when seen in the context of a suffering church. Those

19

who receive this letter need to know above all else that Jesus will vindicate his name and his people as he ultimately calls the nations to account. As we read through this book we shall see this theme surfacing frequently. Those who seek to destroy the church of Christ should know that he is sovereign and his rule will be clearly seen (6:15; 17:14; 18:3-10; 19:15-16; etc.).

Thus the scene is set. This revelation is the revelation above all of Jesus: who he is and how he will reveal himself as history progresses. He is in control and is the ruler even of the kings of the earth. And so John pauses to rejoice in the Lord and Saviour Jesus Christ and to ascribe praise and thanksgiving to God for his wonderful grace.

ii) John ascribes praise to Jesus

To him who loves us and has freed us from our sins by his blood, and has made us to be a kingdom and priests to serve his God and Father – to him be glory and power for ever and ever! Amen. Look, he is coming with the clouds, and every eye will see him, even those who pierced him; and all the peoples of the earth will mourn because of him. So shall it be! Amen. 'I am the Alpha and the Omega,' says the Lord God, 'who is, and who was, and who is to come, the Almighty' (1:5b-8).

Ascribing glory and power to God is to acknowledge all that is true of him. Such 'doxologies' are quite common in Scripture. But this one is a little different, for it is specifically applied to Christ. To him alone belongs glory and power, for he has brought about the salvation of his people. Four glorious statements about what Christ has done for his people summarise why praise and glory should be offered to him.

a) Jesus loves us. The love of Christ has surrounded and directed his people through all time, but above all it has been seen in his death on the cross on our behalf.

b) Jesus has freed us. His death redeemed his people from their sins, freeing them from their captivity or bondage to death, which is the righteous judgment of God upon sinful people. Thanks to **his blood** (his sacrificial death on the cross), Christ has dealt with sin and the penalty for sin. We are now freed to serve God.

c) Jesus has made us to be a kingdom and priests to serve. Drawing on the Old Testament, Christians are reminded that the reason for their redemption is that they should be God's special people reflecting God's holiness back to this world. As we read in Exodus 19:5-6, God commands the people of Israel: 'Now if you obey me fully and keep my covenant, then out of all nations you will be my treasured possession. Although the whole earth is mine, you will be for me a kingdom of priests and a holy nation.'

Much of what follows in this book of Revelation is helping Christians work out what it means to be God's people. It is not that the church is *like* God's people in the Old Testament, but the church is now seen to be God's true Israel.[6] We are to serve as a kingdom in the sense that we serve the one true King, Jesus Christ. We are to serve as priests as we live in a world which persecutes the faithful. This will involve following Christ as faithful witnesses of God's revelation to a sinful world, and living a life of holiness as was required of priests and is seen in all its perfection in Christ himself.

d) Jesus will come again.[7] The greeting comes to an end by again pointing to Christ as King over all the nations (see verse 5) and to the Father who is eternal (see verse 4). The emphasis on Jesus again reminds God's suffering people that Jesus is King and will return in glory, which is what **with the clouds** means. This return will be seen even by those who **pierced him.**

The Old Testament provides the background

John uses several Old Testament references and allusions to make his point here. First, he draws on Daniel, a prophet to whom he owes much, as we shall see later. In Daniel 7:13 we read: 'In my vision at night I looked, and there before me was one like a son of man, coming with the clouds of heaven. He approached the Ancient of Days and was led into his presence.'

What Daniel prophesied about the judgment of evil rulers, we are now told is to be fulfilled in Christ's second coming. Then Zechariah 12:10 is used further to emphasise God's judgment on those who surround Israel and also to show Israel's own mourning for having rejected God: 'They will look on me, the one they have pierced, and they will mourn for him as one mourns for an only child, and grieve bitterly for him as one grieves for a firstborn son.'

Glory speaks of Christ's divinity. **Cloud** is linked with God's glory in the Old Testament, for example, in Exodus 16:10. We may also remember the appearance of God in his glory in the pillar of cloud over the Tabernacle (Exodus 40:34) and later at the opening of Solomon's temple (2 Chronicles 5:13-14). But it also reminds us of Christ's own predictions of the revelation of his divine glory[8] and, of course, of the majestic glory of Christ that was seen at the Transfiguration.[9]

There will be no doubt that Jesus has returned as King since **all the peoples** will see him. The fact that they will **mourn** probably indicates that John has in mind particularly those who have rejected Christ. They will now fear his judgment as they clearly do in 6:15-17.

iii) God identifies himself

Tragic as this day will be for so many, its anticipation is a great comfort to those who currently suffer for Christ's sake. Since Christ will come and God is the **Alpha and the Omega** (the First and the Last, 1:17; 22:13) and **the Almighty**, suffering Christians need to be assured of the ultimate vindication of their faith and of their Lord before the nations of this earth. It is worth noting how this title, which indicates God's great and sovereign power over all, is used in 4:8 and 11:17 in a similar context of praise and doxology.[10] Here God identifies himself as the one who really is sovereign and really does know the end from the beginning.

Summary

In various ways, this introduction has emphasised the trustworthiness, power, sovereignty and love of Christ and of God. These are all vital truths for God's people as much in our day and age as in John's. These are the great truths that remind us that we remain ourselves in the midst of a suffering world in which God's people will often be persecuted. They also remind us of the context within which we live and work and serve. It is a context in which Christ has freed us from the penalty of sin to serve him in this world while we await his return in glory.

2. John's commission to write

In the verses which follow, John, a fellow sufferer for the gospel, tells us of his commissioning by God to write what he sees.

> I, John, your brother and companion in the suffering and kingdom and patient endurance that are ours in Jesus, was on the island of Patmos because of the word of God and the testimony of Jesus. On the Lord's Day I was in the Spirit, and I heard behind me a loud voice like a trumpet, which said: 'Write on a scroll what you see and send it to the seven churches: to Ephesus, Smyrna, Pergamum, Thyatira, Sardis, Philadelphia and Laodicea' (1:9-11).

i) John's own situation

It is appropriate that John should be commissioned by God for the work of recounting this revelation because he too has experienced **suffering** as a member of Christ's **kingdom** and is a Christian **brother** of those to whom he writes. He too knows the need of **patient endurance** which is to be characteristic of those who are **in Jesus**, that is, of those who belong to him. Later John will use these words again as he calls for patient endurance from suffering Christians in 13:10 and 14:12. The island of Patmos where he received this revelation was one of a number of small islands off the south-west coast of Asia Minor (see the Introduction).

ii) A voice speaks

The first day of the week rapidly became the day on which the early church gathered for worship, thus replacing the Jewish Sabbath day worship. This soon became known as **the Lord's Day** for it was the day on which Jesus was raised from the dead. On one such Sunday, as we often call it, John was **in the Spirit**. This indicates that he was receiving some special revelation from the Holy Spirit that gave him full prophetic authority. We find something quite similar in the prophecy of Ezekiel to which there are many allusions to this work of the Spirit (see, for example, Ezekiel 2:2; 3:14, 24). The reference to **a loud voice like a trumpet** adds to the impression of God's special revelation, reminding us of the very loud trumpet sound that accompanied God's message to Moses on Mount Sinai (Exodus 19:18-19). This experience clearly does not refer to the constant presence of the Spirit with God's people, but to a special work of the Holy Spirit in inspiring this particular prophecy. Whether John was asleep or awake is not clear at this point.

Thus it is that John's commission to **write** all that he sees and hears and send it to the seven churches begins. He is confronted now in his vision by the one who has been introduced as the Alpha and Omega in verse 8.

I turned around to see the voice that was speaking to me. And when I turned I saw seven golden lampstands, and among the lampstands was someone 'like a son of man', dressed in a robe reaching down to his feet and with a golden sash around his chest. His head and hair were white like wool, as white as snow, and his eyes were like blazing fire. His feet were like bronze glowing in a furnace, and his voice was like the sound of rushing waters. In his right hand he held seven stars, and out of his mouth came a sharp double-edged sword. His face was like the sun shining in all its brilliance (1:12-16).

iii) The one who speaks

John does not immediately see the source of the voice, rather he sees **seven golden lampstands**, but someone **like a son of man** is there among the lampstands and **in his right hand he**

held seven stars. All of this sounds very strange to our ears but their meaning is explained to John in verse 20. The lampstands represent the seven churches to which he is writing. Again the figure seven is no doubt seen as a sign of completion and perfection. This person is standing among the churches of Christ. In his hand he holds seven stars which we are told are 'the angels of the seven churches' (see below).

a) Like a son of man

This person **like a son of man** is clearly the resurrected and glorified Lord Jesus, but the picture language used here draws upon the book of Daniel, particularly chapters 7 and 10. We noted Daniel 7:13 earlier when talking of Christ 'coming with the clouds'. There 'one like a son of man' was seen, and the passage continues: 'He was given authority, glory and sovereign power; all peoples, nations and men of every language worshipped him. His dominion is an everlasting dominion that will not pass away, and his kingdom is one that will never be destroyed.'

It is a passage well suited to describe what John sees, for it talks of one who is fully sovereign, eternal and surrounded with glory. It reminds us of all that we have learned so far of Jesus before whom the nations will bow (note especially verse 7). But the allusions to Daniel continue, no doubt because his visions were so similar; his message was also about the last times and the sovereignty of God, and his writing was also filled with apocalyptic imagery. Thus we find a description of this person's dress which calls to mind Daniel 10:5-6, with its portrait of one who comes to speak to him in a vision who was 'dressed in linen, with a belt of the finest gold around his waist'. Daniel 10:6 sounds so similar: 'His body was like chrysolite, his face like lightning, his eyes like flaming torches, his arms and legs like the gleam of burnished bronze, and his voice like the sound of a multitude.'

The description of his clothing and his feet all build a picture of one who is pure and holy, perhaps one who is like a priest who comes into God's presence representing his people. And yet, though the priestly identity is surely there, it is at the same time clearly a royal description. Here is a picture of power and authority. This is strongly reinforced by mention that his **head and hair were white like wool, as white as snow, and his eyes were like blazing fire.** Here the picture is drawn from Daniel 7:9-10, not of the son of man but rather of God the Father himself seated on his heavenly throne: 'As I looked, thrones were set in place, and the Ancient of Days took his seat. His clothing was as white as snow; the hair of his head was white like wool. His throne was flaming with fire, and its wheels were all ablaze. A river of fire was flowing, coming out from before him. Thousands upon thousands attended him; ten thousand times ten thousand stood before him. The court was seated, and the books were opened.'

This description of Jesus indicates his supreme authority but also points to his role as judge when he returns in glory. The **sharp double-edged sword** coming from Jesus' mouth intensifies this impression of Jesus Christ as the warrior and judge who will fight for his people and speak words of judgment on all others. Again an Old Testament prophecy, this time about the coming Davidic king, helps us understand the point. Isaiah 11:4 refers to this king who is to come and will judge with righteousness and 'with the breath of his lips he will slay the wicked'.

The whole impression of the vision in these verses helps build a picture for us of Jesus representing his people before the throne of the Father, watching over them and protecting them, but also of Jesus who is truly sovereign and will return to judge those who have rebelled against him.

> When I saw him, I fell at his feet as though dead. Then he placed his right hand on me and said: 'Do not be afraid. I am the First and the Last. I am the Living One; I was dead, and behold I am alive for ever and ever! And I hold the keys of death and Hades' (1:17-18).

There is surely only one response to such an awesome revelation of Jesus Christ and it is to be utterly fearful. In view of Jesus' words, **Do not be afraid**, John's falling down **as though dead** is not an act of worship but rather a fainting with fear. It is the sort of dread that we see elsewhere in Scripture when people are confronted by the glory of the living God (even in a visionary experience).[11] But the one who speaks 'grace and peace' to his people (verse 4) and who 'loves us' (verse 5) **placed his right hand** on John in a gesture of comfort. He then speaks words of comfort, giving three reasons why John should not be afraid. He begins with the words 'I am', a reminder of his divinity.

b) I am the First and the Last: Jesus draws attention to his eternal sovereignty and divinity.

c) I am the Living One. Though he died, now he is alive forever. It is the greatest comfort to the believer that the one who did indeed die has conquered death and is now alive, thus guaranteeing resurrection for those who have faith. For those called by God, there is no need to fear death for Jesus is the Living One.

d) I hold the keys of death and Hades. Through his death and resurrection Jesus has conquered death and so those with faith in Christ can be assured of life themselves, for Jesus will raise them too. This particular encouragement will be vital when Jesus addresses the church at Smyrna. In that letter, 2:10-11, he says, 'Do not be afraid of what you are about to suffer.... Be faithful, even to the point of death, and I will give you the crown of life.... He who overcomes will not be hurt at all by the second death.'

There is enormous comfort for us all as we ponder who Jesus is. As sovereign Lord and God he has conquered death for his people so they need not fear it. Just as he is alive, so we as his people will be made alive and the final judgment (second death, 2:11) will have no sway over us. Far from looking upon Jesus as God who is most to be feared, we look on him as Saviour and Lord who brings us his love, grace and peace.

27

iv) Write to the seven churches

And so the commission is summarised.

> Write, therefore, what you have seen, what is now and what will take place later. The mystery of the seven stars that you saw in my right hand and of the seven golden lampstands is this: The seven stars are the angels of the seven churches, and the seven lampstands are the seven churches (1:18-20).

John is to write both about the present experience through which he is going and the descriptions which follow of the present world scene, as well as writing about the revelation he has concerning the future. In other words, this verse is really a key to the book as a whole. While John here is being asked to write down the immediate things he sees, he is again being asked, as he was in verse 11, to write down all his experiences and visions for together they contain God's word for his suffering church.

The final verse explains the meaning of the lampstands and stars. The reference to the **stars** being **the angels of the seven churches** is not clear. Since the word 'angel' can refer to a 'messenger', this reference could simply be to the messengers or perhaps leaders of the various churches. The 'angels' would thus be human representatives or ministers of the churches. Nevertheless, on other occasions in John's book when the word 'angel' is used, it refers to heavenly beings who work at God's command. It is thus more likely here that a particular angelic being is in mind who is given responsibility for each church. This angelic being would therefore be seen as 'representing' the church or standing for the church being addressed. This is what seems to be happening as we turn to chapter 2.

Special lessons for today

Many Christians over the years have given up reading this book because, beyond the first four chapters, they feel they can neither understand much of it, nor see its relevance to them. These short sections of **special lessons** will occur from time to time in this commentary simply to remind us that this book is in fact written for all the churches of all ages as God's word. They are not by any means intended to be exhaustive of what God is saying through Revelation to us in the twenty-first century, but they will remind us that what is said is useful and profitable for all Christians.

First, a suffering church. We cannot help but note that John writes to a suffering church or one which will suffer, just as he is suffering for the gospel. More Christians were put to death for their faith in the twentieth century than in all the preceding centuries put together, and there is no evidence that this century will be much different. The church of Christ will suffer in all sorts of ways, and this book speaks to us of the comfort, love and discipline which the Lord Jesus, Lord of the church, brings to his people in the present. It also points to the time when such suffering will cease. If ever we want to understand the context in which the church today suffers, then this book is one of our greatest helps and as we read it we need to bear this in mind.

Secondly, Jesus is right there in the midst of his churches. He has not neglected his suffering people nor left them to suffer on their own. More than that, one day he *will* vindicate his name and his people. This truth about Jesus is both a comfort and a challenge as we shall see in chapters 2–3. On the one hand, we need to know for today that even in our churches the same Lord Jesus is present among us and watching over us and caring for us. He 'comes' among us with blessing. On the other hand, we are reminded that if we turn from him, or follow unbiblical teaching or practices, then the same Lord will 'come' not to bless but to judge. The need for modern churches to be faithful to the God of Scripture and to Scripture itself as God's word, could never be greater. As we shall see later, the problems of syncretism, and the pressures of the world around, are acute for us all. We must remember that Jesus is among us, encouraging and comforting us but also commanding obedience.

Thirdly, we must ask how we view Jesus. In verse 17 John's initial reaction, like that of many of the prophets, is to fall down, probably from fear. Very quickly Jesus picks him up and

29

encourages him not to fear. However, in a modern church which spends much time encouraging Christians to regard Jesus as 'friend and brother', this passage reminds us that if the Son of Man appeared to us right now we would fall at his feet before his glory – and until he picked us up, we would surely be fearful. Scripture never compromises the glory and majesty of Christ, while also describing him as one of us. It is all too easy to forget his 'majesty'. We no longer stand in awe at the thought of the King of Glory returning with the clouds to judge and to save. Our worship should incorporate, where possible, the whole teaching about Christ. We should at one and the same time stand in awe of who he is, the one who holds the keys of death and Hades, and yet also enjoy the love and care and comfort of Jesus our friend and brother.

Revelation 2–3

Letters from Jesus to Seven Churches

The next two chapters contain specific letters from Jesus, via John, to the seven churches mentioned in chapter 1. As we shall see, they develop some of the ideas present in chapter 1, but they also anticipate the content of the revelation that is given in chapters 4–21. (Chapter 22 then contains the concluding comments of the whole book.)

These letters are, as it were, letters within a letter. It is clear from the concluding remarks of each that they were intended for all the churches, though addressed to one. We must be careful therefore not so to limit the meaning of these letters that we fail to see how they relate both to the whole book and to ourselves as part of the church of Christ. As each letter is examined, therefore, we shall deliberately look for links to the rest of the vision, but we shall also pause in places to ask how some of the lessons these churches are being taught by Jesus can and should be taken on board by the modern church.

1. The letter to Ephesus

> To the angel of the church in Ephesus write: These are the words of him who holds the seven stars in his right hand and walks among the seven golden lampstands: I know your deeds, your hard work and your perseverance. I know that you cannot tolerate wicked men, that you have tested those who claim to be apostles but are not, and have found them false. You have persevered and have endured hardships for my name, and have not grown weary (2:1-3).

Whether **angel** here is the human leader or presbyter of the church or an angelic being who represents the church has been discussed earlier. It seems more likely that it is an angelic being standing before God representing this church. Thus, the churches are represented in heaven itself. Although the church has not yet been glorified, the angelic leaders of the churches remind Christians that their true home is not on this earth with those who do not believe, but rather in the heavenly realms. The apostle Paul captured this idea very clearly in Ephesians 2:6-8: 'And God raised us up with Christ and seated us with him in the heavenly realms in Christ Jesus, in order that in the coming ages he might show the incomparable riches of his grace, expressed in his kindness to us in Christ Jesus. For it is by grace you have been saved.'

Although the angel representing the church is addressed, it is clear, therefore, that the actual church and its leaders and members are to take heed of all that Jesus has to say to them.

Ephesus was a major port city on the east coast of Asia Minor. It looked out across the Aegean Sea in the direction of Greece. No doubt boats regularly travelled from various islands like Patmos to this city and so it would have received the letter first.

i) Jesus' self-description

Jesus now addresses this church as the one **who holds the seven stars in his right hand and walks among the seven golden lampstands**. He thus identifies himself as the one referred to in 1:13, 16. In 1:20 we learned about these figures. Jesus holds the angels (**seven stars)** in the sense that they are constantly in his presence and upheld and supported by him but, more than that, he **walks among the seven golden lampstands** (the churches). The fact is emphasised that there is nothing Jesus does not know about them because he is right in their midst. This is obviously a challenge to the churches both to live as he would have them live and to be true witnesses or **golden lampstands** for him, but it is also of immense comfort to those who struggle to witness to their Lord in the midst of great suffering and persecution. That Christ is with his churches – watching, helping, upholding them in their witness to the world and providing the grace for perseverance – should provide glorious encouragement to his people through all ages.

ii) The encouragement

First, Jesus begins with some positive comments about the church. As the one who is in their midst, he insists **I know your deeds.** Nothing escapes his eye, which turns every way for the sake of his people (1:14; 5:6). He first comments on their **hard work** and their **perseverance.** As we see in verse 3, this hard work has to do with their witness for Christ. In spite of enduring many **hardships** they **have not grown weary.** They have had to stand for Christ in a way that has called for 'patient endurance'.[12] Back in 1:9 John had written that he was a 'companion' with them in suffering and in having this perseverance for Christ. It is a common experience of all who belong to Christ that they have to live through hardships while standing as witnesses for Christ – and, in this, the Ephesian Christians have excelled.

Secondly, Jesus comments that they **cannot tolerate wicked men.** Here Jesus is probably referring to those who have been recognised by the church as false teachers, in other words, to those they **have tested** and **have found false.** They are **wicked** in that they have no concern for holiness and godliness of life. Clearly some have arisen, perhaps from within the congregation (see Acts 20:30), who are claiming **to be apostles but are not.** They claimed a wider church authority, but they had been tested by the church leaders and had been proclaimed to all as **false.** They did not uphold Christ. They are probably to be identified with the Nicolaitans who are mentioned in verse 6 where Jesus returns to complimenting the Ephesian church for hating evil **practices.** The fact that the Ephesian church had seen these false teachers for what they were may certainly be seen as an answer to the apostle Paul's prayer for this church and his warnings to the elders about false teachers (Acts 20:17-38). That they have endured so much for Jesus' **name** shows that their lives were indeed focused on Jesus, and on promoting him, and living for him. Thus they have endured all these things *because of* who Jesus is, their Lord and Saviour.

iii) The problem

> Yet I hold this against you: You have forsaken your first love (2:4).

Jesus now confronts the church with the main problem he wants them to address. They have forgotten their **first love**. We all understand the picture Jesus uses here. The passion of falling in love for the first time, or the intensity of the first experience of love often far outshines any further feelings of love. The problem for this church is that they started off well enough as a *lampstand*, a witness for Christ, but they have since lost their enthusiasm, their love for Christ. They do what is required of them but their heart is no longer in it and so their effectiveness as a light to the world is diminished.[13] What Jesus says here is a reminder of his words in Matthew 24:11-14: 'many false prophets will appear and deceive many people. Because of the increase of wickedness, the love of most will grow cold, but he who stands firm (Greek – perseveres, patiently endures) to the end will be saved. And this gospel of the kingdom will be preached in the whole world as a testimony to all nations, and then the end will come.' As with this church in Ephesus, Jesus is concerned that the love his people have for him must continue and that it is best demonstrated in carrying the light of the gospel to the nations. Only with a 'first love' will the church be the witness it should be to the world around.

iv) The remedy

Jesus now suggests three things they should do which will help restore that 'first love' and thus further their effective witness for him.

> Remember the height from which you have fallen! Repent and do the things you did at first. If you do not repent, I will come to you and remove your lampstand from its place (2:5).

a) They are to **remember**. They should recall the honeymoon, as it were, and this should motivate them to seek afresh that love that will lead them to tell others about Christ.

b) They are to **repent**. They are to change their whole life before the Lord and turn it around to face the other way. True repentance will lead to action, Jesus tells them...

c) They are to **do the things they did at first**. This does not mean they are to earn their way back into favour and love. Rather, true repentance involves showing the fruit of repentance. Their life will need to be changed in practice and not just in theory. If they are to continue as a lampstand in Ephesus, then they must regain their first abundant enthusiasm for the Lord Jesus and especially for sharing the gospel message with those around.

v) The warning

Only this repentance will keep their flame alight. The church's first love is desperately needed if they are to be an effective witness to the world around. If they fail in that task then they are failing as a church and the warning comes: **I will come to you and remove your lampstand from its place.** The threat is that the church in the area will cease to be. While it is possible that John looks forward here to Jesus' second coming, it is unlikely. More probably, John envisages the real possibility that this church will be judged by God so that it simply does not survive or continue to exist. We must recognise here that, while we are told in Matthew 16:18 that 'the gates of Hades will not overcome' the church, an individual church or congregation may indeed so extinguish its lamp that Jesus removes it **from its place**. God's church will, of course, continue through to the end but individual congregations, as with individual Christians, cannot so presume upon the grace of God that they take the continuation of their witness as inevitable. The call to a 'first love' that witnesses to the world is a vital call concerning not just the health of the church but the nature of the church.

But you have this in your favour: You hate the practices of the Nicolaitans, which I also hate (2:6).

For a moment Jesus returns to their good practice. Their hatred of **the practices of the Nicolaitans** is specially noted. Just what these people taught or believed is not clear, though they are mentioned again in 2:15 in the letter to Pergamum, and there their teaching is linked directly to the 'teaching of Balaam'. Balaam had encouraged the Israelites to 'sin by eating food sacrificed to idols and by committing sexual immorality'. Since it is their **practices** that are singled out, it may well be that the Nicolaitans taught that it was possible to be part of the church and at the same time enjoy the promiscuity of Ephesian life, a life which was dominated by worship of their pagan gods. All who belong to Christ should hate any such behaviour and teaching, for it denies the uniqueness of Christ's Lordship and God's call to holiness of life. It also diminishes the impact of the church's gospel witness. This clearly becomes a sober warning for all time to the church that a failure to stand against sinful practices and a toleration of evil will lead to a church's demise. Accommodation with the world must eventually lead to the disappearance of a church's lampstand, as its light of witness eventually fails altogether.

vi) The promise

> He who has an ear, let him hear what the Spirit says to the churches. To him who overcomes, I will give the right to eat from the tree of life, which is in the paradise of God (2:7).

The final verse of this letter contains an exhortation which is the same in all seven letters. It has the ring of the Old Testament prophetic exhortations to listen to the voice of God. But it also recalls the words of Jesus. For example, we read in Mark 4:9, 'Jesus said, "He who has ears to hear, let him hear."' Here indeed is the **Spirit** *of Christ* speaking and it is vital that all seven of **the churches,** and indeed all churches of all generations, should stop and listen for, by his Spirit, Jesus knows everything about them. Any church at any point in history will have to look carefully at these letters and see what Jesus is saying through them, for he is certainly speaking. However, the application here is also to individuals within these congregations. **He who has an ear, let him hear** implies that there will be some within a church who will respond and some who will not. Every church on this earth is a mixed community. There are those who believe and will respond to the call of the Lord, and those who ultimately do not respond. Here is a challenge and a promise for all to hear.

This church has been genuinely faithful. While it needs to restore its first love and, hence, its witness to the world, it has a genuine commitment to right teaching and practice. The Ephesian Christians need to continue in their hard work and perseverance. If they do this they will **overcome** and will inherit the great promise of **the right to eat from the tree of life**. In all the seven letters there is a promise to the one who **overcomes** (2:11, 17, 26; 3:5, 12, 21). Those who 'overcome' are those who continue to persevere in following and trusting Christ through all the vicissitudes and sufferings of this life. While each letter promises something slightly different to such people, there is no doubt that each promise represents an aspect of the whole inheritance that awaits the people of God.[14] In this instance the promise of eating from **the tree of life** recalls the Garden of Eden (Genesis 2:9). Access to this source of life was cut off after Adam and Eve sinned and were thrown out of the Garden. Jesus' death and resurrection, however, led to his 'triumph' (same Greek verb as 'overcome') over sin and death (5:5), and so the way was opened up again for all who believe and follow him to enjoy eternal life in **the paradise of God.**

This great promise from Jesus to his people looks forward to us sharing with him in a new Eden. And yet, as we shall see in the last two chapters of this book, what we shall actually inherit is far superior even to that glorious picture of **Paradise**. What greater encouragement could there be than this reminder of what our Lord Jesus has accomplished for us and the goal towards which we are headed? What an incentive to recover our 'first love' and to witness fervently for him.

2. The letter to Smyrna

To the angel of the church in Smyrna write: These are the words of him
who is the First and the Last, who died and came to life again (2:8).

Smyrna is a city about 60 kilometres north of Ephesus.
Nowadays it is known as Izmir, Turkey's third largest city. In
ancient times it was renowned for the beauty of its architecture.[15]
During Roman times it became a centre for emperor worship
and was a centre of learning and writing. The description of
this church contains no warning. No 'problem' is highlighted,
rather they are exhorted to continue firm in their faith as
persecution gathers pace.

i) Jesus self-description

In this letter Jesus identifies himself again as **the First and the
Last.** We noted the title in 1:17-18 where its significance was
discussed. It is a title that will not recur until 22:13 where Jesus
is describing how he will shortly return and all that has been
promised will come to pass for God's people who will truly be
'blessed'. How vital this title and the affirmation of Jesus'
resurrection will prove to be to this church, which Jesus will
ask to be 'faithful, even to the point of death' (verse 10). Christ's
resurrection becomes the evidence and guarantee of the
Christian's own resurrection at the last day.

ii) The encouragement

I know your afflictions and your poverty – yet you are rich! I know the
slander of those who say they are Jews and are not, but are a synagogue
of Satan (2:9).

Once again the Lord of the church says **I know**. What Jesus
knows of this church is very special. He has seen that they are
poor in terms of worldly possessions and also afflicted and
persecuted for their faith. The word translated **afflictions** carries
with it the specific idea of the tribulations of the church under

persecution in the last days. Jesus used the same word to describe what would happen to Christians in the 'last days' (the days between his ascension and his second coming) in Matthew 24:9: 'Then you will be handed over to be persecuted (to affliction) and put to death, and you will be hated by all nations because of me.'

Their **poverty** could have come about for various reasons. It could be that some of their property and possessions had been confiscated or ruined by those who were persecuting them. Perhaps they refused to take part in religious ceremonies in the trade guilds of the day and so were unable to take part in normal economic activity and trade. This refusal may have been caused by their Christian desire not to become caught up in a pagan society in which the various trade guilds so often required members to participate in idol worship. Thus in their desire to remain a holy people, they suffered economically. Either way, they are the only church where Jesus takes note of their poverty and this suggests they were suffering severely in this area. (See comments on 13:16-17.)

The main antagonism to this church came from persecution by Jews, who are called here **a synagogue of Satan.** This is strong language indeed. But we know from many places in the New Testament that Jewish persecution of Christians was rife in the early church. From the Roman perspective, Christianity was, for quite a while, seen simply as an offshoot and division of Judaism (Acts 18:14-16). Since Judaism had a measure of protection under Roman law, so did Christians. They were thus not obliged to worship the Emperor as a god but could bring him sacrifices that would honour him. However by the mid Sixties the persecutions under Nero had done away with that protection and it seems that as time went on the Jews were often prepared to denounce Christians to the Roman authorities. The Jews believed that worship of Jesus as Messiah was a blasphemy and so felt further reason to denounce and slander Christians. Smyrna itself was a city renowned for its commitment to Rome and to the Emperor, so Christians who would not bow the knee to an emperor or a Roman god were no doubt subject to the sort of persecution that we read of here.

In talking of those **who say they are Jews and are not**, Jesus is making a very significant theological point to the church. It is one that is made in various other parts of the New Testament. We need, in this case, to understand that the claim to be Jewish is seen as a claim to be the people of God. These people who were persecuting Christians were claiming to be the people of God and children of Abraham. The New Testament perspective since the coming of Christ is altogether different. The true people of God are those who have recognised the Messiah and worship him, that is, the Christians. They are the true inheritors of all the covenant promises of the Old Testament. They are the true 'children of Abraham'. This very radical distinction is now applied here to the Jewish persecutors. They claim to be God's people but are not. In fact, because they are persecuting the real people of God they must be a **synagogue of Satan.** In the Gospels John the Baptist points in this direction when he calls the Pharisees and Sadducees a 'brood of vipers' and then continues: 'Do not think you can say to yourselves, "We have Abraham as our father." I tell you that out of these stones God can raise up children for Abraham' (Matthew 3:7-9). The apostle Paul makes a similar point several times specially in Romans 2:28-29 and Galatians 3:26-29: 'You are all sons of God through faith in Christ Jesus.' 'If you belong to Christ, then you are Abraham's seed, and heirs according to the promise.' Of course, this does not mean that the Jews who are being referred to are any worse than other people, but in their actions they make it clear that their attitude to the truth of the Christian faith is no better than that of the pagans. Meanwhile, this church suffers very seriously under their attack.

Having said all of this, though, there is a great paradox in their real position for Jesus says, **yet you are rich!** The truth of the matter is that though they are materially poor and are heavily persecuted, yet spiritually they are profoundly rich. They inherit all God's covenant promises, for they belong to him. This richness will be summarised in verse 11 when Jesus tells them they will neither face judgment nor 'the second death', meaning, of course, that the fulness of eternal life with their Lord and Saviour will be theirs. With Christ in their midst watching them and protecting them and leading them, they are heading towards the time when 'He will wipe every tear from their eyes and there will be no more death or mourning or crying or pain, for the old order of things has passed away' (21:4). In Christ, Christians are truly rich.

iii) The exhortation

> Do not be afraid of what you are about to suffer. I tell you, the devil will put some of you in prison to test you, and you will suffer persecution for ten days. Be faithful, even to the point of death, and I will give you the crown of life (2:10).

So Jesus now exhorts them to **be faithful** in the suffering that he knows is yet to come their way. Following on from the idea that the synagogue is of Satan, he tells them that it will be **the devil** who will put them in prison. The source of all evil against God's people is the devil. Nevertheless, they are urged **not** to **be afraid** of what is coming even if it leads to their death, probably at the hands of the Romans by execution for so-called disloyalty to the Emperor. The significance of the titles (in verse 8) at the beginning of this letter now becomes apparent. Because Jesus is the sovereign Lord, **the First and the Last,** and because he **died and came to life again**, Christians can know that he has the power to look after them and bring them through death to life. So sovereign is the Lord that even Satan's attempts to dislodge the church are used by God **to test** his people and thus reveal to everyone those who are the genuine believers and those who are not. In other words, all that **the devil** can throw at these people simply confirms their eternal status as the true people of God and inheritors of his promises in Christ. How wonderful is God's grace as it shines through his sovereignty!

Now they are told, **you will suffer persecution**[16] **for ten**

41

days. This specific mention of time has caused much debate as Christians have tried to determine what it means. It could simply mean a literal period of ten days. However, in chapter 1 we saw that some of the description of Jesus was framed with words from the prophet Daniel. Here too it is likely that the book of Daniel forms the background to what Jesus is saying through John. In Daniel 1, Daniel and his friends are making a stand against the pagan rulers, seeking to serve King Nebuchadnezzar, and yet not compromising with his pagan world and its standards. They refuse to eat the meat served. They then set *ten days* as the time for a 'test' to see if they would survive well without eating meat. In many ways Daniel and his friends serve as an example of all believers who withstood the pressures of pagan life and stood for the Lord in spite of the threat of death. They have been tested and withstood the test. The persecution of these Christians from Smyrna can therefore be seen as part of God's 'test', and yet the period of testing is limited. It is not necessarily ten periods of twenty-four hours, but it will certainly come to an end, just as it did for Daniel and his friends, because Christ is in sovereign control. For some in Smyrna, and some Christians throughout the ages, the test may end with death, but the joy is that in God's time there will be a great reward.

iv) The promise

The reward that Jesus promises is particularly suitable for those who may die for their faith: **I will give you the crown** (or wreath) **of life**. The town of Smyrna was famous for its athletic games, and thus a reward of the 'crown of life' would have reminded these Christians of the 'wreath' prize given only to the best athletes and citizens. In life in Smyrna these Christians were considered the lowest of the low, but the Lord of life will reward them with **life** itself, as we see in the promise which follows.

> He who has an ear, let him hear what the Spirit says to the churches. He who overcomes will not be hurt at all by the second death (2:11).

The opening sentence is the same as in verse 7. It reminds us that this is a message for us all. As in verse 7, the promise is to the one who **overcomes**. This time the promise is that the Christian **will not be hurt at all by the second death.** What irony! The world may put these Christians to death, but they will receive the crown of life. The 'second death' is mentioned again three times in the last two chapters (20:6, 14; 21:8). In the last two of these verses it is clear that it refers to eternal punishment ('the lake of fire'). The great promise to the suffering church in Smyrna, where some will probably die for their faith (the first death), is that they will have life for evermore and need have no fear at all of the judgment of God. It is a wonderful reminder that whatever we may have to face for our Lord in this life, what is to come is an eternity of life in the Lord's presence.

3. The letter to Pergamum

To the angel of the church in Pergamum write: These are the words of him who has the sharp, double-edged sword. I know where you live – where Satan has his throne. (2:12-13a)

Pergamum was another important and large city. It was a cultural centre with one of the ancient world's great libraries, but it was very pagan, being the first city to encourage worship of the emperor. One of the gods particularly associated with the city was Asklepios, a serpent god believed to heal people. His serpent form would have reminded the early Christians of Satan. It was also a city where, as Christians died for their faith, it would *appear* that Satan was in control. Thus, it was fittingly called the place **where Satan has his throne**.

i) Jesus' self-description
Yet, to this church Jesus comes using one of his titles used in 1:16 (see comments there). As the one **who has the sharp, double-edged sword,** Jesus has the power to judge everyone who rejects his name.

ii) The encouragement

> Yet you remain true to my name. You did not renounce your faith in me, even in the days of Antipas, my faithful witness, who was put to death in your city – where Satan lives. (2:13b)

This church has already suffered great persecution. **Antipas** has died for the faith in Pergamum and yet this church has remained faithful. Jesus calls Antipas **my faithful witness**. He had truly followed Christ, who is called in 1:5 '*the* faithful witness', even to death. Throughout the ages many parts of the world have seen people die for their faith in Christ. It is the ultimate witness[17] for Christ that we can make on this earth and it is indeed to follow in the footsteps of Jesus himself. In spite of this horror, this church has not renounced Christ. The pressure was on and yet they kept the faith. They still **remain true** to Jesus himself. Satan may appear to be on the throne in this city, but appearances are not what they seem for, even if the power of the sword has been used against Antipas, it is actually Jesus who holds the sword.

iii) The problem

> Nevertheless, I have a few things against you: You have people there who hold to the teaching of Balaam, who taught Balak to entice the Israelites to sin by eating food sacrificed to idols and by committing sexual immorality. Likewise you also have those who hold to the teaching of the Nicolaitans (2:14-15).

In spite of their faithfulness in the midst of persecution, Jesus raises two serious issues with them with which he finds fault. He uses an Old Testament account to explain the problem of accommodation to the world around. In the midst of such antagonism to the Christian faith, no doubt Christians were trying to minimise the way they stood out from the surrounding society. They had not given up their faith, but they no longer stood out from the crowd, and had begun to compromise in various ways with the pagan society. The account of **Balaam** and **Balak** is found in Numbers 22–25. Israel's sexual immorality and involvement with pagan gods is then described in Numbers 25:1-3, and in 31:15-18 we see that Balaam was responsible for leading them astray in this way. Balaam had given way to the pressures of the surrounding societies.

In Greek cities of John's time there were many temples to the gods. Gods dominated the culture in such a way that, even in order to trade, people would need to be part of trade guilds which usually involved worshipping a particular god and perhaps joining in eating meals within the temples. The level of compromise had probably led to the sort of sexual immorality that would have been taken for granted in Greek society on those semi-religious occasions. It is not clear the exact extent to which these Christians were prepared to accommodate for the sake of a more peaceful life or to save their own skin, but perhaps they were even offering sacrifices to images of the emperor feeling that it didn't really matter, for their faith in the true God was still firm.

Jesus also mentions **the teaching of the Nicolaitans.** See the comments above on verse 6. It is likely that they specifically taught that practices which involved sexual immorality and eating meat offered to idols in a temple were not important and simply didn't matter. The problem for this church was that they were prepared to live with people who held to these teachings. They were not taking any disciplinary action against such false teaching. Jesus therefore blames the church for not taking action against those who hold to such false teaching and yet continue to worship.

This is the way in which we, as Christians, so easily find ourselves accommodating to the world around us. We end up excusing behaviour or a way of living that does not take proper account of the fact that we are called to be God's *holy* people. False teachers whose practices in life contradict the calling of God must not be tolerated in a church.

iv) The remedy

> Repent therefore! Otherwise, I will soon come to you and will fight against them with the sword of my mouth (2:16).

There is only one remedy, says Jesus, and that is to **repent.** They need to deal with this situation straight away by asking for God's forgiveness and throwing these people out of the church.

v) The warning

If they are unwilling to repent as a church for not dealing with this heresy, then Jesus himself **will soon come.** That is, he will quickly bring some kind of judgment on this church, no doubt similar to the removing of the lampstand which was the warning for the church in Ephesus. This is not the final judgment so much as Jesus coming to sort things out himself because the church has not done so. The words **with the sword of my mouth** communicate the authority that Jesus has as judge of all.

vi) The promise

> He who has an ear, let him hear what the Spirit says to the churches. To him who overcomes, I will give some of the hidden manna. I will also give him a white stone with a new name written on it, known only to him who receives it (2:17).

On this occasion the promise for those who remain faithful and do repent and continue to remain true in this evil city is that they will receive two gifts. First, they will be given **some of the hidden manna.** Manna was God's gift to the people of Israel who needed food when travelling through the wilderness after escaping from Egypt. Here the promise is that they will receive God's 'hidden' blessing. In other words, it is not yet seen but will be revealed at the last day when they will receive all they need. Meanwhile they must trust in God for this provision, something the Israelites had failed to do when they followed Balaam.

Secondly, Jesus will give them **a white stone with a new name written on it.** Many have speculated on the stone and its name. The 'white' stone may indicate a verdict for the person of 'not guilty' before God. It seems that the name will be a secret between God and the one who overcomes, who perseveres in the faith. Perhaps it will describe the victor's character, and will be a special and very personal reward. The background for this may lie in Isaiah 62:2, in which Israel's status of being a people without a land and apparently deserted will be completely reversed by the Lord in the last days. This closely parallels the situation of these Christians in Pergamum who no doubt seemed to others to have been deserted by their God and to have nothing by way of possessions. But the Lord Jesus promises a complete reversal of these appearances on the last day when he will give them a **new name**, not in the sense of a new name for each individual Christian, but a new name for the people of God. The same idea can also be seen in 3:12, and is surely the same as the name written on the foreheads of Christ's people in 14:1.

4. The letter to Thyatira

> To the angel of the church in Thyatira write: These are the words of the Son of God, whose eyes are like blazing fire and whose feet are like burnished bronze (2:18).

Thyatira was the least significant of the seven towns. Some here remained faithful, and there is an interesting contrast with Ephesus in that its current works are better than the first!

i) Jesus' self-description

Jesus introduces himself with the title **Son of God**. He alludes to Psalm 2:7 and looks forward to the reward (verse 27) where the same Psalm is quoted. No doubt the title was specially relevant to Christians who lived in a town where coins circulated that showed the deification of Domitian's son, 'seated on a globe surrounded by seven stars'.[18] The description that follows of Jesus' eyes and feet was discussed earlier when the words were applied to him in 1:14-15. Again it is Jesus' position as judge which is being stressed here, as with Pergamum. The similarities with Pergamum are interesting. Like Pergamum, many are indeed persevering, and yet there is a toleration of evil which is completely unacceptable in Christ's church. The reference to **burnished bronze** may also have rung a chord with people whose city was known for its trade in metal work. The choice of titles and allusions is an interesting reminder of just how closely Jesus knows his churches.

ii) The encouragement

> I know your deeds, your love and faith, your service and perseverance, and that you are now doing more than you did at first (2:19).

These words must have been of great encouragement. Reference to their **perseverance** again suggests that Jesus is interested in how they function as a 'lampstand'. Their **love** and **faith** and **service** are no doubt seen among themselves as they look after each other and build each other up in the Christian faith, but they also have to do with outreach and standing as a light in the midst of a dark, pagan world. They are even getting better at this task!

iii) The problem

> Nevertheless, I have this against you: You tolerate that woman Jezebel, who calls herself a prophetess. By her teaching she misleads my servants into sexual immorality and the eating of food sacrificed to idols. I have given her time to repent of her immorality, but she is unwilling (2:20-21).

As in the church at Pergamum, people are being misled (literally, 'led astray') **into sexual immorality** and into a wrongful accommodation with idolatry in eating temple meat, probably in the temple context as part of trade and social gatherings. We know nothing about who this woman Jezebel was, though she was passing herself off as a **prophetess**. False teachers will always seek to claim some level of authority for what they want to get across, and so the claim to be a 'prophet' is one that will always be appealing and will often lead people astray. In the Old Testament **Jezebel** was the evil wife of King Ahab, King of Israel. She drew her husband and the nation away from the Lord and encouraged them to worship Baal. She also killed many of Israel's true prophets (1 Kings 16:29-33; 18-21).

When people come claiming to have a special revelation from God or some inner hidden knowledge which they can share with others, there will always be, sadly, some well-meaning Christians who will be led astray. Time and again in the New Testament we read warnings about this. Jesus himself points out the dangers: 'Many false prophets will appear and deceive many people' (Matthew 24:11). Such must be recognised for who they are. In this case, as so often, they will be recognised by their works. This woman is compromising the faith and has no real concern for holiness. Of course, her option would have been much more attractive to some Christians than the route of holiness and separation from paganism, for her way of doing things would have minimised persecution.

iv) The remedy
In spite of her sin, the Lord had been gracious with her and **given her time to repent**. But this way forward had been refused and so judgment is to follow. This is also the only remedy for those who have followed her teachings, as we now see.

v) The warning

> So I will cast her on a bed of suffering, and I will make those who commit adultery with her suffer intensely, unless they repent of her ways. I will strike her children dead. Then all the churches will know that I am he who searches hearts and minds, and I will repay each of you according to your deeds (2:22-23).

In the Old Testament one of the pictures often used of those who turn from the true God and begin to worship idols is that of **adultery.** This is the idea here. The sin she commits will, as God judges her, return to cause her **suffering** and death. Just as sexual immorality can lead to some terrible illnesses, so the sin of leading God's people astray will lead to its own consequences which God shows are part of his judgment on the matter. Those **who commit adultery with her** are those who have been led astray by her teachings. They too will suffer but, under the grace of God, their suffering is designed to be restorative and to help them **repent of her ways**, that is, to turn away from following her teachings. If this doesn't happen, the warning stands for them. They become not God's children but **her children**, and the sovereign Judge **will strike** them **dead.** This judgment will be completely just. Not only has God been gracious in giving time to repent, but if they do not repent then he **will repay each** according to their **deeds**. They can hide nothing from the eyes that are like a 'blazing fire' (verse 18) for he **searches hearts and minds**.

vi) The promise

> Now I say to the rest of you in Thyatira, to you who do not hold to her teaching and have not learned Satan's so-called deep secrets (I will not impose any other burden on you): Only hold on to what you have until I come. To him who overcomes and does my will to the end, I will give authority over the nations – 'He will rule them with an iron sceptre; he will dash them to pieces like pottery' – just as I have received authority from my Father. I will also give him the morning star. He who has an ear, let him hear what the Spirit says to the churches (2:24-29).

Some, however, have not yet been led astray by this prophetess and they are not yet compromising with the pagan society around. They **have not learned Satan's so-called deep secrets**, which suggests that they have not yet been drawn into her Satanic teachings. Jesus promises these people that he **will not impose any other burden** on them. In other words, Christ is not suggesting a whole new legalism that true Christians should follow. In reaction to the ways of the world, Christians have often resorted to a new form of legalism, banning things that actually are not banned by Scripture. Here we see that Jesus will not ask of these Christians any more than is already asked of all Christians everywhere, that they serve the Lord their God with all their heart, soul, strength and mind (Luke 10:27). What they need to do is to **hold on** to what God has already given them until Christ returns. They need to continue in their 'deeds', 'love', 'faith', 'service' and 'perseverance' (verse 19).

Those who continue in this way are those who **overcome**, and the great promise to them is, first, **I will give authority over the nations**. This is an authority that Jesus tells us he has received from his Father. Psalm 2:9 is then used to describe this authority. Originally in Psalm 2 this authority was given by God to Israel's King. As we saw earlier, this is where the title 'Son of God' (verse 18) finds its background. The fulfilment of the promise of Psalm 2 is found in Jesus, but as King of God's people he represents them before the Father. As the King rules, so his people rule. In 3:21 we see that those who overcome are given the right to sit on the throne with Jesus, a point picked up by the apostle Paul in 1 Corinthians 6:2: 'Do you not know that the saints will judge the world?'

Secondly, Jesus promises he **will also give him the morning star.** The morning star stands as a symbol of messianic victory (see 22:16). Thus these Christians who persevere are reminded again that one day they will share in the Messiah's rule, no matter how small a number they appear at the moment, and no matter how much the darkness of the surrounding pagan society seems, for the time being, to have the upper hand. God has made promises to his people and so the whole church of all ages is called upon to take note.

Special lessons for today

As we complete the letter to the fourth of the seven churches, it is worth pausing again and pointing to just a few of the many lessons there are here for the modern church and individual members of the church.

First, Christians must take the way of the cross. Against a

51

modern theology that seems so often to emphasise a Christian's prosperity, or health or wealth or simply good feelings, we have learned much of the need for a theology of the cross, one that seeks to imitate Christ who died for his people. The call for patient endurance and hard work as witnesses for Christ, the reminder of some who have already died for the faith and others who may yet give their lives for the faith, all serve to remind us of the cost of true discipleship. To what extent does our 'first love' for Jesus drive us forward as individuals or as a gathered church community? Are we prepared to let our 'lamp' shine in witness for Christ to the extent that we may find ourselves persecuted?

Secondly, compromise with our society is unacceptable. These letters have also drawn our attention to the devastating effect of false teaching. The churches then, as today, were specially vulnerable to teaching which led to a compromise with the pagan society around. Such compromise would allow Christians to be better thought of by their neighbours and would probably reduce their isolation and even prevent some of the persecution they might otherwise have expected. The need to be on guard against such syncretistic theology or theology that is greatly influenced by the world's values is vital for the church of all generations. In the modern age, we can see how society easily influences Christian attitudes to sexual ethics, to marriage, to the roles of women and men, and so on. It is perhaps especially ironic that the western church is particularly influenced by a society which denies absolutes. With this denial goes a condemnation of anyone who thinks that there may be judgment for those who do not follow the one way God has given us for approaching him – through Jesus Christ our Saviour. How often do we hear church leaders denying final judgment or preaching what we call 'universalism', that is, that all will eventually be saved. Such teaching denies entirely the warnings of this passage and the awesome and sometimes frightening teaching of this book. Can we actually see the ways in which we may be drawn away from the truth? Can we recognise any false teachers in our own churches? In Pergamum we are shown the need for disciplinary action to be taken against false teachers. There is a great need for this to be taken seriously once again, not in terms of a 'witch hunt', but always with a view to bringing the false teacher back to the truth and the ways of Christ.

Thirdly, true Christian riches often belie appearances. When we looked at the church of Smyrna we saw that the church was called 'rich'. They were spiritually rich in spite of their outward appearances. Do we regard ourselves in this light in spite of the problems we may face in life?

Finally, we must heed the call to 'overcome'. We must learn from these letters and the ones which follow just how important this theme of 'overcoming' is for the Christian church and the individual Christian life. 'Overcoming' sin will lead to persecution and suffering and to apparent defeat. But this defeat is only apparent for, in fact, those who 'overcome' are the ones who receive all of God's richest promises. In the end they will 'overcome' not just the sin of this life but will come to the place where once and for all Jesus has 'overcome' (or 'conquered') all that is evil.

5. The letter to Sardis

> To the angel of the church in Sardis write: These are the words of him who holds the seven spirits of God and the seven stars. I know your deeds; you have a reputation of being alive, but you are dead. Wake up! Strengthen what remains and is about to die, for I have not found your deeds complete in the sight of my God. Remember, therefore, what you have received and heard; obey it, and repent (3:1-3a).

Sardis was a wealthy city situated in the valley of the river Hermus. It was on five important trade routes. Sardis also had a thriving, wealthy and large Jewish community in the city. Although there is no clear opposition to the gospel here, Jesus calls a sleeping church back to the apostolic faith.

i) Jesus' self-description

Again picking up from the first chapter, here Jesus calls himself the one **who holds the seven spirits of God** (1:4) and who holds **the seven stars** (1:16, 20; 2:1). The seven spirits refer to the Holy Spirit[19] and the **seven stars** are the angels of the seven churches. This description serves to remind the church that in Jesus Christ is all the power they need to be the church they should be. They have heavenly help available from the Spirit of God himself and from the angels. However, sadly, there is no initial encouragement as Jesus writes this letter, though we do see in verse 4 that there are just a few people who still honour the Lord in their life and behaviour.

ii) The problem

Jesus again clearly sees and understands the inner workings of this church and knows its **deeds**. The church seems to have a reputation for being **alive** spiritually. Perhaps this is the reputation they have among themselves. If it is, then they are deceiving themselves, for Jesus says **you are dead**. He goes on to say, **I have not found your deeds complete in the sight of my God**. They are not living out the gospel. And so, as God looks on them to assess them and judge them, they are found wanting. Since the problem is described in similar terms to that in the church at Ephesus, it is likely that the key area of concern has to do with their witness and outreach for Christ. They are not functioning properly as a 'lamp'.

iii) The remedy

The remedial action is to obey five commands that are given here.

a) **Wake up** (verse 2). The congregation is called to be alert to what is happening. They are sleeping through their own gradual demise. In fact much about them is already spiritually dead. Time is short and so they need a good shake to get them to realise how urgent things really are.

b) **Strengthen what remains**. So urgent is the situation that they must begin by focusing on the things that do remain and are still are profitable, that is, the deeds that still do reflect their missionary purpose as a lampstand for Christ.[20] Perhaps some of those who claim to be Christians in the church will thus be found out and it will be seen that they are not true believers.

c) Remember what you have received (verse 3). Not only are they to remember what it was like when, as a whole church, they seized every opportunity to live for the Lord and work for him and witness for him, but they are specifically to remember what they **have received**. This is most likely a call to return to the original apostolic teaching on which their church was founded. It is vital for every church that recognises its need to 'wake up', to look backwards before looking forwards. Christians are continually to move forward, but on the basis of the once and for all foundation of the apostles and prophets (Ephesians 2:20).

d) Obey it (keep it). Once they have looked back to the teaching of Scripture and of the apostles, then they must move forwards in obedience to this revealed will of God. Obedience is the key to discipleship and showing the fruit of the Spirit in the life of the church and of the individual.

e) Repent. In one sense this final command could have come first, but in fact it amply summarises all that has been said. Repentance will cause the church to turn around and begin to wake itself from its stupor, strengthen what remains, study their received doctrine again and begin to live it out for Christ in obedience. Without repentance, there will be no change and the church will completely die.

iv) The warning

> But if you do not wake up, I will come like a thief, and you will not know at what time I will come to you (3:3b).

Again, Jesus talks of 'coming', not with the final judgment, but with judgment on this particular church at this stage in its history.

Such judgments remind us of the final judgment that will come at Christ's return. It is for this reason that Jesus picks up a picture that is used elsewhere of the final judgment itself (see Matthew 24:42-44). A **thief** never announces his coming. He takes the household by surprise. One day the time will be up for this church and Jesus **will come**. Meanwhile, in God's grace, they have time for repentance and for a new start.

v) The promise

> Yet you have a few people in Sardis who have not soiled their clothes. They will walk with me, dressed in white, for they are worthy. He who overcomes will, like them, be dressed in white. I will never blot out his name from the book of life, but will acknowledge his name before my Father and his angels. He who has an ear, let him hear what the Spirit says to the churches (3:4-6).

Here promise for the future and encouragement for what already exists are rolled together. First the Lord points to those **who have not soiled their clothes.** They are examples for the church and will be commended by the Lord, for they are unstained with idolatry and pagan compromise. They will **walk with** the Lord himself and so experience the greatest of all the promises, that God will be with his people. They will be with him, and they will be **dressed in white, for they are worthy**. Jesus has been their example for he is **worthy** (5:2, 9, 12). As he had served his Father against the antagonism of the world, so they have done the same and will be dressed, like him, in white.

White is a colour of purity and holiness and thus points to the fact that they will be declared 'not guilty' on the Last Day as the Lord **acknowledges** them. Later in this book, white is the colour of the robes of all who gather in the Lord's presence (4:4; 6:11; 7:9). As we see in 7:9-14 the white robes do not indicate that their good works have achieved their salvation, as if they could somehow *earn* this favour from God. Rather they are dressed in white because Christ has died for them. The promise is re-emphasised as we are told that those dressed in white will never have their names blotted out **from the book of life**. Their eternal security is without doubt. Rather Jesus will **acknowledge** (or confess) the names of these people before the Father and the angels. This is a most wonderful promise to the faithful believer that Jesus himself will bring him or her right into the Father's presence, not for judgment and condemnation but for recognition and blessing.

The phrase **book of life** is used five times in Revelation[21] and reveals the names of those who are true believers and God's elect people. Their names have been written in the book of life *from the foundation of the world* (17:8). This contrasts with those books in which the sins of unbelievers are recorded and which will provide the basis for their judgment (see 20:12-13 and Daniel 12:1-2).

What joy to hear these words spoken to a church in which only a few were remaining faithful to the Lord. The challenge, warning and promises must be heard by all Christian people and all churches, for it comes from the Spirit of God.

6. The letter to Philadelphia

> To the angel of the church in Philadelphia write: These are the words of him who is holy and true, who holds the key of David. What he opens no one can shut, and what he shuts no one can open (3:7).

Philadelphia lies around 120 kilometres east of Ephesus, and is situated in a fertile area of volcanic soil – excellent for vineyards. Like so much of that area even in modern times, the city suffered frequent earthquakes. It was damaged in the earthquake that destroyed Laodicea in AD 60. But it was the earthquake of AD 17 that lived on in memory. Emperor Tiberius was not renowned for generosity, but he had given Philadelphia five years of relief from taxes to help them rebuild after that terrible earthquake. Following this generosity, the town was renamed 'New Caesarea', though the name never really stuck.

In AD 92, their relationship with the emperor reached rock bottom as Domitian ordered Philadelphia's vineyards destroyed, apparently to encourage production of corn at a time when Asia Minor was suffering from a food shortage. In this political and economic context[22] the church has **little strength** and is small and suffering, but Jesus says they **have kept** his **word**. That is, they have been faithful to him in practice. They have obeyed Scripture (primarily the Old Testament) and the teachings of Christ that would have been handed down to them from the apostles or through the Gospels, which would have been in circulation by this stage. Furthermore they **have not denied** his **name**. They had stood firm for Christ throughout.

Smyrna and Philadelphia were the only churches to receive no condemnation or discipline from their Lord. Other similarities between the two churches are notable. They both suffered persecution at the hands of the Jews. Both are told that this opposition is of Satan. Both churches are told that they will inherit a 'crown'. Yet Christians in this church at Philadelphia will need to endure further persecution and so they need encouragement. This is what Jesus now gives them.

i) Jesus' self-description

Jesus here describes himself as **true**. Undoubtedly this stands in direct contrast to what the Jews of the synagogue of Satan would have said of him (verse 9). But it is also in direct contrast with their experience of the emperor Domitian, who had proved himself untrustworthy. Jesus is also **holy,** a term applied frequently in the Old Testament to God himself. Here, then, is a claim to divinity as well. Whatever the Jews may have been saying, or however untrustworthy Domitian was, Jesus is the holy and true (or 'trustworthy') God.

Jesus holds the **key of David** because he is the promised Davidic king whose throne lasts forever. Isaiah 22:19-22 gives rise to the idea of the key. In that passage Eliakim replaced Shebna as steward of the palace and became the one who controlled entry to the king's household. This is who Jesus is. He alone can give access to God's kingdom (**What he opens no one can shut**) and to an inheritance of God's covenant promises. He can also shut people out: **what he shuts no one can open.** This self-description itself is full of encouragement to this suffering but faithful people. Jesus is the sovereign King and in control whatever may appear to be true at times on the ground in Philadelphia.

ii) The encouragement

> I know your deeds. See, I have placed before you an open door that no one can shut. I know that you have little strength, yet you have kept my word and have not denied my name. I will make those who are of the synagogue of Satan, who claim to be Jews though they are not, but are liars – I will make them come and fall down at your feet and acknowledge that I have loved you. Since you have kept my command to endure patiently, I will also keep you from the hour of trial that is going to come upon the whole world to test those who live on the earth. I am coming soon (3:8-11a).

Once again Jesus says **I know** what this church is doing and everything about it. But he now moves on. This church is struggling in its mission, and so he shows how his sovereignty is being used to their great benefit.

a) Jesus opens the door for mission

First, he promises, **I have placed before you an open door**. While it may be that the 'open door' here continues the same idea of the previous verse, that is, of an 'open door' for believers into the kingdom of God, it seems more likely that the idea has moved on and the 'door' that Jesus has now **placed before** this church is a door that will enable them to carry out their witness in the world. Their 'lampstand' is given the opportunity by Jesus to shine, for he has opened up opportunities for them to witness. This understanding of an 'open door' being placed in front of believers so that they can witness is quite common in the New Testament. For example, in 1 Corinthians 16:8-9, Paul writes: 'I will stay on at Ephesus until Pentecost, because a great door for effective work has opened to me.' Again in 2 Corinthians 2:12 we read: 'I went to Troas to preach the gospel of Christ and found that the Lord had opened a door for me.'[23]

Here is a lovely picture for us to grasp. Jesus not only opens the door to the kingdom of heaven for his believers (verse 7), but he also opens the door for gospel opportunities in front of his often weak and disheartened church. In a day of a strong Jewish mission and antagonism to Christians, Jesus will open up the opportunities for his church. G. B. Caird well sums up the message: 'If Christ opens the door, no one can shut it, not even Satan.... He has opened a door in front of his loyal followers.... Christ holds the key to earthly opportunity as well as to heavenly glory.'[24] How encouraging, not just for the Philadelphian church but for all churches down through the ages, to know that the work of the gospel is ultimately the work of Jesus who opens the door for his people and that their eternal security is safe in the hands of the one who holds the keys of the kingdom!

b) Jesus will overcome the church's enemies[25]

Trying to stop people entering the kingdom of God is the whole purpose of Satan. The Jews were seeking to undermine Christian confidence in being the people of God. Very sadly, there will come a time when these people of Satan will recognise, too late, that it is Christians, and not them, whom Jesus has **loved** (verse 9). They will all **acknowledge** the truth of this fact as Jesus makes them **come and fall down at** the **feet** of Christians. Christians will thus find their commitment to Christ is publicly vindicated.[26] As Sweet says, 'Christians must *know* that God has set his love on them, and that arguments which disparage their standing are the work of *Satan*, if they are to bear their witness in face of the *trials* and suffering which lie ahead.'[27]

c) Jesus will protect his people.

They have kept the word of Christ part of which is **to endure patiently** (perseverance). They have been through some troubles already at the hands of the Jews, and Christ has upheld them thus far. But there is **the hour of trial that is going to come**

upon the whole world and they need to hear Jesus say clearly to them, **I will also keep you**. Jesus will protect his people even through this time of suffering and persecution that is to come.

Trial in the Bible can be used of testing and refining God's people (as in 2:10 in the letter to Smyrna), or it can look towards the judgment of God on unbelief. Here it is judgment and the wrath of God that are in mind because **the whole world** is mentioned. There is great debate, however, about the particular time of trial. There is no reason to assume that these Christians will be *removed* from the situation before the trial occurs (some suggest that the 'rapture' is in mind). It is more likely that Jesus will continue to protect his people *in* and *through* this time.[28] This **trial** thus becomes a time of judgment for unbelievers, and a time of further sanctification and spiritual growth through *testing* for believers. Whether the time refers to particular tribulations just before Christ returns or to specific problems that Philadelphia and perhaps the churches in Asia Minor were about to face is not altogether clear. Given the context of this specific letter, the latter is probably more likely. However, the promise of protection through tribulation that comes on the world as part of God's judgment is a promise for all churches throughout the ages and once again should serve as further encouragement. The fact that the Christians are commended for having 'kept Christ's word of patient endurance' suggests they have already experienced some of this **trial**. Jesus promises to be with his people and keep them while this judgment takes place.

We should note here that **the whole world** ('those who live on earth') in the book of Revelation refers to evil people (6:10; 12:9; 13:3 etc.) and they are to be the subject of this particular trial, but God's people will get caught up in it and its effects and so will need God's protection throughout.

d) Jesus is coming soon

Finally, by way of encouragement Jesus says in verse 11, **I am coming soon**. This is the greatest news of all for all Christians.

Christ, as we have seen in other letters, 'comes' to his people in a special way. Here his coming is clearly to encourage and uphold and keep these faithful Christians. But this statement also points forward to the great description of that future time, described in chapters 21–22, when Jesus will finally bring to an end all the persecution, suffering and time of trial as he returns in glory to rescue and save his people.

iii) The exhortation

> Hold on to what you have, so that no one will take your crown (3:11b).

These Christians have so much. They are already keeping God's word and refusing to deny him even under great pressure. Now Jesus exhorts them to continue in the same way. He says, **hold on to what you have**. They are doing well, but greater trials have yet to come. **No one** must be allowed to **take** their **crown**, so they must remain faithful to God's word (see on 2:10).

iv) The promise

> Him who overcomes I will make a pillar in the temple of my God. Never again will he leave it. I will write on him the name of my God and the name of the city of my God, the new Jerusalem, which is coming down out of heaven from my God; and I will also write on him my new name. He who has an ear, let him hear what the Spirit says to the churches (3:12-13).

Once again Jesus makes promises to those who **overcome**. That is, to those who overcome sin, refuse to compromise with the world and hold on to Christ. Jesus knows how precious to them personally will be the picture of a **solid pillar in the temple**. Such pillars will not fall. Of course there is no temple in the **new Jerusalem**, but that is not the point here; rather the point is about stability and firmness, about the contrast with their current living conditions. Jesus knows they come from a city where they had tried to change the name to New Caesarea, but he promises they will be part of a new city whose name will last forever, **the new Jerusalem**. **Never again** will Christians need to **leave it**. Never again will they find themselves being evacuated and having to live outside in the road for fear of falling walls. Earthquakes will not come to this great city any more than sin or trial will be seen in it. On **coming down out of heaven from my God**, see comments on 21:2, 10. On **I will also write on him my new name**, see comments on 2:17.

The promises are once again so appropriate to this particular people. In the midst of insecurity from earthquakes on the one hand, and attacks on their faith on the other, Jesus promises final stability and protection for ever in his presence in the heavenly city which will come one day.

7. The letter to Laodicea

No other church receives such condemnation as this; yet, of all the seven letters, this letter reveals most clearly how intimately Jesus knew his churches both in their spiritual activity and in their socio-political circumstances. Laodicea was situated about 160 kilometres east of Ephesus and a little south-east of Philadelphia. It was a wealthy and prosperous city, and it is worth drawing attention to some facts about the city that will help us understand more clearly what Jesus is saying to this church.[29]

a) Laodicea was renowned for water that tasted bad and which could make one sick. This contrasted greatly with the medicinal hot springs of Hierapolis, visible across the valley, or the cold refreshing waters of Colossae up the road. ('Hot' and 'cold' are thus both *positive* attributes, verse 15.)

b) The Laodiceans were both proud and wealthy. In AD 60 they had suffered a great earthquake but had refused to accept financial help from Rome for reconstruction work: 'I do not need a thing' (verse 17) was their attitude.

c) Laodicea was a renowned medical centre, and it seems even to have been famous for a particular eye ointment. They did not think of themselves as 'blind' (verse 17)!

d) This prosperous town also had a reputation for good clothing. They were known specially for black wool clothing from black sheep in the area: a contrast with their 'nakedness' and the 'white clothing' that Jesus supplies.

e) Local superstition possibly believed that the wearing of white garments would lead to death, as corpses were buried in white. Again this would provide a vivid contrast with the white robe given by Jesus to those who will live for ever.

f) Laodicea was a city where the Romans had billeted their soldiers and requisitioned hospitality from the locals: a contrast with the way Christ gently approaches them (verse 20).

i) Jesus' self-description

> To the angel of the church in Laodicea write: These are the words of the Amen, the faithful and true witness, the ruler of God's creation (3:14).

The word **Amen** describes what is to be trusted and is certain. As **the Amen** Jesus is the God who is absolutely trusted. He is also the **faithful and true witness** (reminding us of 1:5). Jesus faithfully proclaimed God to this world, persevering through suffering and even to his death on the cross. His testimony was true and faithful to his calling. In this he is, of course, an example to the Laodiceans who are not being faithful or true to their calling. Jesus is also the **ruler** (perhaps better translated as the 'beginning') **of God's creation**. Again the emphasis is on Jesus' sovereignty, for he is the source and beginning of all creation, and alone can be the source of life for the Laodicean Christians. Sadly, there is no immediate encouragement offered to this church, rather Jesus goes straight into defining their problem.

ii) The problem

> I know your deeds, that you are neither cold nor hot. I wish you were either one or the other! So, because you are lukewarm – neither hot nor cold – I am about to spit you out of my mouth. You say, 'I am rich; I have acquired wealth and do not need a thing.' But you do not realise that you are wretched, pitiful, poor, blind and naked (3:15-17).

Using the picture of drinking water that tastes bad, Jesus says that their witness as a 'lampstand' tastes foul! Hot water from springs can be used for medicinal reasons, and cold water tastes good and is refreshing, but they are more like the nasty tasting and very hard water that had been transported across the plain to reach their city. They are so far removed from God's purposes for them as a church that the danger is that he will **spit** them **out of** his **mouth**.

The essence of the problem, however, is one of spiritual arrogance. Like the city of which they are part, these Christians believe they have 'arrived'. They cannot imagine that they lack anything at all, they **do not need a thing**! Like their fellow citizens, the people in this congregation were probably well-off, and they may actually have regarded this economic prosperity as proof that they were in a good state spiritually as well. The sad thing is that this church simply refused to look at itself and realise what it really was. So Jesus continues, **But you do not realise that you are wretched, pitiful, poor, blind and naked.** Everything that Laodicean Christian and non-Christian alike would have said about themselves is here denied by Jesus as he disciplines this church. Good black clothing, good eye ointment, material prosperity, none of this could hide the fact that the church was disobedient to its calling to be a 'lampstand' and 'witness' following the one 'faithful and true witness', Jesus Christ.

iii) The remedy

> I counsel you to buy from me gold refined in the fire, so you can become rich; and white clothes to wear, so you can cover your shameful nakedness; and salve to put on your eyes, so that you can see (3:18).

At the beginning of this letter Jesus identified himself as the source or beginning of all creation. Just as he brought life to the world, so he alone can be the source of life for this church or any church. So Jesus calls upon them to turn to him for **gold refined in the fire**. Being truly **rich** as a Christian involves recognising our complete dependence upon God.

Come to me for true wealth, the most precious sort, the

65

refined sort, says Jesus. The refining of a Christian's life has to do with being purified from the sin of the world. Coming to Jesus is thus the direct opposite of what was happening in this church which was becoming more and more merged into the surrounding life of materialism and paganism. **White clothes to wear** reminds us of the reward that the few real Christians at Sardis were to receive precisely because, unlike the Laodiceans, they had *not* 'soiled their clothes' (3:4, see there the comments on white clothes). They also need spiritual discernment and for this they should turn to Christ for his ointment (**salve**). The fact of the matter is that they cannot at present even see the problem, let alone look for a remedy. For this, too, they must turn back to Jesus himself.

The point is simple. They felt so good and so proud as a church that they had begun to exclude Jesus from their actions and plans, and were no longer functioning as a 'lampstand' of witness. Jesus knew that he had to speak sharply and in a way which would really sting and hurt. The Laodicean church was proud and no proud person likes to be put down like that. So the warning which follows is also couched in compassion.

iv) The warning

> Those whom I love I rebuke and discipline. So be earnest, and repent (3:19).

Right in the middle of such dreadful and hurtful condemnation from Jesus, we see him extending the hand of mercy and love. He is reproving them and chastening them but he does it as a Father who loves his children. The time is not too late, yet. The warning that follows the remedy is thus summarised with two commands: **be earnest, and repent**. Once again the key to it all, repentance, is put last. They must turn round and ask for forgiveness and be **earnest** in doing what they should have been doing all along – witnessing as a 'lamp' to a world of sin and evil.

v) The promise

Here I am! I stand at the door and knock. If anyone hears my voice and opens the door, I will come in and eat with him, and he with me. To him who overcomes, I will give the right to sit with me on my throne, just as I overcame and sat down with my Father on his throne. He who has an ear, let him hear what the Spirit says to the churches (3:20-22).

These people must first and foremost turn back to Christ as the source of their life. It is as though they have become so self-satisfied that they have excluded Christ altogether from his church! And it still is his church, that is why he is still prepared lovingly to rebuke and discipline them. But when all is said and done, they are behaving like people who have closed the door on Jesus. It is almost as if he were outside the church looking in, for they seemed to have no need of him or of anything at all. This is the context of this very famous verse 20.

Here I am! I stand at the door and knock. It is one of the saddest pictures imaginable. In spite of so many evangelistic sermons about the need for people to open the door of their heart to let Jesus in so that they can become Christians, this is not the primary meaning here. Jesus is speaking primarily to the church, though also to individuals within the church, and so he is speaking to those who at the very least consider themselves to be *Christians*. It is Christians to whom Jesus speaks here and whom he now rebukes. They *must* repent and involve him in their lives and mission and witness. If they do this, then Jesus says, **I will come in and eat with him, and he with me**. Here again Jesus promises to **come**. He is not thinking at this moment of the final coming of Christ but of a 'coming' in which he will once again bring them *his* blessings and his fellowship and presence with them – **I will come in and eat with him, and he with me**. The meal is a symbol of the restoring of full and close communion between the Lord and his church.

This promise is for the whole church and the call is to the whole church. But Jesus has made the appeal in the singular (**If anyone hears**), and it may well be that only a few will respond to this call and so receive the promises. It reminds us that we come before God both as part of a local church but also as individuals responsible to him for our own service and commitment.

Once again the letter concludes with comfort for those who **overcome**. Jesus himself was the faithful and true witness even in his death on the cross and as such continues to be the example for his church (**just as I overcame and sat down with my Father on his throne**). To those, therefore who overcome, Jesus says, **I will give the right to sit with me on my throne** (see also on 2:26). This latter promise reminds us of the Lord's words to his disciples in Luke 22:28-30: 'You are those who have stood by me in my trials. And I confer on you a kingdom, just as my Father conferred one on me, so that you may eat and drink at my table in my kingdom and sit on thrones, judging the twelve tribes of Israel.'

This promise of sitting on the throne is a reminder that we are members of the kingdom of God over which Christ is Lord (Colossians 3:1-4). As he represents us now on his throne, so already we are 'seated with him' (Ephesians 2:6-7). But there will come a time when we shall see the King face to face and he will be among his people and we shall be reigning in glory with him. (See also 2 Timothy 2:11-12).

Special lessons for today

Some of the points we noted in chapter 2 continue to be made in chapter 3. But it is worth noting a further very important teaching here for the modern church and individual Christians.

Firstly, Christians must understand what constitutes an 'alive' church. It is sad but true that churches all over the world have a tendency to think they are 'alive' when in fact they are all but 'dead' spiritually. All sorts of different circumstances can cause them to have an over-optimistic self-assessment. There can be the small traditional church that believes it is still alive because some people still come to church and they still say the same services year after year. There can be the middle of the road sort of church that has a reasonable profile and is well liked in the community and so thinks it is 'alive'. There can be the large and even very large church that thinks it is alive just because of the numbers of people who come each Sunday. But Jesus says to his churches that none of these things is what makes an 'alive' church.

An 'alive' church is one that is awake and alert to doing what God wants of them by way of witness to the gospel. It is a church which constantly remembers what it has received in the gospel and the word of God in Scripture, and above all in the grace of God in Jesus Christ. When a church continues to come back to Christ and his word in Scripture and continues to rely on his grace and seeks constantly to shine as a 'lampstand' in this world, then we may say that it is 'alive'. Though this is primarily applied here to local church congregations, the truth remains the same in an individual's life as well. We are to be alert all the time to follow the Lord's will, and we can only know that as we rely on his grace, study his word and 'remember' what we have received.

Secondly, Christ opens the door of mission for his churches. Sometimes as we think of mission and outreach to those around we can become thoroughly disheartened, particularly if we seem to be so few and the world around so large. But this chapter has offered such great encouragement to us, for Jesus says he has placed before his church an 'open door' for mission. We need to realise, whether in a persecuted setting or a comfortable setting where the temptation is to sit back and relax, that Jesus goes before us into this world as one who is *the faithful witness*, and he opens the door that we too may become faithful witnesses.

Thirdly, the church must avoid conceit and complacency. The letter to Laodicea offers a number of challenges for us all. However, there is a particular challenge to churches that feel they are more 'successful'. They may have been built up in all the right ways, but as God has prospered them so they have become self-reliant and considered themselves 'successful' and well off. Perhaps they have a large staff, multiple 'programmes', and many lay people involved in all the things that are going on, and yet it seems that Christ has been excluded from his church. It is surprisingly easy for such a church to become self-deluded and not realise that it is poor and blind. Unless our churches focus on Christ and look continually to his word for sustenance and rely always on his grace, then we too shall stand condemned as 'wretched, pitiful, poor, blind and naked'.

Revelation 4

The Heavenly Throne Room

In chapter 4 John is transported in his vision from earth and the present scene of the seven churches to a heavenly place. Here he sees God's heavenly throne room and those who are gathered round the throne. The impression of the whole scene is one of sovereignty, majesty and awe. Here John takes us, his readers, with him to the place from which the sovereign God rules over everything and everyone. Nothing has happened, nor does it happen, nor will happen that is not under God's oversight and within his purposes. Here in chapter 4 there is a special emphasis on the lordship of God in *creation*, while in chapter 5 we see the lordship of God in *redemption*.

These chapters are of fundamental importance to all that the apostle has to say. He will go on in his vision to tell of the great destruction that God brings, of judgment and of death and the wrath of God, but it is first set in this wonderful context of the creating and redeeming purposes of God. Certainly we shall see God as judge as the vision goes on, but these two chapters remind us that he is also utterly faithful to his promises and does redeem his people.

1. The throne room in heaven

> After this I looked, and there before me was a door standing open in heaven. And the voice I had first heard speaking to me like a trumpet said, 'Come up here, and I will show you what must take place after this.' At once I was in the Spirit, and there before me was a throne in heaven with someone sitting on it (4:1-2).

John is now transported, **in the Spirit,**[30] to the heavenly throne room so that he can be shown **what must take place after this**.

He is summoned by the same voice he had heard back in 1:10, the glorified Christ. The **throne** itself is central to the room he now sees, for it is the great symbol of God's sovereign power. There is **someone sitting on it** but John makes no attempt to describe that person in detail, except to give us a picture of extraordinary splendour.

> And the one who sat there had the appearance of jasper and carnelian. A rainbow, resembling an emerald, encircled the throne (4:3).

John describes **a rainbow** completely surrounding the throne. Here is the most wonderful picture of the sovereign judging Lord surrounded by the very symbol of his own covenant faithfulness to his people. Here, in picture form, is a warning not to interpret the disasters which will be talked about in the next part of the visions as if God had forgotten his promises to Noah. Even while God sits on the judgment throne, he is surrounded by his own covenant promises. The picture of this rainbow is probably drawn from Ezekiel, as is so much of the imagery that follows. Like John (verse 6), Ezekiel sees the four creatures, one like an ox, one like a lion, one like an eagle and one like a man (Ezekiel 1:10). The talk of fire and thunder and lightning also creates a similar impression to John's vision (verse 5), and to the impressiveness of being confronted by a God who judges. What the prophet then sees is the appearance of the likeness of the glory of the Lord, and in Ezekiel 1:25-28 we have another wonderful description of a vision of the glory of the Lord: 'brilliant light surrounded him. Like the appearance of a rainbow in the clouds on a rainy day, so was the radiance around him. This was the appearance of the likeness of the glory of the LORD. When I saw it, I fell face down, and I heard the voice of one speaking.'

This picture of the throne room and a vision of the glory of the Lord was given to Isaiah and Daniel as well. In Isaiah 6 the prophet saw the Lord seated on the throne high and exalted, being worshipped by the heavenly creatures who called, 'Holy,

holy, holy is the LORD Almighty, the whole earth is full of his glory.' Each of these visions of the glory of the Lord leads to worship, as it does here in 4:11.

2. The picture around the throne
As John looks, so his eye moves beyond the throne itself to what surrounds it. Here again the picture is one of awe and majesty but also of worship.

i) The twenty-four elders

> Surrounding the throne were twenty-four other thrones, and seated on them were twenty-four elders. They were dressed in white and had crowns of gold on their heads (4:4).

The number twenty-four could be derived from a number of sources. Perhaps it most likely represents the patriarchs (the twelve tribes of Israel) and the twelve apostles. They are seated on thrones, which indicates that they too have a ruling function. They are **dressed in white** and wear **crowns of gold**. It is important to remember that we have already heard of the promises God has made to his people if they remain faithful witnesses to him. In the letter to Sardis we were told that those who remain faithful 'will walk with me, dressed in **white**, for they are worthy' (3:4). A **crown** has been mentioned as a reward for the faithful in 2:10 and 3:11. More than that, we have been told that God's redeemed and faithful people who 'overcome' and do God's will 'to the end' (2:26) will be given 'authority over the nations'. Finally, at the end of the letters in 3:21, we read: 'To him who overcomes, I will give the right to sit with me on my throne, just as I overcame and sat down with my Father on his throne.'

It thus seems most likely that in seeing the twenty-four elders John sees figures who, just as has been promised, represent all God's redeemed people who will rule with him. This is how it will be for all the redeemed. They will be in the presence of God and will reign with him and with Jesus.

ii) The noise and light

From the throne came flashes of lightning, rumblings and peals of thunder. Before the throne, seven lamps were blazing. These are the seven spirits of God (4:5).

The **seven spirits of God** are the Holy Spirit (see on 1:4; 3:1). The full effect of this extraordinary vision is now felt because it is not just what John sees that makes an impression, but also what he hears. No doubt the fire points towards the purifying work of God's Spirit, but it also points towards the work of judgment (see Matthew 3:11). The noise also reminds us of God's awesome power and authority. The description is not unlike what the Israelites experienced as Moses led the people out of the camp to meet with God and the cloud of God's glory descended on Mount Sinai. There we read 'the people trembled' (Exodus 19:16-19).

iii) A sea of glass

Also before the throne there was what looked like a sea of glass, clear as crystal (4:6a).

This sea of glass, of the perfection of crystal, separates God in his holiness from everything else. It probably looks back to the creation itself with the waters above the earth and to the releasing of the waters in the flood of Noah's day. It is this sea which will disappear later (see 21:1). In other words there will come a time when sin and sinful people have been judged and God's people will no longer experience this sea which separates them from their God.

iv) Four living creatures

In the centre, around the throne, were four living creatures, and they were covered with eyes, in front and behind. The first living creature was like a lion, the second was like an ox, the third had a face like a man, the fourth was like a flying eagle. Each of the four living creatures had six wings and was covered with eyes all around, even under his wings (4:6b-8a).

As John continues to survey the scene, he sees **four living creatures** at the heart of the picture, **around the throne**. We said at the start of this chapter that here we see God as primarily the sovereign over all *creation*. These angelic creatures represent the universe of God's created order, all of which worships him and centres itself around him. The lion is perhaps symbolic of the whole animal creation, being the greatest example. The ox may represent all domestic animals, and the eagle represents the birds, while the figure of a man represents human creation. All that God has created is represented here before his throne. It is the most amazing picture. More than that, they are pictured as **covered with eyes**.

Since the picture of the living creatures draws upon Ezekiel's description of the heavenly cherubim in Ezekiel 1:5-9,[31] it is likely that reference to the eyes **in front and behind** also comes from Ezekiel where he further describes the cherubim: 'The cherubim went in whatever direction the head faced, without turning as they went. Their entire bodies, including their backs, their hands and their wings, were completely full of eyes, as were their four wheels' (Ezekiel 10:11-12). As God's agents they are forever looking this way and that way in order to serve him and worship him.

3. United worship before the throne

Day and night they never stop saying: 'Holy, holy, holy is the Lord God Almighty, who was, and is, and is to come.' Whenever the living creatures give glory, honour and thanks to him who sits on the throne and who lives for ever and ever, the twenty-four elders fall down before him who sits on the throne, and worship him who lives for ever and ever. They lay their crowns before the throne and say: 'You are worthy, our Lord and God, to receive glory and honour and power, for you created all things, and by your will they were created and have their being' (4:8b-11).

Now John sums up the totality of what he has seen so far, and it is a scene of worship.

i) God who is worshipped

The thunder and fire and sea and the magnificent creatures and the thrones have all pointed towards the holiness of God Almighty, his magnificent creative power, and his eternity. The worship that is now described centres on these three great attributes of God.

a) The Holy God. God's holiness describes both his perfection and lack of any sin, but also his separation from all that may be tainted with sin, and so he is praised here with words which again draw on Isaiah 6:3: **Holy, holy, holy.**

b) The Lord God Almighty. Represented by the four **living creatures**, we are reminded that the whole of God's creation was designed to bring praise and glory to its Maker. He is the all-powerful Creator, who is utterly sovereign over his creation and rules over all. He is worshipped and praised with words which speak back to God his glory with the words, **for you created all things, and by your will they were created and have their being.** There is nothing that exists that has not come into being **by [his] will.** More than that, all things continue to **have their being** by God's will. In other words, he not only brings all things into being but sustains all things.

c) The Eternal God. God's eternity is mentioned three times in this short paragraph. We are told that he is the God **who was, and is, and is to come.** Then twice repeated we have the words **who lives for ever and ever.** The stress on God's eternity reminds us that all creation, including all the worshippers around the throne, are *not* eternal but are created by God. This attribute of eternity thus brings us back to the essential difference between God and all else. We are created and not eternal. Since our eternal creator is sovereign over us, we are *not* almighty.

So it is that the assembly before and around the throne worship the most wonderful creator God.

ii) The worship he receives

It is difficult for us, who still have the sad tendency to think of worship as largely about what we do on Sunday, to grasp what we see as happening here in heaven.

a) This worship is ceaseless. Here before the throne of God we have the reminder that the whole of life is to be about bringing glory and honour and praise to God. We read **they never stop saying...** It is part of the sadness of our fallenness and sin that we find ourselves so often falling short of living for God's glory. Yet when we finally enjoy life in all its fulness before the sovereign Lord, we too shall find that this is indeed at last our natural inclination, for it is what we have been created for.

b) The worship is spoken. Worship of God is verbal. We read that they never stop saying, and that the elders **say ...** God has created us to communicate with each other and with him. It is useful to remind ourselves that when these crowds speak the praises of God they do so to him but they also hear each other. So they remind each other that they are all part of this magnificent creation designed to communicate with the Lord God Almighty.

c) The worship is active. The elders **lay their crowns before the throne**. This action is, of course, symbolic. Here they are acknowledging the one true God and the one who sits on *the* throne. Nevertheless, such an action reminds us that these elders, who themselves have thrones and are involved in the work of the Lord, do that work to his glory. Even the rule they have (represented by their crowns) is a rule which must be subordinated to his rule. As we fulfil the work that God has called us to do in his service, we learn from this heavenly assembly to make sure that we do all, as it were, with our crowns laid before him. We are to live and work to his praise and glory.

4. Summary

This chapter has spoken of the creator God. It reminds the suffering church of what **must take place after this**. There is no doubt about this heavenly scene. For those of us who are part of the present church on earth, we are given an eternal perspective which we must hang on to at all times. We are reminded that, when we face hardships and even sufferings, God is still almighty and eternal. We are reminded that, whatever our circumstances, God has created us to worship him and to speak his praise and to work for his glory. Furthermore, we are shown that as our lives are lived before God we are to consider our worship to be ceaseless. There is nothing we do or think or say that should not be directed towards our God and for his glory.

Earthly worship is to be modelled on this heavenly scene. It involves us, at all times, as individuals and as a gathered church in giving ourselves wholly to God. It also calls upon us to have a proper regard to who our God really is. He is the eternal, holy and almighty Lord. Praise his name.

Revelation 5

The Scroll that is Sealed

Then I saw in the right hand of him who sat on the throne a scroll with writing on both sides and sealed with seven seals. And I saw a mighty angel proclaiming in a loud voice, 'Who is worthy to break the seals and open the scroll?'[32] But no one in heaven or on earth or under the earth could open the scroll or even look inside it. I wept and wept because no one was found who was worthy to open the scroll or look inside (5:1-4).

The scene of the throne room continues in this chapter. As John watches, he sees that the Lord God on the throne has in his **right hand a scroll**. This would have been a papyrus document wrapped around a pole. Usually such scrolls had writing only on one side and were read by simply unwinding the document. But in this case it is heavily **sealed with seven seals**. Once again the figure seven suggests perfection and completeness and no doubt here implies that God himself has sealed the scroll. Official documents were often sealed, as happens even today, in such a way that only the authorised reader would be allowed to break the seal.

1. The challenge to open the scroll
The question thus faced and so loudly posed by the angel is whether anyone has the right to open this particular scroll: **'Who is worthy to break the seals and open the scroll?'**

As we shall see later, the content of the scroll concerns God's whole plan of salvation and judgment for this earth, from the cross through to the final culmination of his purposes in the new heavens and the new earth. Indeed its contents will be revealed through the rest of this book of Revelation (chapters 6–22). Once this scroll is opened John will indeed be shown 'what must take place after this' (4:1). But for now the question posed is whether there is anyone with the authority to open this scroll. The opening of the scroll of God's purposes is not just about finding someone morally good enough to do this job, but about finding someone with the authority to open the scroll in the sense of putting it into effect.

The answer comes back that **no one** at all could be found who **could open the scroll or even look inside it.** The purposes of God for human beings in this world are laid out in his gracious plan, but no man or woman is able to implement this plan for none is able to accomplish the redemption of which it speaks, and none has the authority to carry out the judgment of which it speaks. It is not until verse 9, however, that we come to understand this. For there we see that the reason Christ is indeed worthy is because he has set in motion the plan of redemption.

2. The human reaction

As yet, though, John has not seen this and so he says, '**I wept and wept.**' This weeping is like the laments of prophets such as Jeremiah as they see God's people facing judgment, apparently without hope in their unworthiness and sin. It is the weeping of one who wonders whether God's people will ever finally be saved and receive their promised inheritance. It is the weeping of one who feels his sin and the unworthiness of all humanity before a holy God, and the weeping of one who is concerned for the suffering church and wonders whether in fact there will be any protection at all for God's people if the seals are not opened.

3. Christ can open the scroll

> Then one of the elders said to me, 'Do not weep! See, the Lion of the tribe of Judah, the Root of David, has triumphed. He is able to open the scroll and its seven seals' (5:5).

one of the elders who represents mankind (see on 4:4) now speaks words of great comfort, revealing to John that there is, after all, one who is worthy. And so he points to Jesus, the Messiah.

In fact this verse is one sentence in Greek and says that **the Root of David has triumphed** *in order to open* **the scroll and its seven seals**. In other words, Jesus' victory on the cross through his death and resurrection is precisely what was required for the revelation of God's redemptive purposes. What will shortly be revealed as the seals are opened, therefore, describes the situation following the death, resurrection and ascension of Christ. Though much lies in the future, the main context is the *present* age of the church with Christ as the exalted Lord and Saviour.

The only person able to open the scroll is thus the Messiah who is here referred to by two great titles of power, and then described as **a Lamb** (5:6).

i) Christ is the Lion of the tribe of Judah

This is a title drawn from Genesis 49:9 where Jacob pronounces a blessing upon his sons. To Judah, Jacob says: 'You are a lion's cub, O Judah; you return from the prey, my son. Like a lion he crouches and lies down, like a lioness – who dares to rouse him? The sceptre will not depart from Judah, nor the ruler's staff from between his feet, until he comes to whom it belongs and the obedience of the nations is his.' As time went on, it was from the tribe of Judah that King David came and the fulfilment of Judah's descendants becoming rulers was revealed. In God's covenant with David, he promised that David's descendant would inherit an eternal throne (2 Samuel 7:12-13), and so we see how this blessing is fulfilled that 'the sceptre will not depart from Judah'. Ultimately Jesus, son of David, was born as the Messiah of the tribe of Judah. The title he is given here thus sees him as the ultimate fulfilment of the blessing Jacob promised to his son Judah. It specially emphasises his authority over the nations. Jesus has the authority as King.

ii) Christ is the Root of David

This is also a title drawn from the Old Testament references to the messianic king who would come as a descendant of King

81

David. The great messianic passage from Isaiah 11 is specially informative here. In verse 1 we read: 'A shoot will come up from the stump of Jesse; from his roots a Branch will bear fruit'. And verse 10 says: 'In that day the Root of Jesse will stand as a banner for the peoples; the nations will rally to him...' Jeremiah 23:5-6 picks up a similar theme providing still further background for what John hears from the elder: '"The days are coming," declares the LORD, "when I will raise up to David a righteous Branch, a King who will reign wisely and do what is just and right in the land. In his days Judah will be saved and Israel will live in safety."' But strangely and of great significance, the title implies that the Messiah who comes *after* David was in fact David's *root* and thus was also *before* him. As P. E. Hughes reminds us, 'this is a pointer to his [Christ's] pre-existence as the eternal Son of God.'[33]

These two great and magnificent titles pull together themes from the Old Testament showing how God's promises to his people all come to focus in the person of Jesus Christ. They specially emphasise the Messiah's conquering rule over the world, and point to his role as the deliverer of his people. Thus, he alone is the one who can open and put into effect the redemptive plan of God found in the scroll.

iii) Christ is the Lamb

> Then I saw a Lamb, looking as if it had been slain, standing in the centre of the throne, encircled by the four living creatures and the elders. He had seven horns and seven eyes, which are the seven spirits of God sent out into all the earth. He came and took the scroll from the right hand of him who sat on the throne (5:6-7).

As John looks up to see what the elder is referring to, he says he **saw a Lamb, looking as if it had been slain.**[34] The one who has the right to open the scroll because he has conquered and is the messianic King is now seen, but he appears not as 'Lord of lords' but as a slain lamb. Again John draws pictures from the Old Testament. Two backgrounds are probably in mind. The first draws upon Isaiah's prophecy in chapter 53 that talks of God's servant who is to come. In verse 7 he says: 'He was oppressed and afflicted, yet he did not open his mouth; he was led like a lamb to the slaughter, and as a sheep before her shearers is silent, so he did not open his mouth.' The picture of a lamb is deliberately pointing to sacrificial imagery and thus recalls also the Passover lamb of Exodus 12 where the lamb is sacrificed so that the people are protected from the destroying angel. Paul had spoken of how Christ's death on the cross was a fulfilment of the Passover when he wrote in 1 Corinthians 5:7: 'Christ, our Passover lamb, has been sacrificed.'

The picture we immediately recognise as Christians, therefore, is of Jesus who died on the cross giving his life like a sacrificial lamb and so achieving our forgiveness and salvation. He took our sin upon himself so that we could be redeemed. He did so by becoming a sacrificial lamb and taking our sin upon himself. Now this Jesus who died for us is seen **standing in the centre of the throne.**

Christ is now the focus of attention, though his precise location is not that important. First, we see that he is alive, the slain lamb clearly lives. Secondly, he is 'in the midst of ' or very close to the throne where he is to be enthroned. Third, as ruler and king, he has those who are in attendance upon him, namely, the **four living creatures and the elders.** But the picture is not yet complete for the lamb also has **seven horns and seven eyes, which are the seven spirits of God sent out into all the earth.** Horns were a symbol of strength and power and the repetition of **seven** here is again symbolic of completeness and perfection. The seven eyes (drawing on imagery from Zechariah 3–5) are a picture of Jesus' sovereign power and knowledge that extends everywhere,[35] and which specially seeks to protect his people. As we saw in 1:4 the **seven spirits** stand for the perfection of God's Holy Spirit who is the Spirit of Christ (see Romans 8:9; 1 Peter 1:11) and who reveals the purposes of God to us and applies the work of Christ's salvation to us. Given the way the picture links the seven spirits to the slain lamb, it is likely that the reference to them being **sent out into all the earth** is an allusion to the Day of Pentecost when the Spirit came upon the disciples and empowered them to take the gospel to the whole world (Acts 1:8; 2:32-33). This incorporation of the whole earth under the sound of the gospel of the Lamb slain for sins is amplified in verse 9.

The vision so far

The complex imagery should not make us feel we cannot understand what John sees. In fact, once we put together the pictures drawn from a variety of Old Testament verses, it all becomes surprisingly clear. We can summarise it in this way. John has been shown one person who has the authority to open the scroll and implement the purposes of God for this world. He is the Messiah, Jesus Christ, who is full of power and authority, having conquered sin (verse 5). But as John looks, he sees there is more to this Jesus, and what he sees points to the way in which Jesus actually did triumph over sin and death. He did this through his sacrificial death on the cross (led like a lamb to the slaughter). However, what is amazing is that this lamb, with all the marks of his death upon him, is in fact standing and has the great figures of heaven in attendance. Indeed, as John looks closer, he sees that the lamb has horns indicating his strength and power, and his eyes are looking everywhere as his Spirit searches out his people, saving them and protecting them. The vision is, in other words, a summary of the core gospel message. Jesus is Saviour and Lord: he died to save his people but was raised from the dead to be exalted on high. Thus, he alone has the right to take the scroll from God the Father.

In the context of the seven churches and the churches as we know them today, John's vision reminds us of the gospel in which we trust, and it further serves as a guarantee of its truth for it is the Spirit himself who reveals all this to John for the sake of the churches.

4. Christ takes the scroll

> And when he had taken it, the four living creatures and the twenty-four elders fell down before the Lamb. Each one had a harp and they were holding golden bowls full of incense, which are the prayers of the saints. And they sang a new song: 'You are worthy to take the scroll and to open its seals, because you were slain, and with your blood you purchased men for God from every tribe and language and people and nation. You have made them to be a kingdom and priests to serve our God, and they will reign on the earth' (5:8-10).

In a picture that recalls Daniel's prophecy in Daniel 7:9-14,[36] it is Jesus, the Lamb, who thus approaches the throne and takes the scroll. The link between the Lamb and Daniel's 'son of man' who approaches the throne, further emphasises that this Lamb is the ruler. He has the authority to take the commission from the Father to implement his plan for the world – the plan found in the words of the scroll. As he does so, all in heaven fall down and worship him.

5. Christ is worshipped

As they worship in song, using their harps to accompany the music, they bring to God **the prayers of the saints** which are represented by **bowls full of incense**.

i) The prayers of the saints

These prayers are not the prayers of some very special 'saints', in the sense that they are somehow more special than other Christians (as, for example, we might talk of *Saint* Paul), but rather they are the prayers of all God's people. The picture recalls the ritual of the Tabernacle where 'fragrant incense' was to burn morning and evening. Psalm 141:2 also helps us understand what is going on here: 'May my prayer be set before you like incense; may the lifting up of my hands be like the evening sacrifice.' In that passage King David's prayer is that God should deal with evildoers (141:5). That is precisely what these prayers of the **saints** are here. They are prayers from all God's people, both those who have already died for the faith, and those who are suffering. The prayer becomes explicit in 6:10: 'How long, Sovereign Lord, holy and true, until you judge the inhabitants of the earth and avenge our blood?' (see also 8:3-5). To put it another way, it is the same prayer that we pray as we say, 'Your kingdom come, your will be done on earth as it is in heaven'.[37] Here is the heart-felt prayer of all God's people who long to see an end to suffering and persecution and the coming of the new heavens and the new earth. John's vision will take us right through to that wonderful future when our prayers will be answered with Christ's return in glory. But for now we pray, and our prayers come right into the throne room of the Father.

ii) The new song

A **new song** is now being sung while these prayers are presented. It is a 'new' song because it is the song sung to Christ in praise of the redemption he has achieved through his death (**blood**). The song again reminds us that he is **worthy** because he has **purchased men for God**. Just as God the Creator is **worthy** to receive praise and glory for his work of creation in 4:11, so Jesus is **worthy** to receive praise for his redeeming work which will eventually lead to a 'new creation' (21:1-5). The 'new song' thus fits the new work which Jesus has done and is doing, and it is a song with which the church should join. How much we should enjoy singing praises to our Lord Jesus Christ! He has died for our salvation, and has called us to himself, and is with us by his Spirit. He alone can bring us into our eternal inheritance of a new heavens and a new earth. He alone (by his Spirit) has enabled us to become a 'new creation' (2 Corinthians 5:17), fitted and suited for the inheritance we await. The churches of Asia Minor faced many problems, but they needed to join in praising their Lord Jesus, the Lamb who was slain and yet who had conquered sin and death.

Christ's work of redemption is universal in that, through his death on the cross, people from **every tribe and language and people and nation** are able to inherit eternal life. No longer are the covenant promises seen only in terms of one people or race, the Jews. Here is the ultimate fulfilment of God's promise to Abraham that through him 'all peoples on earth will be blessed' (Genesis 12:3). The song continues by reminding us that Christ has made these redeemed people **a kingdom and priests to serve our God** (see comments on 1:6). It is interesting to see that we are told Christ has **made them to be....** The implication is that this is the continuation of and climax of creation itself. This is what it has all been driving towards: a people who are there **to serve our God**.

However, more is added: those whom Christ has purchased **will reign on the earth**. Christ's achievement on the cross and as sovereign Lord is rightly described as the *redemption* of his people, recognising the sacrifice of his death and the people's being freed from sin and death. It is also rightly described as *salvation* for his people, since he has saved them from the judgment and death they deserve for their sin. But his work on the cross accomplishes even more, for in his 'triumph' (verse 5) his reign is established. As Jesus reigns, so his people **will reign on the earth.** In one sense, the people of Christ who are already a 'kingdom' and already 'priests' are also already 'reigning'.[38] What is true of their Lord (who already reigns, 1:5) is true of them. Just as the appearance of the Lamb who was slain is not indicative of the reality of his lordship and sovereignty, so the suffering church that looks so weak does not actually portray the heavenly realities – that it shares Christ's rule on earth.

This rule is exercised as Christians speak of Christ, pronounce the gospel of grace and the danger of judgment, and as they pray for their world. Nevertheless, though there is a sense in which the redeemed already rule, there is no doubt that they still await the fulfilment of that great privilege when they will rule with Christ on the **new earth** (21:1).[39]

iii) Thousands upon thousands worship

> Then I looked and heard the voice of many angels, numbering thousands upon thousands, and ten thousand times ten thousand. They encircled the throne and the living creatures and the elders. In a loud voice they sang: 'Worthy is the Lamb, who was slain, to receive power and wealth and wisdom and strength and honour and glory and praise!' Then I heard every creature in heaven and on earth and under the earth and on the sea, and all that is in them, singing: 'To him who sits on the throne and to the Lamb be praise and honour and glory and power, for ever and ever!' The four living creatures said, 'Amen,' and the elders fell down and worshipped (5:11-14).

At this point it is as if the whole of the throne room, indeed the whole of heaven, opens up with the glorious sound of praises to Christ. **Angels** in their tens of thousands encircle **the throne,** joining with **the living creatures and the elders** in praising Jesus. They praise him in his role as the one who is counted **worthy** and who has received authority because of his sacrificial work upon the cross as **the Lamb.** But the praise extends still further as the whole of creation recognises what the Lamb has achieved and will achieve by taking hold of the scroll.

iv) Jesus Christ is worshipped as divine

One of the most interesting aspects of the end of this chapter is the way it helps us recognise Jesus as divine, as God. A quick comparison between 5:9-10 and 12-13 (where praise is directed to Christ) with 4:11 (where praise is directed to God on the throne) provides clear evidence for this. Note the number of words in common and specifically the use of **glory** and **power** and **honour.** We can also see how both the Father and the Lamb are shown to be eternal in their existence in the words **for ever and ever**. Above all, **the elders fell down and worshipped** both the Father and the Lamb (see also 7:10-12).

As we see Christ receiving such praise from **every creature in heaven and on earth**, we are again reminded of the prophet Daniel's vision in which he saw 'one like a son of man' coming before the Father where 'He was given authority, glory and sovereign power; all peoples, nations and men of every language worshipped him. His dominion is an everlasting dominion that will not pass away, and his kingdom is one that will never be destroyed' (Daniel 7:14).

6. Summary

Jesus Christ, the Lamb who died and is now alive, is the one and only person who can 'open the seals' of a scroll that contains God's will for this world. Jesus both reads and puts into action the great purposes of God. We shall see later that these purposes involve the judgment of sin and evil and sinful people, as well as the salvation of all who trust in Christ. It is vital as we read the chapters ahead that we keep in mind that Christ is sovereign and Lord. As we read much about judgment, we are called upon to remember chapters 4 and 5 as the backdrop for all that happens. There is a Lamb upon the throne who has already taken upon himself the judgment of those who trust in him. They are his people and they come from all the nations upon earth. What lies ahead may be disconcerting and may even appal us. Such is the nature of the effects of sin and the judgment that must take place. But what comfort and joy for those who worship the Father on the throne and who worship the Lamb. They are already represented there in the heavenly places and, as we shall see, they will be kept safe until finally they reach the new Jerusalem and the new heavens and the new earth.

For no groups of people are such truths more vital than for the suffering church. Christ is sovereign in spite of appearances as they suffer at the hands of evil people. Evil will be judged by God. Justice will one day be done. The suffering will not be in vain, for just as Christ was *the faithful witness* who 'overcame' by becoming the Lamb who was slain and who rose again, so these Christians will follow their Master and will indeed 'overcome' and will reign with him. The church of this age must keep constantly before it this perspective, relying entirely upon the Lamb who is opening the seals and working out the plan of God for the salvation of his church.

An Introduction to the Visions of Wrath

As has been seen, chapters 4 and 5 have set a framework for the destruction that is going to dominate the visions in chapters 6–20. God has created (chapter 4) and is to be worshipped. Jesus is victorious and has suffered to redeem fallen men and women and so is to be worshipped. Now we see the 'wrath of the Lamb' (6:16).

Three main visions follow:

1. the breaking of the seals;
2. the seven trumpets;
3. the seven bowls of wrath.

Each, in different ways, seems to describe similar things. There is great debate about the precise meaning of aspects of these visions, but it is best to start by reminding ourselves of some basic teaching in the Bible about the time that culminates in the second coming of Jesus. We live in the 'last days', which are the days between Christ's first and second comings. Many parts of the Old and New Testaments indicate that during this period God's people (the elect) will suffer, and the world will see considerable trials and tribulations. Some of those prophecies do not seem to have any particular time in mind within that period, while others possibly indicate that there will be an increase of trials towards the end, perhaps with one period of intense tribulation immediately before the Lord's return.

As we might expect, in the picture we are given here, with the opening of each seal, there is a distinct feeling that we are getting nearer to the final judgment day or second coming. 'Come!' (chapter 6), repeated by each of the four living creatures, is the cry echoed down through the ages by the church pleading for the Lord's return.[40] The four creatures represent the whole of the created order which is involved in this cry of the church (see Romans 8:22-23). The breaking of each seal brings that day closer.

The opening of the seventh seal reveals the book itself in which more details of God's judgment are given through further visions.

The successive disclosures closely parallel the words of Jesus in Mark 13:7-27, where the last days are indicated by the appearance of false Christs, wars, earthquakes, famines, general persecution of Christians, darkening of the sun, stars falling and the shaking of powers in heaven, and the coming of Christ.

Revelation 6

A Scroll with Seven Seals

It is now time to join John and watch as the Lamb opens the seven seals of the scroll. As Christ opens the scroll, we discover that heavenly evil forces are released upon the earth. This helps explain the experiences of the seven churches as they suffer and are persecuted and even die for their faith. The work of these evil forces therefore brings punishment on some but also works to refine the faith and works of those who belong to Christ. In an amazing way, what is now revealed demonstrates that Christ is already sovereign King over all. If people have been asking whether he is really sovereign as they are persecuted for their faith or whether he had any control over such devastating earthquakes as some of them had recently experienced, the answer is 'yes'. The need for God's people now is to understand how it is that Christ is in control, and what is going on through all the troubles and uncertainties and difficulties of life.

> I watched as the Lamb opened the first of the seven seals. Then I heard one of the four living creatures say in a voice like thunder, 'Come!' (6:1).

Christ now opens the first of the seals and one of the **living creatures** summons forth a rider. The summons **in a voice like thunder** indicates that he speaks for the one on the throne. What is about to happen, however terrifying, is indeed under the control and will of God.

> I looked, and there before me was a white horse! Its rider held a bow, and he was given a crown, and he rode out as a conqueror bent on conquest. When the Lamb opened the second seal, I heard the second living creature say, 'Come!' Then another horse came out, a fiery red one. Its rider was given power to take peace from the earth and to make men slay each other. To him was given a large sword. When the Lamb

opened the third seal, I heard the third living creature say, 'Come!' I looked, and there before me was a black horse! Its rider was holding a pair of scales in his hand. Then I heard what sounded like a voice among the four living creatures, saying, 'A quart of wheat for a day's wages, and three quarts of barley for a day's wages, and do not damage the oil and the wine!' When the Lamb opened the fourth seal, I heard the voice of the fourth living creature say, 'Come!' I looked, and there before me was a pale horse! Its rider was named Death, and Hades was following close behind him. They were given power over a fourth of the earth to kill by sword, famine and plague, and by the wild beasts of the earth (6:2-8).

1. The first seal
The first seal is broken to reveal a **white horse**, and a **rider** with a **bow**. He wears a crown which **he was given**. He rides out as one **bent on conquest**. Because of the reference to a 'white horse' and to his 'crown', some have thought this refers to Christ. Certainly in 19:11 we see Christ riding a white horse. But here the rider cannot really be Jesus. He is, after all, the one opening the scroll. In fact, the horsemen bring evil. They remove peace and cause wars, famines and ultimately death. Here, then, is a false Christ who is determined to conquer. Following Mark 13, where Jesus lists false Christs as the first of the trials to appear for believers (13:6), followed by wars (13:7), it would appear that here we have a false Christ or antichrist. This explains the similarity between this rider and Christ in chapter 19. **He was given** his power by God and God controls what he will be able to perform and what he will not be able to do. Ultimately, of course, God will never allow him to conquer.

The four horsemen
The background to this description of the four horsemen riding on different coloured horses is to be found in Zechariah 1:8-17 and 6:1-8. The horsemen are used as God's instruments to bring judgment on his people's enemies. The colours (Zechariah 6:6) stand for the four points of the compass, and it is likely that the same idea is present in Revelation 6 where the whole earth is subject to the horror inflicted by the riders. The first rider may

be something of a summary of the three which follow. Since he holds a **bow**, we understand he will fight with arrows. In Deuteronomy 32:23-25 we read of the arrows of God's judgment thus: 'I will heap calamities upon them and expend my arrows against them. I will send wasting famine against them, consuming pestilence and deadly plague ...'

It is worth noting that the horsemen bring all these things upon this world. As these horsemen ride out, so Satan and his forces bring suffering and trials to God's people in an attempt to break them and 'conquer' them. We have already seen that the seven churches are urged to 'overcome'. It is precisely against this attack, which Satan and his horsemen will throw at them, that they are to 'overcome'. It is an indication of God's sovereignty, even over these horrific events, that ultimately Satan's work proves to be judgment and punishment on unbelievers and yet a refining and strengthening of faith for those who trust in Christ.

2. The second seal

Another living creature summons forth this rider on a **fiery red horse**. This rider **was given power** to cause wars and destroy peace among the nations. We are reminded of Christ's second warning in Mark 13:7 of events that will happen. For those in the seven churches, and to us of the church on earth, here is a vivid reminder that God's people may indeed have to endure to death (2:10), but they should not take this as a sign that somehow God is no longer in control. Throughout these last days, what God's people need to see is that God's purposes include even an 'interim' judgment on those who rebel against him, and God's people get caught up in all this; but for them, victory and true conquest lies ahead.[41] The judgment talked of here, therefore, precedes the final judgment which has yet to come.

3. The third seal

The next rider comes forth on a **black horse** (verse 5). This rider brings economic hardship to the world. With **a pair of**

scales in his hand, he will not measure out proper amounts of food to the world. (**A quart of wheat for a day's wages** indicates how tough life will be.) Famine will be part of what happens. This too is being experienced by some of the seven churches (2:9), and so they need to be comforted by the fact that even these events are under the divine Sovereign. Later, in 13:16-17, famine is specifically aimed as a persecution of Christians, because only those marked by the evil one will be allowed to buy food. It is good to remember that on the last day, at Christ's second coming, Christians will find that 'never again will they hunger; never again will they thirst' (7:16). However, the limitations upon the evil works of this rider are clearly seen. Although life will be severe, barley will still be available, though most won't be able to afford very much of it at all, and wine and oil will continue to be available.

4. The fourth seal

The fourth rider comes forth on a **pale horse**[42] (verse 8). This one is given the name **Death**, and **Hades**, the place where the dead are kept, is said to follow him. Very often these words go together as we have seen in 1:18 and will see again in 20:13, 14. The rider brings death by sword, famine, plague and by wild beasts, as he passes through the world. Few other forms of death can be imagined and this is probably acting as a summary of the evil done by the riders who have been sent out. Once again it is ironic, though, to see that such evil powers find they are limited and end up working to the orders of the God against whom they are striving. **They were given power over a fourth of the earth** indicates that God both gives that power and limits it. In fact, what we see here is precisely an exercise of the sovereign power that has been given to Jesus and has been described in 1:18: 'I am the Living One; I was dead, and behold I am alive for ever and ever! And I hold the keys of Death and Hades.'

In Ezekiel 14:21, God tells Ezekiel that he will send these same four forms of death in judgment upon idolatrous peoples, but also insists that the righteous will be saved in the end. Here John receives the same message and draws upon Ezekiel for help in describing what he sees.

5. The fifth seal

> When he opened the fifth seal, I saw under the altar the souls of those who had been slain because of the word of God and the testimony they had maintained. They called out in a loud voice, 'How long, Sovereign Lord, holy and true, until you judge the inhabitants of the earth and avenge our blood?' Then each of them was given a white robe, and they were told to wait a little longer, until the number of their fellow servants and brothers who were to be killed as they had been was completed (6:9-11).

With the fifth seal the scene changes somewhat. The first part of the revealing of God's purposes, the first four seals, has shown his judgment, but now we learn a little of God's purposes for believers who have died and are yet to die under these judgments. What is to become of them? The evil that has been released upon earth has led to Christians dying for their faith: **because of the word of God and the testimony they had maintained**. We are reminded of those who have been addressed in chapters 2–3 (particularly in 2:9-11, and 2:13 where we hear that Antipas had died). The fifth seal thus brings an explanation to those of John's day, as well as to the generations that follow, who will suffer death for their trust in Christ.

In our own day and age we may well think of those who have died under Islamic persecution in northern Nigeria, the Sudan or parts of Indonesia. We are asked to join John in this vision and to see their souls **under the altar**, in other words, they are under the protection of the Lamb who was sacrificed. In heaven they are kept and protected by Christ himself. And yet they cry out with the same call that has been the cry of God's people in both the Old and New Testaments. It is the cry in Isaiah 6:11 and Zechariah 1:12: **How long, Sovereign Lord...?**[43] It is alright to have some understanding of what God is doing in judging the world and ordering evil to carry out judgment on *unbelievers*. But the *saints* are caught up in this. They are suffering and dying for their faith. Even in heaven and under Christ's protection, though the martyrs understand something of what is going on, still they ask, **How long?**

Their concern is twofold. First, they are concerned for those who will continue to suffer. Will this go on for long? How many more Christians will have to die, whether under the plagues, famines, war or directly under persecution? In other words, they want to know how much longer this age will continue, and when the new age with no more wars or rumours of wars will begin.

They are also concerned for God and his honour. **How long ... until you judge...?** When will God's justice be clearly seen? When will evil be finally destroyed? How long will God ask evil forces like these four riders to do his work for him? When will he destroy them as well? The believers know from God's word that all judgment and vengeance on the enemies of God must be left in God's hands. They know that 'it is God alone who avenges himself and his people' (Psalm 94:1). They know 'it is he who takes vengeance' (Isaiah 61:2). They know what the apostle Paul wrote: 'Do not take revenge, my friends, but leave room for God's wrath, for it is written: "It is mine to avenge; I will repay," says the Lord' (Romans 12:19). They have left it in God's hands, but when will the day come when he will vindicate his name?

These are questions that all Christians ask at some time in their lives. Perhaps it is as a result of particular sadnesses and deaths in our own family or perhaps because we have heard of yet another Christian dying for his faith, and so we are caused to ask again for the very thing for which we so long: 'Lord, how long until Christ returns and all this suffering and evil is dealt with once and for all?'

The answer is that **they were told to wait (rest) a little longer**. Meanwhile each is given the reward of a **white robe**,[44] thus confirming their worthiness and purity in the presence of God. The reason for this delay is now given: **until the number of their fellow servants and brothers who were to be killed**

as they had been was completed. God's purposes are not yet fulfilled. More will yet have to die or suffer the hardships of this world in which the four horsemen are on the loose, before finally the end will come. This delay is talked of from another perspective in 2 Peter 3:9. Here we see that it is also a time in which God's grace remains available to those who will repent: 'The Lord is not slow in keeping his promise, as some understand slowness. He is patient with you, not wanting anyone to perish, but everyone to come to repentance.'

6. The sixth seal
The sixth seal brings us back to the stark age under the influence of the four horsemen.

> I watched as he opened the sixth seal. There was a great earthquake. The sun turned black like sackcloth made of goat hair, the whole moon turned blood red, and the stars in the sky fell to earth, as late figs drop from a fig tree when shaken by a strong wind. The sky receded like a scroll, rolling up, and every mountain and island was removed from its place. Then the kings of the earth, the princes, the generals, the rich, the mighty, and every slave and every free man hid in caves and among the rocks of the mountains. They called to the mountains and the rocks, 'Fall on us and hide us from the face of him who sits on the throne and from the wrath of the Lamb! For the great day of their wrath has come, and who can stand?' (6:12-17).

Here we are reminded again of the language that Jesus himself used in Mark 13:7, 8 and 24. Here, as Christ continues to open the scroll of God's will and purposes, we look forward to the answer the question 'How long?', and to the time when the Lord's name will be vindicated and those who have caused such pain to God's people and who have remained unrepentant (see 9:20) are dealt with by God. This is the time of the great judgment. A great shaking and destroying of all that is evil will take place. Evil will fall as buildings fall in an **earthquake**. **Stars** fall from the sky like **figs** dropping from trees in a **strong wind**. The **black** of the covered sun points to the final withdrawing of God's light from the realm of Satan and those who follow him, while the **blood red** of the moon points to the blood of their judgment. Everything in the natural order as we know it will be affected, even those things that have seemed so stable and seemed to go on for ever, like mountains and islands.

So frightening will this time be that even the **kings of the earth** and the **mighty**, along with everyone else, will seek to hide. They will flee to **mountains** and hide, no doubt in caves. They will plead for it all to come to an end. But they will be aware that this is not just some further natural disaster, for they recognise that they are now facing the very thing they never believed in: **the wrath of the Lamb**. So just and righteous is God's judgment that no distinction is made among different types of people. Whether **kings** or **generals**, whether **rich** or **slave**, all will experience this judgment. It is indeed a frightening and terrible thing to fall into the hands of an angry God! **For the great day of their wrath has come, and who can stand?**

The descriptions of these great cataclysmic events are probably figurative. Elsewhere in the Bible similar picture language is used of the destruction of nations.[45] But the fact that many descriptions in this book are figurative does not in any sense diminish their horror or reduce their seriousness. In fact the reverse is true. Figurative language is used to describe the worst scene we can imagine. The actual fact of God's judgment will be even worse, for we really cannot imagine properly, whatever pictures we use, just how terrible will be that day. No wonder the section ends with the question, **who can stand?** The question is vital. Is there actually anyone who can stand before the mighty wrath of God as he judges?

The sixth seal has pointed ahead. We are invited to look beyond this age, in which we cry out 'How long?', to the time when Christ finally comes to judge. For those who read this passage, and are believers, here is what we await. We shall see an end to the suffering of this world, whether as a result of earthquakes such as those the churches in Asia Minor had experienced, or at the hands of persecutors. The church throughout the ages is not being asked to wait for ever. The

99

Lord in whom she trusts is guarding her at present, limiting the work of these Satanic forces, but he will one day redeem her and avenge his name and the name of his people. But will even the church **stand** in the face of God himself?

7. The 'wrath' of God

It is important to note that the Bible talks of the 'wrath' or the 'anger' of God on a number of occasions. In the common usage of English, 'anger' and 'wrath' are generally rather arbitrary human emotions that we consider to be sinful. This is what they are with us. When used of God, however, they are never arbitrary. Nor, in fact, are they emotions in the sense that we think of them. Rather they describe part of the perfect justice of God which will always seek out and ultimately destroy evil. Here is a perfect and righteous judicial 'anger'. Though there is no clear parallel in modern society, the closest we might approach the idea would be to say that when a just verdict has been rendered on a criminal in our court system, the punishment reflects the judicial 'anger' of the legal system.

Special lessons for today

It is one of the most difficult problems of our age, just as it must have been for the seven churches, that Christ seems to delay in his return. Our cry too is, ' How long, O Lord?' Whether it is because we see the evil being unleashed on the world that leads to people being hurt in war or through ethnic tensions, or the horror of illness and people around us dying of painful diseases, or the persecuted church and those who give their lives for the faith, the question remains a problem for us all. We long to see Christ return. This passage, however, helps us understand that, in spite of appearances, Christ is sovereign Lord and does control the seals. He works out the will and purposes of the Father on the throne. Even the evil around us works for God to bring judgment on unbelievers. The effect of such evil on believers, however, will be to refine them and help them grow to be more Christ-like, for Christ himself also suffered at the hands of evil. That evil too was at the command of God and, in spite of the fact that the cross seemed to be the place of Satan's victory, it was actually precisely there that God's victory was won and most clearly seen. This is the route we have to follow and it is the path of Christ. It doesn't sit easily with the 'comfort religion' being pedalled by so many who claim to be gospel people. It doesn't sit easily with those who would claim that God is not really fully sovereign in all things, but it is the great message of hope and encouragement that Jesus brings to his churches and that he brings to us.

Much of today's church is, sadly, not asking, 'How long?' Much of the church in today's world is sitting far too comfortably, often blissfully unaware that other parts of the church are suffering for the faith. There is a call in these chapters for every church to see itself as living in the last days. If we are content and happy and see no real need to ask the Lord to come soon, then we are ignoring other parts of the body of Christ. If we fail to recognise that parts of the church, even at the start of the twenty-first century, are fiercely persecuted, suffer famine or economic hardship, or are caught up in war, then we have failed to recognise the truth of Scripture that, when one part of the body suffers, all suffer (1 Corinthians 12:26). These are pointers that we are indeed in the last days, just as they were pointers for the seven churches. Perhaps things will yet get worse for us, but the coming of the Lord will be like a 'thief in the night'. Are we prepared?

Excursus: Can God really be the ultimate master of the evil perpetrated by the four horsemen?

If the four horsemen are, as the passage suggests, emissaries for Satan and for evil, and if they are summoned forth with the word 'Come!' at God's own command, then we are right to ask how God, who is 'holy' in his perfection and separation from all that is evil, can seemingly be so involved with evil.

First, we must recognise that this question actually arises in other places in Scripture as well. As we have shown, what is being asked of us is little different from what Christ himself went through. Satan was so under God's ultimate control that God was able to bring salvation to men and women around the world as he over-ruled that work for his eternal and good purposes and to his great glory.

Secondly, this passage is not suggesting that God is the author of evil itself. God does not create sin and evil. But because he is completely sovereign, God can use even evil for his ends, apparently without the understanding of Satan and his minions that that is in fact what God is doing!

Thirdly, in his great justice, God is, within very carefully defined limitations, commanding the evil angelic forces to carry on with what they most want to do, to seek to uproot and destabilise the faith of believers. This, however, is not what God intends as he commands them to go forth and do their work. From the same events in which they seek to destabilise faith and overthrow God's people, God intends to bring glory to his name. At the same time, it is God's intention to bring ruin to those who follow Satan and to bring rewards and a refined faith to those who do believe. As Christians are attacked in this way and yet remain under the protection of their Lord, they will suffer, they will die in persecutions and natural catastrophes like earthquakes, but God will see to it that they come through to eternal life with him, and that they are rewarded with the white robes of the righteous and that they will walk with God himself.

Perhaps one of the most interesting incidents in the Bible where this over-arching sovereignty of God, even over evil, is most clearly stated is the story of Joseph. Joseph's brothers sold him into slavery in Egypt. Their intention was utterly evil. Joseph rose to power in Egypt and later saved his father and brothers from starvation. When his father Jacob eventually died, the brothers were afraid that Joseph would now take his revenge on them. But Joseph responded in Genesis 50:19-20: 'Don't be afraid. Am I in the place of God? You intended to harm me, but God intended it for good to accomplish what is now being done, the saving of many lives.' Surely we are obliged to say that God took the evil that the brothers were wanting to do to Joseph and used it for his own ends of saving his people from starvation.

This is the wonder of God. It is not that he is the source of evil or our evil actions or thoughts but that, in his most extraordinary sovereign power and his great grace and love towards his people, he will even use that evil to our eternal good. This is the way we saw him work with the cross. The result was salvation and mercy for people of all nations. This is how we must understand him working as we live in today's world and sometimes fail to understand what is going on, and as we plead with him, 'How long, O Lord, how long?'[46]

Revelation 7

The Servants of God are Sealed

Now we await the opening of the seventh and final seal and the completion of God's purposes. But the question of 6:17 must first be answered, **who can stand?**

1. God's protection of his people
The answer appears in verse 3. The ones who stand will be those who are sealed. And so in chapter 7 we have a pause in the opening of the seals. It is a pause in which we learn more about how those mentioned as the fifth seal was opened (6:9-11) are to be preserved. There will indeed be people from all nations **standing before the throne and in front of the Lamb** (7:9).

> After this I saw four angels standing at the four corners of the earth, holding back the four winds of the earth to prevent any wind from blowing on the land or on the sea or on any tree. Then I saw another angel coming up from the east, having the seal of the living God. He called out in a loud voice to the four angels who had been given power to harm the land and the sea: 'Do not harm the land or the sea or the trees until we put a seal on the foreheads of the servants of our God' (7:1-3).

The next thing (**after this**) John sees is four angels and their duty, as we are immediately told, is to hold back the evil being poured out in the world while **a seal** is put **on the foreheads of the servants of our God.**

i) The figure 'four'
The figure four is a symbol for the whole world or for universality. It probably originally comes from the phrase used here: **the four corners of the earth.** We often refer to the *four* points of the compass: north, south, east and west.

ii) Angels and winds

These **four angels** who watch over the whole earth (its **four corners**) are **holding back the four winds.** These winds are the same figures as the evil riders that we have learned about in chapter 6. Zechariah 6:1-8, which has provided much of the background for John's description of what he sees, helps us understand this.[47] There the four horsemen are described in verses 5-6 as 'the four spirits (winds) of heaven, going out from standing in the presence of the Lord of the whole world. The one with the black horses is going towards the north country, the one with the white horses towards the west, and the one with the dappled horses towards the south....' Soon John discovers the reason for the work of these angels.

Therefore what John is witnessing in this vision is, as it were, a step back in time 'to a point before the release of the four horsemen or winds, when they were still being held under restraint until the **servants** of God should be sealed'.[48] The successive opening of the scroll has revealed God's judgment as it takes place in this world even in this age, the age of the seven churches and the age in which we live. But frequently we have read of how God will preserve his people, his churches, through this time. Now we see how this preservation takes place. Another **angel** brings a command from God to the four angels: **Do not harm the land or the sea or the trees until...** These four angels are not themselves evil, but have the power to **harm the land** in the sense that they can release the four winds on God's command. We have already seen at some length in chapter 6 how it is that God himself releases the four riders to carry out their evil purposes. So the winds, the riders, are restrained by God's angels. And thus believers are sealed by God.

iii) The seal of the living God

The idea of sealing God's people for their protection reminds us of the Passover and its sacrifice, when blood was placed on the doorways of the houses of the Israelites so that the oldest son would not die as the destroying angel passed over (see

Exodus 12). We read in Exodus 12:13: 'The blood will be a sign for you on the houses where you are; and when I see the blood, I will pass over you. No destructive plague will touch you when I strike Egypt.' God's people were protected with a seal made in blood as God sent an evil angel of judgment upon the Egyptians. Now, once again **the servants of God** must be sealed with **a seal on the foreheads** for their protection against this judgment. They are not taken out of the scene to some secure place, any more than the oldest sons of the Israelite families were taken away on the Passover night. Rather they remain on the scene and in the midst of the horror, but they are protected spiritually by God with his own special seal.[49]

In ancient times slaves would have been marked as a sign of being owned by a particular household. This is the idea here. These people are 'owned' by God and so given his seal as his **servants** or 'slaves'. The same idea is picked up in 14:1: 'Then I looked, and there before me was the Lamb, standing on Mount Zion, and with him 144,000 who had his name and his Father's name written on their foreheads.'[50] They belong to God and have the name of the Father and the Lamb placed on them as a seal.

iv) The seal and the Holy Spirit
Elsewhere in the New Testament we learn that this seal is specifically to be equated with the gift of the Holy Spirit who comes upon all believers. As the Spirit of God and the Spirit of Christ, he brings the name of the Father and of the Lamb to God's people. In 2 Corinthians 1:21-22 Paul writes this: 'Now it is God who makes both us and you stand firm in Christ. He anointed us, set his seal of ownership on us, and put his Spirit in our hearts as a deposit, guaranteeing what is to come.' In Ephesians 1:13-14 we read of this sealing again: 'Having believed, you were marked in him with a seal, the promised Holy Spirit, who is a deposit guaranteeing our inheritance until the redemption of those who are God's possession...' And finally in Ephesians 4:30: 'Do not grieve the Holy Spirit of

God, with whom you were sealed for the day of redemption.'

The Holy Spirit, who is God with us, is indeed the **seal** of the living God. As the riders, the trumpets and bowls of God's anger are successively revealed in this book, we are asked to remember that, through it all, God's people are preserved spiritually right now and even through the final judgment day until the full inheritance is received in the presence of God's glory. But before the vision reminds us of that great future of glory that belongs to God's people, John learns who is being sealed.

v) The 144,000

> Then I heard the number of those who were sealed: 144,000 from all the tribes of Israel. From the tribe of Judah 12,000 were sealed, from the tribe of Reuben 12,000, from the tribe of Gad 12,000, from the tribe of Asher 12,000, from the tribe of Naphtali 12,000, from the tribe of Manasseh 12,000, from the tribe of Simeon 12,000, from the tribe of Levi 12,000, from the tribe of Issachar 12,000, from the tribe of Zebulun 12,000, from the tribe of Joseph 12,000, from the tribe of Benjamin 12,000 (7:4-8).

The 144,000 that John now hears about are **those who were sealed**. Their precise identity has provoked considerable discussion. Some suggest that they represent the remnant of physical Israel, that is, faithful Jews. However, to this point all that we have read has concerned the seven churches and the church generally. It thus seems more likely that the 144,000 represent the church. For the New Testament writers, the concept of a distinction between Jew and Gentile had been challenged. All people who are faithful to Christ, whether Jew or Gentile, are one in Christ and are God's people. The promises once thought by some to apply only to physical Israel have been shown to apply to all Christians. A 'real' Jew is one 'inwardly', said Paul in Romans 2:28-29. He called the church 'the Israel of God' in Galatians 6:16. But in Revelation 2:9 we have learned the same truth: 'I know the slander of those who say they are

Jews and are not, but are a synagogue of Satan.'[51] It is Christians who are now called by the old Jewish term: a kingdom of priests (1:6; 5:10).

The figure of 144,000 is symbolic of completeness.[52] It is 12x12x1000. The figure of 1000 seems to confirm this aspect of completeness, while the figure of 12x12 is probably drawn from the twelve tribes of Israel, mentioned here, combined with the twelve apostles. In chapter 21 the figure twelve is repeated many times in the description of the new Jerusalem. There, twelve gates have the names of the twelve tribes inscribed upon them and the wall has twelve foundations, each with the name of an apostle inscribed on it.

It is interesting to note that the tribe of Judah is mentioned first, though this is rarely true elsewhere. This is probably to remind us that it was through Judah that the promises of the Messiah are realised. The original prophecy in Genesis 49:10 also points to the inclusion of people of all nations, thus reaffirming our view that here the mention of the tribes of Israel must be seen as including all who belong to Christ and excluding both Jew and Gentile who do not belong to him.

Thus, in this first part of chapter 7, John's vision takes us back to answer how God's people are protected as judgment is about to be released in the opening of the scroll. This will happen as God's people are sealed by the Holy Spirit. The number who are sealed is 'complete'. In other words, everyone who will be saved and who will persevere through the trials and tribulations of this age is protected by God. Not a single one can be harmed spiritually. What amazing comfort this must have been for those suffering already within the seven churches! But how much comfort, as well, is brought by this passage to each of us who profess faith in Christ but are worried and disturbed by all the evil going on around us in this world. God has sealed us and, even if we may have to suffer to the point of death, our reward is certain for we belong to the Father and are 'owned' by him. John turns now to see the future and the reward that awaits those who are 'sealed'.

2. The heavenly reward

The picture that John now sees is nothing short of amazing. The remnant of people who belong to God and have been sealed by him and eventually stand before him is not some small number, but an enormous throng from across the world.

> After this I looked and there before me was a great multitude that no one could count, from every nation, tribe, people and language, standing before the throne and in front of the Lamb. They were wearing white robes and were holding palm branches in their hands. And they cried out in a loud voice: 'Salvation belongs to our God, who sits on the throne, and to the Lamb.' All the angels were standing around the throne and around the elders and the four living creatures. They fell down on their faces before the throne and worshipped God, saying: 'Amen! Praise and glory and wisdom and thanks and honour and power and strength be to our God for ever and ever. Amen!' (7:9-12)

i) How many will share in this salvation?[53]

If by the end of the opening of the sixth seal, we have begun to ask **who can stand?** (6:17), it is because the wrath of God seems so severe as it is poured out on this earth that perhaps no one will survive. But there has been a pause in the visions during which we have been shown that God himself has sealed his servants, his faithful people, and they are the ones who will survive. But this can still raise questions. Are many likely to be saved by God? Perhaps some thought it would be only the very righteous and most spiritual of people who would be saved. But we have seen that in fact, in God's infinite wisdom and grace, the complete number of his people will persevere. Lest Christians are tempted to think that they are such a small minority in this evil world, that the final number will be just a small remnant, we are now shown the throne room in the future, after it is all over. And there John sees **a great multitude that no one could count**. More than that, if some had been tempted by the teachings of the 'synagogue of Satan' (3:9), they may have wondered deep down whether perhaps it would be necessary to be a Jew in order to be saved. John sees people **from every nation, tribe, people and language** and they are indeed **standing** before the throne and **the Lamb**.

As we look forward in John's vision, we see those in **white robes** (see comments on 3:4). In effect, we see those from Sardis (3:4) who have remained faithful. We see those from Laodicea who have repented and turned back to Jesus (3:18). And we see hordes of God's people from many different ages standing there in the throne room praising God for his **salvation**. God's angels are there and all the other figures we have seen before: the **elders** representing all of redeemed humanity, the **four living creatures** representing the whole of the created order. The praise that they offer to God is the same as that being offered in 4:9, 11 and 5:12.

However, lest there be any remaining doubt about the identity of the 144,000 who are dressed in white robes, one of the **elders** raises the question in order to offer an answer.

ii) Who are they?

Then one of the elders asked me, 'These in white robes – who are they, and where did they come from?' I answered, 'Sir, you know.' And he said, 'These are they who have come out of the great tribulation; they have washed their robes and made them white in the blood of the Lamb' (7:13-14).

John listens to the elder to hear the answer to his unvoiced question. The elder then tells him that these in **white robes** are **they who have come out of the great tribulation**. The reference here to **the great tribulation** has caused a number of problems in defining who these people are. Some have suggested that these are the final number of martyrs anticipated by the opening of the fifth seal (6:9-11). The great tribulation, it is said, is a period of particular persecution that breaks out just before the coming of Christ (see on 3:10; Daniel 12:1). This is possible, and yet, as we have worked through the passage thus far, it seems rather unlikely, for the vision has pointed to something much more general. These are surely the company of all believers, for all believers, as we have just seen, have been sealed. By definition, believers are those who **have washed their robes and made them white in the blood of the Lamb**. In other words, they are the ones who have turned to Christ and trusted in him and his sacrifice for their forgiveness, righteousness and salvation. This is the company of which we, too, are part. We actually catch a glimpse here of ourselves in the future. We will be in that company if we trust in Christ.

Once again, then, this text provides immediate comfort for those in the seven churches who are or will be going through serious trials and tribulations. Their reward is guaranteed by the seal that has been placed upon them. As the apostle Paul put it:

> Who shall separate us from the love of Christ? Shall trouble or hardship or persecution or famine or nakedness or danger or sword?... No, in all these things we are more than conquerors through him who loved us (Romans 8:35, 37).[54]

iii) The reward that awaits them all

We now hear a description of the wonderful peace and eternal reward that is enjoyed by those who are the Lord's people, once they have come through the tribulation they face in this life:

> 'Therefore, they are before the throne of God and serve him day and night in his temple; and he who sits on the throne will spread his tent over them. Never again will they hunger; never again will they thirst. The sun will not beat upon them, nor any scorching heat. For the Lamb at the centre of the throne will be their shepherd; he will lead them to springs of living water. And God will wipe away every tear from their eyes' (7:15-17).

Each part of this description of glory in which believers rejoice has a background in the Old Testament. Here is the ultimate destiny of God's suffering people, to be with God and with the Lamb for ever. Here, too, we see people experiencing what has been promised in various places to the seven churches. Here is a shortened description of what is described in more detail in chapters 21 and 22.

a) Before the throne

We have already seen the vision of God on the throne in chapter 4. We have seen the Lamb in the midst of the throne in chapter 5. This is the glory that greets the redeemed as finally they are brought right into the presence of the one they have worshipped through many trials and tribulations. As Psalm 103:19 puts it, 'The LORD has established his throne in heaven, and his kingdom rules over all.' Throughout history God's people have worshipped God Almighty, the Creator and Redeemer God who is King from all eternity and for ever.

b) In God's temple

As God revealed himself to his people, so he had them build a tabernacle or 'tent of meeting' (Exodus 36-39) and then, once settled in the Promised Land, he had King Solomon build a temple (2 Chronicles 3–6). These places of worship symbolised the place where God dwells, where he is on his throne. They were placed at the very centre of God's people. Thus the tabernacle was placed at the centre of the tribes who all camped in their set places around it (Numbers 2). The symbolism is clear. God is at the heart and centre of his people's activities and it is to him they must always look and him they must always serve and worship. The temple too was at the heart of God's capital city, Jerusalem. It was in these two buildings that God's glory was specially revealed so that the people would understand the significance of the tabernacle and the temple in their midst. The pillar of cloud and of fire descended on the tabernacle, symbolic of the glory and presence of God himself (Exodus 40:34-38). And the same thing happened at the dedication of Solomon's temple (2 Chronicles 5:14).

Thus the temple and the throne are drawn together. The holy God who sits on his eternal throne demands worship and, for the protection of his people, provides the means and the place for them to do this. In Isaiah 6:1 we see precisely this in Isaiah's vision: 'I saw the Lord seated on a throne, high and exalted, and the train of his robe filled the temple.' Jeremiah, likewise, barely distinguishes between the throne and the temple as he says in 17:12: 'A glorious throne, exalted from the beginning, is the place of our sanctuary.'

Thus in the Old Testament, the temple becomes the place where God's presence, and thus his throne, is symbolically represented on earth. Though people could come close to the Lord as they worshipped in the temple, only the high priest could enter right into the Most Holy Place where the ark of the covenant was located. To do this he had to perform many ceremonies; not least, he had to 'wash his robes'.

So much more could be said here. We could mention how the coming of Christ to this earth ended in the tearing down of the curtain covering the Most Holy Place in the temple; how Christ now reveals God in human and accessible form; how as we worship Christ, we come to the one who is on the throne; and so on. Such themes are developed at length through the New Testament (specially in 2 Corinthians 3:7-18 and Hebrews 9).

However, as we look at what John sees here, we realise that all the symbolism, all the temporary means of worship, all the symbolic pictures of the holy God on his throne, have once and for all disappeared. Now the people of God worship, in the temple of his presence, the God who is on the throne. Now at last they *see God* (Matthew 5:8), they see *face to face* (1 Corinthians 13:12), indeed they *see his face* (Revelation 22:4).

c) Covered by God's tent
Furthermore, **he who sits on the throne will spread his tent over them**. Here is a reminder of the tent of the tabernacle in the wilderness. But more than that, there is a specific reference back once again to Ezekiel. This time it is Ezekiel 37:26-28 that provides the background. There the prophet speaks of the time when their numbers will be great and he will put his sanctuary *among them forever*. These people now find indeed that they are safe forever in the presence of the King of kings. They are truly his people and he is their God.

d) No more tribulation and trial

In a reference back to the great end-times prophecies in Isaiah (49:10), John now sees that all trials and tribulations have gone: 'They will neither hunger nor thirst, nor will the desert heat or the sun beat upon them. He who has compassion on them will guide them and lead them beside springs of water.' Imagine the joy of those who are suffering among the seven churches! Imagine their excitement as they see that the promises that have just been made to them will indeed come true! Their suffering and their struggle has not been in vain. The promises of Jesus to his churches are not empty words, but will receive real and substantial fulfilment. As Jesus had said to the Philadelphia church (3:12): 'Him who overcomes I will make a pillar in the temple of my God.' (See 2:3, 9; 2:13, 17, 19; 3:4-5, 8, 10 etc.)

e) The Lamb on the throne is the shepherd

In a wonderful mixture of metaphors we see that the **Lamb** is their **shepherd.** Note that the Lamb, Jesus Christ, is exalted and seated on the **throne**. Time and again in the Old Testament God has been referred to as a shepherd of his people.[55] Now here is the divine Lord Jesus, seated upon the throne, and tending his people in a full and perfect completion of all that he has ever done for his people through history. In Psalm 80:1 we see a clear reference to the enthroned God who is the shepherd: 'Hear us, O Shepherd of Israel, you who lead Joseph like a flock; you who sit enthroned between the cherubim, shine forth.' But here too we are reminded of the words of John's Gospel where Jesus is identified as 'the Lamb of God, who takes away the sin of the world' (1:29). He also identifies himself in John 10:11: 'I am the good shepherd. The good shepherd lays down his life for the sheep.'

f) They drink the water of life

It is a natural extension of this picture that the good shepherd who is on the throne gives water to his sheep. Once again it is Isaiah 49:10 that is in mind as John describes what he sees.

(See d) above.) ...**springs of living water** speak of the waters that Christ provides for eternal life (John 6:35). Here is the fulfilment of Isaiah 55:1, for these are indeed the people who have answered God's call: 'Come, all you who are thirsty, come to the waters... and your soul will delight in the richest of fare.'

g) Joy replaces sadness and suffering

As eternal life in God's presence takes over from suffering and death and tribulation, so John turns to Isaiah 25:8[56] for his final description, **God will wipe away every tear from their eyes.** The tears of the church of this age are wiped away by God who is on the throne. The great joy of this worship of all God's people, this great multitude from all nations and all generations, shines out from this page of Scripture.

As God's people suffer for the faith, and suffer under natural calamities like earthquakes, as they suffer generally from living amongst those who persistently reject God and his Word, as they suffer the results of the fall, such as illness and tears and pain, so they are to look forward. They are sealed for eternity. Satan and his minions, the riders and winds, will not harm them and no one will take away this glorious inheritance that belongs to all God's people of all ages.

Special lessons for today

Firstly, tribulation and trials are clearly portrayed as the lot of Christians on this earth. (Apart from seeing this so clearly in the opening of the first six seals, the truth is spelled out for us in many other places such as 1:9; Acts 14:22 and 1 Corinthians 12:26.) They occur because this earth, ever since the fall, has been under God's 'curse', his judgment. Such trials are not to be limited only to 'suffering for the faith', but will involve the general suffering and 'groaning' of a whole creation that awaits the return of Christ. There will therefore be times in every Christian's life when such tribulation seems to overtake them. We wonder how much more we can take. We cry and we hurt. In the midst of this, however, we find Jesus' promise to be with us through everything. We find Jesus to be our example and the one we are to follow, for he too has suffered. We continue to hold on to the promises of the coming kingdom and the time when we shall inherit the fullness of all that has been promised to God's people. Here John's vision becomes critical in providing great comfort to believing people, for we see what we all long for, the picture of the throne and the temple in the same place. We see the place where the tears are wiped away and the caring shepherd is seen face to face.

Secondly, we are reminded of the great heavenly picture of the martyrs under the throne, as we hear of Christian brothers and sisters being persecuted for their faith. But we also need to see this picture as we face ill health, poverty, natural disaster and any of the other sad and hurtful effects of the fall in our world. Here is a vision we must take to ourselves. It is only as we lift our eyes to behold the Lamb on the throne, that we shall begin to develop the perspective on life that should be ours. Then and only then, shall we be able to face the future with joy. Only then shall we be able to say with the apostle Paul in Philippians 4:11-12: 'for I have learned to be content whatever the circumstances. I know what it is to be in need, and I know what it is to have plenty. I have learned the secret of being content in any and every situation, whether well fed or hungry, whether living in plenty or in want.'

Thirdly, we must note that we live in an age that wants everything now. We are impatient. We want to own a house or a car. We want more money and better holidays. This is a materialistic age and, as Christians, we are often sucked into this way of thinking. In some parts of the church this attitude has affected its theology and distorted the biblical vision of how and when believers are to receive the fulness of God's inheritance. While there is no doubt that God brings us many blessings in this life, frequently including physical blessings, nevertheless these are always 'passing' and, indeed, some Christians may never really experience much at all by way of physical blessings such as wealth or health. This is not at all to be seen as a result of lack of faith, as some suggest. Much the reverse. If we look carefully at chapters 6 and 7 we begin to realise that patience, endurance and perseverance are to be the marks of Christians living through this age of the church, the last days. The truly joyful Christians will be the ones who persevere with Christ's help and who await his coming for the day when their joy will be fulfilled in the presence of God and of the Lamb. Those Christians who seem to expect it all now need to heed the warning of Scripture here, and other Christians need to take note lest they are led astray by false promises achieved without having to persevere in the way of Christ who suffered and died.

Revelation 8–9

John's vision now returns us to the opening of the seals. In 6:15-17, we saw that the beginning of the final judgment had arrived. The intervening chapter showed us how God has sealed his people for their eternal protection and pointed us forward to our eternal worship in his presence once all these things are over.

The seventh seal

> When he opened the seventh seal, there was silence in heaven for about half an hour. And I saw the seven angels who stand before God, and to them were given seven trumpets. Another angel, who had a golden censer, came and stood at the altar. He was given much incense to offer, with the prayers of all the saints, on the golden altar before the throne. The smoke of the incense, together with the prayers of the saints, went up before God from the angel's hand (8:1-4).

1. Silence in heaven

With the seventh seal being opened, we expect to see the final judgment, and yet we are given a dramatic picture in which everything stops in heaven for a period of **silence. half an hour** is the time, it seems to John, that the silence lasts. But what is the purpose of the silence? It is probably mentioned for two reasons. As the final great day of the *wrath of the Lamb* comes, the whole of heaven stands in silence, in awe of the dreadful event that is about to occur.[57] Perhaps it is a silence like that seen *before* the judgment in Zephaniah (1:7). There we read the command: 'Be silent before the Sovereign Lord, for the day of the LORD is near.' In a passage addressing the people of God, Zechariah looks forward to the last day and says (2:13): 'Be still before the LORD, all mankind, because he has roused himself from his holy dwelling.'

During this period of silence John sees **seven angels** being given **seven trumpets**, but their purpose is not yet explained.

2. Prayers in heaven

Meanwhile **another angel** stands before **the altar**. There he offers **incense.** The symbolism of the temple that we saw in the last chapter continues. Now, through the imagery of incense and the temple, we see prayers rising into the very presence of God himself. There they are mixed with the prayers of all who already worship in his presence. The **angel's hand** that brings the prayers into the presence of God reminds us that each of the seven churches had its angel and that these angels are there to aid God's people and watch over them, carrying out the Lord's will for them. The fact that the angel presents these prayers indicates that God has received them. It does not indicate that the prayers of Christians need to pass through angels before being received in heaven.

These prayers of God's people are the prayers of those who are suffering on earth as well as the prayers of the martyrs *under the altar* (6:9). The prayers of all God's church, those still on earth and those in heaven, are all asking that God will bring an end to suffering and to the time of tribulation and trial. They are praying that God will vindicate his name, that at last justice will be seen to be done, and that they will all come into the full inheritance that has been described in the second half of chapter 7.

It is a sad fact that the church often fails in this sort of prayer. To pray for Christ to come must include prayer for the Lord's name to be upheld in the judgment of all those who have stood against him and his people. Christians in the twenty-first century are often so afraid of mentioning judgment that they would rather forget its existence. But it is our duty to be concerned with the Lord's justice in judgment as well as in salvation. In our prayers we must ask that God will defend his utter holiness and justice. Praying 'thy kingdom come' is asking God to come in judgment on evil, not just that he speed the day of our final salvation.

Then the angel took the censer, filled it with fire from the altar, and hurled it on the earth; and there came peals of thunder, rumblings, flashes of lightning and an earthquake (8:5).

At first glance this verse seems strange, and yet it reflects the fact that God has heard and is now answering the prayers of his people. Here is the answer to the prayer of 6:10: 'How long, Sovereign Lord, holy and true, until you judge the inhabitants of the earth and avenge our blood?' Here, too, is the answer to the prayers which have just been described. God sends judgment from heaven down to earth. This is indeed the seventh and final seal. The judgment of the final day has arrived. The same figures of judgment (**peals of thunder, rumblings, flashes of lightning and an earthquake**) are also used at the end of the series of trumpets (11:19) and bowls (16:18), and in each case describe the final judgment. Once again we are reminded of God's appearance on Mount Sinai in Exodus 19:16-19, and that is the passage that also introduces us to the *sound of a trumpet*. We should also recall the words of Jesus in Luke 12:49, 'I have come to bring fire on the earth, and how I wish it were already kindled!'

The Seven Angels With Seven Trumpets

1. Introduction
John's vision now returns to the angels who **were given seven trumpets.** As each trumpet is sounded, so the judgment of God is revealed. At the end of the sixth trumpet there is another pause, similar to that at the end of the sixth seal. Then comes the final judgment. Later, when we come to the seven *bowls* of God's judgment (chapter 16), there is also a pause before the seventh bowl is poured out, then comes the final judgment.

i) The relationship between seals, trumpets and bowls.
The question that arises as we read on is simply this: 'Do the judgments of the trumpets and the judgments of the bowls represent exactly the same thing (only restated or stated from a slightly different point of view) as was represented by the opening of the seven seals?' There have been many different replies to this down through the ages.

Some have suggested that the seven trumpets are, in fact, the outworking of the opening of the seventh seal. In other words, they take it that, following the silence in heaven, the final judgment of the seventh seal still has to be described and that this is only partially done in verse 5. It is described in full with the blowing of the trumpets. This is certainly possible, though the main problem lies in the fact that so much is repeated from the opening of the seals themselves. As we saw with the seals, so we shall see with the trumpets, the judgment that is revealed is partial and clearly not the final judgment, that is, until the seventh trumpet. It is thus unlikely the trumpets are the outworking of the seventh seal, for that seal, as we have seen, reveals the final judgment.

Certainly we must all be careful not to be overly dogmatic on these questions for we are dealing with visions and prophecies related to us in vivid apocalyptic imagery. Chronological order is not always apparent, and the visions of wrath overlap considerably in their descriptions. However, other commentators have suggested that the trumpets reveal different aspects of the *same* series of judgments as were released by the breaking of the seals. Some have said the seals concentrate on the judgment of the whole world, while the trumpets view the same proceedings from the perspective of the unbeliever. This is certainly possible. It does justice to the fact that the early trumpet blasts introduce partial judgment rather than the final judgement, and it also does justice to the fact that the seventh seal and the seventh trumpet blast reveal final judgment.

Even allowing for the seals, trumpets and bowls revealing essentially the same thing (judgment on this age, protection and sealing of God's people, followed by the final judgment), the following comparison of the last of each sequence of judgments shows there is an apparent intensification in the descriptions.

The seals	The trumpets	Bowls of wrath
Sixth seal	**Seventh trumpet**	**Seventh bowl**
There was a great earthquake. The sun turned black like sackcloth made of goat hair, the whole moon turned blood red, and the stars in the sky fell to earth, as late figs drop from a fig tree when shaken by a strong wind. The sky receded like a scroll, rolling up, and every mountain and island was removed from its place (6:12-14).	'The nations were angry; and your wrath has come. The time has come for judging the dead, ... — and for destroying those who destroy the earth.' Then God's temple in heaven was opened, and within his temple was seen the ark of his covenant. And there came flashes of lightning, rumblings, peals of thunder, an earthquake and a great hailstorm (11:18-19).	Note: 'It is done!' (16:17). Then there came flashes of lightning, rumblings, peals of thunder and a severe earthquake. No earthquake like it has ever occurred since man has been on earth, so tremendous was the quake. The great city split into three parts, and the cities of the nations collapsed (16:18-19).
Seventh seal		Every island fled away and the mountains could not be found. From the sky huge hailstones of about a hundred pounds each fell upon men (16:20-21).
peals of thunder, rumblings, flashes of lightning and an earthquake (8:5).		

ii) The general approach taken here

The general approach we take below is that the seals, trumpets and bowls describe the same thing, that is, a period of judgment in this age that leads inexorably towards the final judgment. Time and again, we return in the midst of these descriptions to see how God protects and cares for his people so that they will eventually share in the inheritance of the saints. We have seen this clearly prefigured in 7:9-17.

As indicated above, we shall also see that the seven trumpets do indeed appear to look at judgment from the perspective of an unbeliever. In this regard, we should notice that the judgments that come upon the world continue to give time for the unbeliever to repent. The final judgment comes upon those who have not turned to God in spite of his many warnings. Thus 9:20-21 provides a vital backdrop against which we come to understand what is going on in the world today for the unbeliever: 'The rest of mankind that were not killed by these plagues still did not repent of the work of their hands; they did not stop worshipping demons, and idols of gold, silver, bronze, stone and wood – idols that cannot see or hear or walk. Nor did they repent of their murders, their magic arts, their sexual immorality or their thefts.'

iii) The seven angels

> Then the seven angels who had the seven trumpets prepared to sound them (8:6).

These angels were introduced briefly in verse 2. The number 'seven' symbolises God's perfection in all his purposes. 'Seven spirits' in 1:4 refers to the Holy Spirit. The seven churches and seven lampstands refer to the real churches mentioned but also represent the complete number of God's churches, which is why everyone is urged to 'hear what the Spirit says to the churches'. In this sense we should not rush to decide who these seven angels are. It is possible, of course, that they are the angels of the seven churches, or perhaps seven archangels such as Gabriel and Michael who are mentioned in Scripture. Either way, they are given the duty of serving God as he judges the world.

iv) The trumpets

The sound of a trumpet is mentioned on many occasions in the Old Testament. It can be a call to battle for God, as we see when the *seven* trumpets are blown at the destruction of Jericho.[58] There the ark of the covenant was led in procession round the city as the trumpets were blown. Certainly the holy war of Joshua 6 has its final counterpart here in Revelation as God wages war against Satan and all that is evil and against those who refuse to repent. John no doubt has Jericho in mind as he specifically mentions the ark, the symbol of the Lord's presence with his people, in 11:19.

Trumpets can also indicate a summons to national repentance, for example, in Isaiah 58:1 and Ezekiel 33:3-4. In the seven trumpets of this passage we see that the summons does not lead to repentance (9:20-21). Then, finally, a trumpet sound is also particularly associated in Scripture with the second coming of Christ. It announces the coming and the great victory of Christ. Thus we read in Matthew 24:30-31: 'They will see the Son of Man coming on the clouds of the sky, with power and great glory. And he will send his angels with a loud trumpet call, and they will gather his elect from the four winds, from one end of the heavens to the other.'[59]

Each of these ideas helps us understand this trumpet sound that issues from the seven angels. God is declaring holy war upon Satan and those who follow him. He summons people to repentance, and he announces the final judgment day and the coming of Christ.

v) The parallels with the plagues of Egypt

As we look through the first four trumpets we shall see that there are obvious and deliberate parallels with the plagues that came upon the Egyptians as a result of their disobedience to the Word of God through Moses. There the pagan people were judged because of their idolatry and works of magic. We suggested earlier that this series of judgments may be the same as those revealed in the first six seals, but from the perspective of their effect upon the unbeliever. These parallels with the plagues of Egypt support this position. 9:20-21 specifically speaks of how, in spite of the trumpet blasts and judgments, people did not repent of their worshipping *demons* and *idols* or of their *magic arts*. As with the Egyptians, we see God's judgment aimed at unbelievers. While it offers opportunity for repentance, it also serves to harden their hearts, for they continue to reject God. Thus the judgments themselves serve to demonstrate the justice of what is happening. Sinful people are continuing to reject even the trumpet blast of God!

If the plagues of Egypt form the backdrop to this, then we need to remember that God preserved the Israelites throughout each one.

2. The seven trumpets

i) The first trumpet

> Then the seven angels who had the seven trumpets prepared to sound them. The first angel sounded his trumpet, and there came hail and fire mixed with blood, and it was hurled down upon the earth. A third of the earth was burned up, a third of the trees were burned up, and all the green grass was burned up (8:6-7).

The catastrophes that come with the sounding of the trumpets roughly parallel the plagues of Egypt when God judged Pharaoh and the Egyptians for their rebellion against his word: 'Let my people go!' There, one after the other, the plagues revealed just how hard Pharaoh's heart really was. These trumpet judgments reveal the same (9:20-21). The link with the Exodus theme helps us see two things.

a) It helps us understand that the judgments are deserved and just because, when confronted by the awesome work of God himself, the people still refuse to repent.

b) It helps us understand a theme that recurs in the New Testament, that the salvation of God's people from and through this judgment is like a new Exodus. Christians will come through these plagues as the Israelites did, and they will come through to a Promised Land, namely, 'the new heavens and the new earth'.

This first trumpet blast recalls the seventh plague on the Egyptians, the plague of hail (Exodus 9:22-25). Here it is even more intense for, as well as **hail**, there is **fire mixed with blood**.

Again, however, this is not the end of the world. God is not yet bringing final judgment, for he still allows time for repentance as only **one third** of the earth is burned up, and only **one third** of the trees and all the grass destroyed.

ii) The second trumpet

> The second angel sounded his trumpet, and something like a huge mountain, all ablaze, was thrown into the sea. A third of the sea turned into blood, a third of the living creatures in the sea died, and a third of the ships were destroyed (8:8-9).

The second trumpet blast reveals further judgment and, like the third trumpet, recalls the first plague (Exodus 7:20-25) when the Nile was turned to blood and the fish died and no one could drink its water. Although these judgments are aimed at inanimate creation, their impact is dramatic among the people who deny the creator God. Once again, the judgment is partial as **a third of the sea turned into blood**, and a **third** of **creatures** are destroyed. Even much of the economy is affected, as **a third of the ships were destroyed**, no doubt by the great waves of the sea created by the catastrophe. While it would not be right to equate this solely with huge volcanic activity, nevertheless, when we read stories about the effects on the world of the eruption of Krakatoa or the devastation of the earthquakes and associated tidal waves so often seen around the Pacific rim, we can capture a partial view of the horror of what is being described.

Such tragedies continue throughout the age we know. As we have seen with the seals, so these trumpets represent God's continuing judgment on a rebellious people in this world. The trumpets cry out for people to repent, and they herald the impending final judgment day.

iii) The third trumpet

> The third angel sounded his trumpet, and a great star, blazing like a torch, fell from the sky on a third of the rivers and on the springs of water – the name of the star is Wormwood. A third of the waters turned bitter, and many people died from the waters that had become bitter (8:10-11).

Here we see, for the first time in this series of judgments, that **many people died**.

a) Background in judgment on Babylon (from Jeremiah).

The background to this judgment and the one that follows is to be found in Jeremiah 51:24-25, 42. There Jeremiah prophesies about how God will judge Babylon. In the book of Revelation we see later that the city of Babylon is taken to represent all sinful and rebellious humanity.[60] So although the city is not mentioned by name at this point in John's vision, it is clearly in mind. Rebellious people are being judged. As Jeremiah puts it: ' "Before your eyes I will repay Babylon and all who live in Babylonia for all the wrong they have done in Zion," declares the LORD. "I am against you, O destroying mountain, you who destroy the whole earth," declares the LORD. "I will stretch out my hand against you, roll you off the cliffs, and make you a burnt-out mountain…. The sea will rise over Babylon; its roaring waves will cover her." '

In the background here, then, we are reminded that the judgment of the trumpets, like that of the seals, is aimed at the rebellious sinful people of this world, while God's people will be protected. **Wormwood** is a bitter herb and makes water undrinkable. Interestingly, the word is used frequently in the Old Testament as a metaphor for the bitterness of God's judgment on unfaithful Israelites, specially their leaders.[61]

b) Background in judgment on Babylon (from Isaiah).

Whether the **great star** is an evil angel being cast down from heaven who, ironically, brings evil to his own people, is not clear. However, it is again most likely to be linked in John's mind with Old Testament references to Babylon.[62] Isaiah 14 describes the judgment on Babylon like this: 'you will take up this taunt against the king of Babylon: How the oppressor has come to an end! (verse 4).… How you have fallen from heaven, O morning star, son of the dawn! You have been cast down to the earth, you who once laid low the nations!' (Verse 12). The **star** thus probably refers to an evil angel representing Babylon (all those who persistently continue in their unbelief). As God's churches have their angels representing them, so those in rebellion against God are watched over by rebellious angels.

Here, the third trumpet, portrayed in pictures and images drawn from a variety of passages in the Old Testament, shows the judgment of God on those who rebel against him. Although as yet this judgment is still not final, in that only **a third of the waters turned bitter**, nevertheless, God continues even now to bring down those who continue to resist him, whether individuals or nations, or even those who claim to be his leaders but refuse to follow him.

iv) The fourth trumpet

> The fourth angel sounded his trumpet, and a third of the sun was struck, a third of the moon, and a third of the stars, so that a third of them turned dark. A third of the day was without light, and also a third of the night (8:12).

The results of this trumpet blast parallel the ninth plague of Egypt in which total darkness covered Egypt for three days (Exodus 10:21-23). Once again, this is not the final judgment, since only **a third** of the sources of light are affected. The effect on the earth is also partial, as the darkness affects only parts of the day and night. The darkness in the plagues of Egypt precedes the final great plague on Egypt. Darkness often points to judgment by God, as it does, for example, when Jesus dies on the cross, carrying our sin on himself.

> As I watched, I heard an eagle that was flying in mid-air call out in a loud voice: 'Woe! Woe! Woe to the inhabitants of the earth, because of the trumpet blasts about to be sounded by the other three angels!' (8:13)

Now, as John's vision continues, **an eagle** flies overhead proclaiming, **'Woe! Woe! Woe...'** As with the trumpet at the last judgment, we are reminded again of Jesus' words about that time in Matthew 24:28-29: 'Wherever there is a carcass, there the vultures[63] will gather. Immediately after the distress of those days the sun will be darkened, and the moon will not give its light; the stars will fall from the sky, and the heavenly bodies will be shaken.' The picture is vivid indeed – birds of prey gather to eat the remains of those who have died. Such is the enormity of the calamity that will fall on **the inhabitants of the earth**. This phrase normally indicates those who do not believe, as in 11:10, 13:8 and 17:8. Taken in this way, it provides a further answer to the question in 6:10 of those who have died for the faith, 'How long, Sovereign Lord, holy and true, until you judge **the inhabitants of the earth**...'.

All who live on earth and will not repent are now again asked to heed the next three trumpets in particular. These trumpet blasts are referred to as **woes** (9:12; 11:14; 12:12). The word 'woe' is regularly found on Jesus' lips as he warns people, specially the Jewish leaders, of the danger of judgment that will come upon them (for example, repeatedly in Matthew 23).

Having heard the eagle mark out the woes that follow for particular concern, John gives much more space to their descriptions.

v) The fifth trumpet

> The fifth angel sounded his trumpet, and I saw a star that had fallen from the sky to the earth. The star was given the key to the shaft of the Abyss. When he opened the Abyss, smoke rose from it like the smoke from a gigantic furnace. The sun and sky were darkened by the smoke from the Abyss (9:1-2).

John saw a **star** which **had fallen** and **was given a key.** The star is an angelic being, probably not Satan, but one of his minions. Even so, just as we noted with the judgment of the seven seals, it is God who controls what this being is about to do. This is clear from the words **was given.** He is allowed by God to open **the Abyss.** To be more precise, we may say that Jesus actually gives the key. For we have read in 1:18 that he holds the keys of Death and Hades. As the angel opens the Abyss, terrible smoke as if **from a gigantic furnace** arises from it. So awful is the smoke that **the sun and sky were darkened**. The opening of the Abyss will lead to the unleashing of a terrible plague of locusts. The picture is not that difficult to understand, but the background once again helps explain things more clearly.

a) **the fallen star.** See comments on 8:10 where we suggested that the fallen star must be an evil angel representing fallen humanity. The idea of the sinful nature of this angelic being is further confirmed by the fact that only evil angels are described as 'falling' or 'having fallen'. Thus Jesus declares of Satan himself in Luke 10:18: 'I saw Satan fall like lightning from heaven.' It is important to note as well that Jesus says this in answer to the comments of the seventy-two disciples who return to Jesus and say: 'Lord, even the demons submit to us in your name.' Jesus continues with a sentence that reminds us that the sting of the scorpions mentioned here in 9:5 is typical of demonic activity: 'I have given you authority to trample on snakes and scorpions and to overcome all the power of the enemy ....'

b) **the Abyss.** This is the place out of which the Beast comes in 11:7 and 17:8, and it is the place in which Satan is ultimately and permanently confined in 20:3. It is the home where all that is evil and demonic is confined by God. So awful is it that demons cast out of the demon-possessed man called *Legion* plead not to be sent there (Luke 8:31). See also Jude 6 where the angels who disobeyed are kept by God 'in darkness, bound with everlasting chains for judgment on the great Day'.

c) **the blanket of smoke.** The smoke that covers everywhere causing a great darkness reminds us, perhaps, of the darkness that follows a big volcanic eruption. The picture would probably have had quite an impact on those in the seven churches who had heard of the eruption of Vesuvius in AD 79 when the sky darkened for three days even as far afield as Asia Minor. Even today people report living through locust plagues which obliterate the light as myriads of the insects cover the sky. So this is very vivid and realistic picture language. It probably specially recalls God's judgment on Sodom and Gomorrah, where smoke rose from the land 'like smoke from a furnace' (Genesis 19:28). That John describes it as smoke from a **gigantic furnace** suggests something even more awful. Clearly the Abyss is the place of God's judgment upon these Satanic and demonic forces.

> And out of the smoke locusts came down upon the earth and were given power like that of scorpions of the earth. They were told not to harm the grass of the earth or any plant or tree, but only those people who did not have the seal of God on their foreheads. They were not given power to kill them, but only to torture them for five months. And the agony they suffered was like that of the sting of a scorpion when it strikes a man. During those days men will seek death, but will not find it; they will long to die, but death will elude them (9:3-6).

d) The release of locusts. Again we are reminded of the eighth plague that fell on Egypt (Exodus 10:12-20). It is clear, however, that here they stand for spiritual forces of evil, demonic forces. They **were told not to harm the grass of the earth**. They are sent to attack and torture people for five months. The fact that the time is limited and that they **were not given power to kill them** reminds us that even though these are evil forces, they are being released by God to carry forward his purposes. The impact of this plague and attack by the forces of evil will be so terrible, and society will become so brutal and violent that people **will long to die**. We are reminded of 6:16 where people seek to flee the wrath of the Lamb, but cannot. Death is no escape for them for it does not lead to the obliteration they long for, for no-one can escape God and his judgment. Those who belong to Christ, however, will remain untouched by the scorpions[64] for they **have the seal of God on their foreheads** (see comments on 7:3).

e) Demonic war is unleashed against unbelievers

> The locusts looked like horses prepared for battle. On their heads they wore something like crowns of gold, and their faces resembled human faces. Their hair was like women's hair, and their teeth were like lions' teeth. They had breastplates like breastplates of iron, and the sound of their wings was like the thundering of many horses and chariots rushing into battle. They had tails and stings like scorpions, and in their tails they had power to torment people for five months. They had as king over them the angel of the Abyss, whose name in Hebrew is Abaddon, and in Greek, Apollyon (9:7-11).

John's vision of these locusts continues as he see them lined up **like horses for battle**. As he struggles for words to describe what he sees, he no doubt remembers not just Exodus 10, but also that a trumpet sound introduces Joel's prophecy of the hordes of locusts that will destroy Israel as God's judgment for her unfaithfulness: 'Blow the trumpet in Zion; sound the alarm on my holy hill. Let all who live in the land tremble, for the day of the LORD is coming. It is close at hand – a day of darkness and gloom, a day of clouds and blackness. Like dawn spreading across the mountains a large and mighty army comes …' (Joel 2:1-2). Later God describes this army as a plague of 'locusts,... my great army' (Joel 2:25). In Joel it was probably a real army from the north bringing God's judgment. Here in Revelation it is a great spiritual battle that is going on.[65] The work of these demonic forces is fearful, yet still we see that it is limited by God to **five months**.

The **breastplates of iron** remind us of the hard shell-like substance that protects the locust. Again it points to the war that will be waged. They are led into that war by **the angel of the Abyss**. The names he is given are in Hebrew and Greek and mean the same thing. **Abaddon** in the Old Testament is the place of death, like Hades, and **Apollyon** in Greek comes from the word 'to destroy'. It reminds us of the destroying angel who killed the first-born sons of the Egyptians. He operated under God's control, for this was God's judgment upon the evil Egyptians. Yet the angel was evil and was not allowed to touch the Israelite families (see Exodus 12:23).[66] That he is here in 9:11 described as the **king** suggests he is almost certainly Satan himself, or one of his senior officers.

f) The end of the fifth trumpet

The first woe is past; two other woes are yet to come (9:12).

The fifth trumpet has revealed terrible judgment upon unbelievers in this world. God's people will not be affected, but demonic forces will battle against the very people who themselves have chosen evil ways. This judgment upon them will work as the plagues worked in Egypt. On the one hand they call out for people to repent, for they have nowhere else to turn. Yet, on the other hand, when they have nowhere else to turn they would still rather choose death than repent, and so they are confirmed in their sinful ways. Only those who are sealed by Christ will not be affected. That includes all those who are Christians and, of course, those who will in the end repent, for their names too are in the *book of life* (13:8; 21:27). Two trumpet blasts, **two other woes** will now be announced.

vi) The sixth trumpet

As this trumpet sounds, we sense, as we did with the sixth seal, that we are very close indeed to the end and the final judgment. What has been kept back is now released. It is the beginning of the end.

The sixth angel sounded his trumpet, and I heard a voice coming from the horns of the golden altar that is before God. It said to the sixth angel who had the trumpet, 'Release the four angels who are bound at the great river Euphrates.' And the four angels who had been kept ready for this very hour and day and month and year were released to kill a third of mankind. The number of the mounted troops was two hundred million. I heard their number. The horses and riders I saw in my vision looked like this: Their breastplates were fiery red, dark blue, and yellow as sulphur. The heads of the horses resembled the heads of lions, and out of their mouths came fire, smoke and sulphur. A third of mankind was killed by the three plagues of fire, smoke and sulphur that came out of their mouths. The power of the horses was in their mouths and in their tails; for their tails were like snakes, having heads with which they inflict injury (9:13-19).

Now John hears another voice. As it comes from the **golden altar that is before God**,[67] the origin of the voice must be God or Jesus, though it may be an angel who actually speaks the words. This altar is where the prayers of God's people are received, and so what follows may well be seen as an answer to their prayers (see comments on 8:3).

a) Four angels released

The command leads to the release of another group of four angels. It is unlikely they are the same angels as were holding back the four winds in 7:1, for these new angels are evil. Since they have to be **released** they have obviously been held back at God's command, and so perhaps they are actually the *four winds* themselves that had been held back. The fact that they are **bound at the great river Euphrates** is also significant. The Euphrates, often mentioned in the Old Testament, was the area from which the great invading, killing and plundering evil forces came against Israel. Here is a picture of invading forces, like the Assyrians and Babylonians, that bring death. In the Old Testament both these nations were understood to bring God's judgment on the unbelieving people of Israel. Given several references to the destruction of Babylon later in the book, it is likely that Jeremiah's prophecy is specially being used to help John with his description. There Jeremiah sees the invading Babylonians coming from across the Euphrates on horses. The fact that John says they **had been kept** for a very specific time indicates this is all under the sovereign purposes and plans of God.

b) An army is ready

The angels are allowed to **kill a third of mankind**. To achieve this they amass an enormous army. The numbers of the **mounted** army are, of course, far too numerous (**200 million**) to be envisaged in literal terms, even in the twenty-first century. Rather this continues to be a description of demonic forces at work in the world, hence their horses appear with **heads of lions** and **their tails were like snakes**. As the horses move forward they breathe the great symbols of judgment that we have already noted, **fire** and **smoke**. **Sulphur** is added for the first time, perhaps specifically recalling the judgment on Sodom and Gomorrah (Genesis 19:24), and thus indicating how close we now are to the final judgment. In 21:8 the final judgment on unbelievers leaves them in a place called 'the fiery lake of burning sulphur'.

c) A third of humanity is killed

This time people are killed. The angels fulfil their commission and **a third of mankind was killed**. These people are the unbelievers and they die physically because they are already spiritually dead. Whereas for the believer death leads into the presence of God, for the unbeliever it leads to the place from which the sulphur and smoke are arising.

d) Those remaining still do not repent

> The rest of mankind that were not killed by these plagues still did not repent of the work of their hands; they did not stop worshipping demons, and idols of gold, silver, bronze, stone and wood – idols that cannot see or hear or walk. Nor did they repent of their murders, their magic arts, their sexual immorality or their thefts (9:20-21).

John still sees those who are unbelievers when he talks of **the rest of mankind**. They have seen their friends and neighbours die and still they have not repented. In fact there was no let up in their sinful activities. These centre on **worshipping demons**. The irony is that they continue to worship the very beings whom

God has released to bring judgment upon them. In their lack of repentance they confirm the justice of God's judgment. If these people want to worship demons, then to demons they will go. As the Bible repeatedly says, their **idols** are nothing of themselves for they **cannot see or hear or walk**. But the worship of idols is not therefore neutral. It is still disobedient worship and it is worship of demons. In 1 Corinthians 10:19-20 Paul puts it this way: 'Do I mean then that a sacrifice offered to an idol is anything, or that an idol is anything? No, but the sacrifices of pagans are offered to demons, not to God, and I do not want you to be participants with demons.'[68]

Particular sins are then mentioned by John. Each sin is appalling in its own way and the people did not even repent of these. Each sin, though only a sampling, indicates how absorbed in sin they are, each seeking his or her own way forward and intent on satisfying their own cravings and lusts.

Thus the second woe (sixth trumpet) comes to an end. There is nothing left to follow after the revealing of such continuing sin and demon worship, except the final judgment itself. And yet, as between the sixth and seventh seals there was a pause, so here. Chapters 10 and 11 are that pause before the seventh trumpet is sounded.

Special lessons for today

One of the first points we have noted is how in these passages, and in what follows, we see that Satan is allowed great power by God. But the end result is that he, Satan, brings *God's* judgment on his own evil followers! There is no doubt that Satan hopes to bring terror to believers, indeed he brings continuous pain to this world. It is surely amazing how God so over-rules that believers need have no fear. They are sealed by God. They will be preserved even through death. Extraordinary as it may seem, God ensures that Satan only succeeds in causing his own people to suffer so much that they want to die. While the description of torture need not be taken so literally that we expect plagues of locusts (though in some countries this may happen), nevertheless we cannot allow ourselves to weaken the impact of this imagery. Sin often leads to physical consequences in people's lives. Thus Paul describes how physical suffering can follow from sin (Romans 1:24-32).

This is the world we live in and in it Satan is alive and active. We see people around us caught up in the pain and suffering of their own sin. The work Satan has started in their lives leads to suffering. Adultery leads to the pain of broken families; lying, cheating and stealing lead to some of the widespread feelings of insecurity we so often meet. We cannot say we sympathise with such people's sufferings if we do not also point them to the cause. To try to deal with the symptoms without pointing to the personal reality of Satan and the seriousness of sin is to deceive people and further the work of the enemy.

Even many church leaders in our day refuse to acknowledge the reality of Satan. There can be few things more satisfying to him than to know that some people will read this fearful description and yet continue to deny his existence. He is truly Apollyon.

Meanwhile for those who believe and do acknowledge Satan's existence and power, we are reminded frequently in John's vision that his power is limited. Where believers suffer alongside the world, it will bring them a refining of the faith. But they will be protected altogether from the effects of the great spiritual attacks that we have read about in the final three trumpet blasts, the three woes.

Another vital lesson, to which G. B. Caird has drawn attention, concerns the way the modern world regards life and death.[69] There is a general feeling, often felt by Christians as well, that life on earth is the key to happiness. Death takes away that joy of life. This is a far cry from what John is saying to us. He calls unbelievers 'the inhabitants of the earth'. This is the only realm of existence they are interested in. For them death is thus the ultimate tragedy. This is one of the idolatries that John fights against. Death and suffering and pain come to us all. As someone has said, death is one of the few certainties most people have in life. John asks us to see this life as transient. He does not deny that it may often be marvellous, for this is God's world, but he is more concerned for the experience of so many of God's people. For them it is more often than not a world of persecution and suffering and natural tragedies. We must live life in the full knowledge that God is with us now and will be with us forever, and above all that he is in control in *all* the circumstances of life which we face, even if we cannot immediately understand what we are going through. Do we hold the vision of chapter 7 before our eyes, or not?

Revelation 10–11

We await the seventh trumpet and the final judgment. But there is a pause now. The account of the seventh trumpet is not picked up again until 11:15. This is not a pause in the actual timing of the final judgment,[70] but a pause here in John's vision as he is first shown something else, as he was in chapter 7 before the seventh seal was revealed. The interlude in chapter 7 took us back to the church and the sealing of God's people so that they should be preserved from judgment. Here again, before the account of judgment is continued, we pause to hear more that is of vital importance for the church to hear. Two extra visions give us further insight into what happens to the church and what the church is to do during these days before the final judgment arrives. The first vision concerns a 'little scroll' (chapter 10), and the second shows us 'two witnesses' (11:1-13).

1. A little scroll

> Then I saw another mighty angel coming down from heaven. He was robed in a cloud, with a rainbow above his head; his face was like the sun, and his legs were like fiery pillars. He was holding a little scroll, which lay open in his hand. He planted his right foot on the sea and his left foot on the land, and he gave a loud shout like the roar of a lion. When he shouted, the voices of the seven thunders spoke. And when the seven thunders spoke, I was about to write; but I heard a voice from heaven say, 'Seal up what the seven thunders have said and do not write it down' (10:1-4).

In 5:2 a *mighty angel* had asked whether there was one who could open the seven seals of the scroll. This is another **mighty angel** and another scroll, **a little scroll.** This angel comes with all the symbols of divine rule.

i) The angel represents Christ

He is Christ's agent as he brings the scroll. See comments on 4:3 for the **rainbow**. The **cloud** is a sign of God's glorious presence. **His face was like the sun** are the same words used to describe Jesus in 1:16 and the **legs** like **fiery pillars** remind us again of the description of Jesus in 1:15. It may be that the reference to **fiery pillars** is expected to remind us of the way God appeared as Redeemer to his people during the Exodus and wilderness wanderings. He judged Egypt but had an altogether different relationship of love with his people – he was their Saviour and Redeemer.

Here, then, is a mighty angel who brings with him a message from the Lord. Because this message is specially given to help and teach the church, the scene now moves back to earth as the angel comes **down from heaven.** The fact that he **gave a loud shout like the roar of a lion** also is clearly intended to remind us that he speaks for Jesus, the *lion of the tribe of Judah.* As he speaks the **thunders** speak, and so we are reminded of the judgment of God and of the Lamb and the great divine power (see Psalm 29:3).

Unlike the previous scroll that was sealed, this lies **open in his hand**. As Christ's representative he puts **his right foot on the sea and his left foot on the land**. This does not indicate his great size so much as the fact that what he has to say involves the whole world. Christ has complete authority over all, and the rainbow reminds us that the message is part of the total fulfilment of God's covenant plans, for his people, in and through Christ.

ii) John is not to write this message down

Thus far John had written down all that he had seen (1:11, 19 etc.). But, tantalisingly, what was spoken remains personal to John and he is specifically told, **do not write it down**. There is little point in speculating therefore about what John did hear. Nevertheless, as we read on, it becomes clear that it probably had yet more to do with the judgment of this earth.

Then the angel I had seen standing on the sea and on the land raised his right hand to heaven. And he swore by him who lives for ever and ever, who created the heavens and all that is in them, the earth and all that is in it, and the sea and all that is in it, and said, 'There will be no more delay! But in the days when the seventh angel is about to sound his trumpet, the mystery of God will be accomplished, just as he announced to his servants the prophets' (10:5-7).

The angel now raises **his right hand to heaven** which is the traditional way of taking an oath, much as we might raise the Bible in our right hand and promise to tell the truth. The background to this is found in Daniel 12:4, where Daniel had also been told to 'seal the words of the scroll until the time of the end'. In Daniel, a heavenly figure then also swears **by him who lives for ever** (i.e. by God), as he responds to the question, 'How long …'.

iii) No more delay

The angel John sees responds, **'There will be no more delay!'** John is no doubt aware that what he is seeing is the ultimate fulfilment of all that had been written before about judgment and salvation, including the fulfilment of Daniel's prophecy. More than that it is the final fulfilment of God's own words to Moses in Deuteronomy 32:39-41 as he spoke about judging those who are evil: 'See now that I myself am he! There is no god besides me. I put to death and I bring to life, I have wounded and I will heal, and no one can deliver out of my hand. I lift my hand to heaven and declare: As surely as I live for ever, when I sharpen my flashing sword and my hand grasps it in judgment, I will take vengeance on my adversaries and repay those who hate me.'

The reminder that God **created the heavens** and **the earth** and **the sea** points to his ultimate authority as he decides to delay no longer. But it also speaks here of the extent of the authority that has been given to Jesus Christ, since his representative angel stands on both **sea** and **land**.[71] So the announcement of final judgment is made. When the **seventh**

angel sounds his **trumpet**, the final day will come. The angel says, **the mystery of God will be accomplished, just as he announced to his servants the prophets** (probably referring to the fulfilment of the words of the prophet Moses and of Daniel, as well as others). But we must be clear that this fulfilment specifically here includes the gospel, the good news. The Greek verb used is from the same root as our word 'gospel'.[72] *We are thus to understand this as about salvation as well as about judgment. This is why, as we shall see, the message is both sweet and bitter.*

The mystery of God has to do with his great purposes for this world and, in particular, his people. In the apostle Paul's writings, *mystery* is a description of the plans of God to save people from around the world. Here in John's vision, it has to do with all that surrounds the time leading up to and including the final day. In fact, we may say more than that, for the mystery concerns all that this book of Revelation is teaching us, and this includes the reasons why Christians have to suffer – it is for the sake of the gospel. When all is thus **accomplished**, the saints will no longer suffer (6:11 is thus brought to completion).

iv) John eats the little scroll

> Then the voice that I had heard from heaven spoke to me once more: 'Go, take the scroll that lies open in the hand of the angel who is standing on the sea and on the land.' So I went to the angel and asked him to give me the little scroll. He said to me, 'Take it and eat it. It will turn your stomach sour, but in your mouth it will be as sweet as honey.' I took the little scroll from the angel's hand and ate it. It tasted as sweet as honey in my mouth, but when I had eaten it, my stomach turned sour. Then I was told, 'You must prophesy again about many peoples, nations, languages and kings' (10:8-11).

John does what he is told, and goes **to the angel** and takes **the scroll**. There are no seals to be removed. This is probably because it is coming directly from Christ himself, through his representative angel, and Christ has already removed the seals on this document.

However, the instructions that come with this scroll sound very strange to our ears. He is told to **Take it and eat it**. The results will be that in his **stomach** it will be **sour**, perhaps suggesting it will make him feel sick, yet as he eats it **it will be as sweet as honey**. The background to this picture is again firmly rooted in the Old Testament. Ezekiel also ate a scroll (Ezekiel 2:9-3:3). The figurative intention of this action of eating is made clear in Ezekiel 3:10, where the prophet is told: 'Son of man, listen carefully and take to heart all the words I speak to you.' As a prophet in the last days, John had a privileged calling. But first he had to take to heart the message for himself. And it tasted **sweet**, for it was a message about the fulfilment of prophecy and about the return of Christ and the protection of God's people. Yet the message was also **sour**, for along with the covenant blessings of Christ's second coming, come all the horrors of judgment and wrath and covenant curses on those who have not repented. John's task will be to tell about the glory of the second coming and the new heavens and the new earth, but it will include also prophesying about the events heralded by the seventh trumpet.

v) John is recommissioned to prophesy

This bitter-sweet message, which by divine commission John **must prophesy**, is one which concerns the salvation and judgment of people of **many nations** and **languages**. No one is omitted from the message of God which John brings. As we near the time of the final judgment, and the descriptions of that time intensify through the seventh trumpet and the seventh bowl of wrath, so John needs to hear **again** that Christ wants him to be a witness to these things and to proclaim loudly for all to hear. John's mission is to the world and the church. While the Old Testament prophets like Ezekiel and Jeremiah primarily prophesied to rebellious Israel, the parallels are clear. The prophets themselves suffered as they proclaimed the truth of God's word. John's will not be an easy calling. As one of God's people he can say with Jeremiah (15:16): 'When your words

143

came, I ate them; they were my joy and my heart's delight.' But Jeremiah also knew what it was to be rejected as God's prophet because his words were God's words of judgment on the people: 'I became the laughing-stock of all my people; they mock me in song all day long. He has filled me with bitter herbs and sated me with gall' (Lamentations 3:14-15).

As we move into the next chapter, we shall find that, just as John's prophetic task will not be easy and will lead to suffering, so it will be for all Christians in these last days.

2. The two witnesses

What we now read about 'two witnesses' as part of this 'interlude' takes place during the age of the church, the last days. This is the time of the first six seals and the first six trumpets. It is the time before the final judgment. What we now read, therefore, is a call to the church to witness faithfully to *the faithful witness*, to Jesus Christ as King. John's recommissioning to prophesy (chapter 10) leads into what follows, and he begins again with an emphasis on how the church is ultimately protected by God.

The first two verses, however, open up a host of questions for us and so we offer a general indication of some of these before looking in more detail at the text.

Some general observations on this chapter

We have already suggested that chapter 11 is designed to help the church know what its duties are during the period prior to the return of Christ and his second coming. However, there are different views about the meaning of the discussion of the temple in these opening verses, and then we are also faced with the problem of the interpretation of the periods of time that are mentioned.

a) On the temple, altar and holy city (verses 1-2).

Some have said that this passage deals with the place of the Jewish people in the last days, and that this is a prophecy of a time when the temple has been rebuilt and the Jews will face the antichrist. Such Jews will be protected by God. The temple, altar and city are thus to be taken literally.

Another view takes the passage symbolically but still as referring to the way in which God will ultimately look after the Jewish people. Jerusalem represents the Jewish people. The temple is 'measured', symbolising their being set apart for preservation by God (see Zechariah 2:1-5). The fact that only the central part of the temple is measured indicates that only a remnant of Jews will be saved.

Others regard this whole section as referring symbolically to the church, all members of which can be called 'the temple of God' (1 Corinthians 3:16).[73] Jerusalem and the outer courts are symbolic of the *nations*. Thus there is a parallel in this passage with the sealing of the saints in chapter 7. Here the church (the temple) is measured for protection. But it will suffer at the hands of the nations. This view, it is said, brings chapter 21 more into line with the thought of chapter 10 and shows that it is following the ideas seen under the previous visions where the church suffers but is protected.

In order to benefit from the teaching on this chapter a decision on these matters is necessary. This is not necessarily easy. Below we argue that this passage makes most sense when taken to refer to the church and the Christians who make up the church. We shall thus see that this chapter is a prophecy telling us that the church must bear faithful witness even while all around appears to be in the hands of Satan. The church is thus a *witness*. And God will protect this witness, but more on this later.

b) Times

Undoubtedly the references in Revelation to specific periods of time are difficult to understand. Are they to be taken literally? Are they some kind of symbol? If they are symbolic, is there any key available to help us understand the meanings, or do they have to remain enigmatic in this age?

Before we attempt an answer to this we should note:

(i) Some of the numbers are repeated in different ways. Forty-two months (a month = 30 days), mentioned in 11:2 and 13:5, is the same period of time as 1260 days (11:3; 12:6). This, of course, is three and a half years. Now in Daniel 7:25 and 12:7, we read of *a time, times and half a time*. If a *time* is a year, then again we have three and a half years. This idea is explicitly picked up in Revelation 12:14.

(ii) Whether or not we take this period of time literally, the background for the idea can be seen in Daniel. There in chapter seven we read of the power and rule, for this limited time, of the 'beast' – a figure introduced to us in Revelation 11:7 as the one who comes up from the bottomless pit.

The nations will trample over the holy city for the three and a half years, which is the time of the beast's authority (see 13:5-17), the length of time during which the 'witnesses' prophesy (11:3), and the length of time for which the 'woman' (church) will be nourished, or 'taken care of' in the wilderness (12:6). The three and a half days (11:9, 11) perhaps reminds us of Jesus' own experience of suffering, the cross and the resurrection.

Certainly it is thus possible to see these numbers symbolically, especially if it is remembered that the number seven is always considered to be a number reflecting God's perfection or completion of his purposes and plans. Three and a half being half of fulness or perfection may indicate, therefore, the fact that all this still remains firmly in God's control and that he will yet bring it to conclusion. The consummation has yet to come, but it will come. Meanwhile the troubles are for a limited time and under the sovereign control of the only one who brings all things to conclusion.

This latter view is the one we take below as we go through the text. It is immediately obvious that this suits the context we have described as we continue to read this interlude before the final judgment with the seventh trumpet. This interlude is looking again at the role of the church during this time leading up to the final judgment, the time in which John lived, the seven churches lived, and you and I still live.

i) John is given a measuring rod

The pictures John uses here are vivid symbols drawn from Ezekiel's prophecy about the new temple in Jerusalem (Ezekiel 40–48). There too, in a vision, Ezekiel sees a person with a 'measuring rod' in his hand, and he sees the temple being measured out (40:4-7).

> I was given a reed like a measuring rod and was told, 'Go and measure the temple of God and the altar, and count the worshippers there. But exclude the outer court; do not measure it, because it has been given to the Gentiles. They will trample on the holy city for 42 months' (11:1-2).

The **measuring** here, as in Ezekiel, has to do with the fulfilment of God's design and purposes. The temple is the gathered people of God and they are measured for their sure protection. Here is the church, those who will forever sing the praises of the Lamb, and yet who will suffer and need the Lamb's protection. This is why John adds **count the worshippers there**. God's elect belong to him and their number is known. As Jesus said in John 10:28-29: 'I give them eternal life, and they shall never perish; no one can snatch them out of my hand. My Father, who has given them to me, is greater than all; no one can snatch them out of my Father's hand.'

The temple has always been the place where God's presence is specially known and the centre of the worship of God's people; and in Jesus Christ, God is with his people and in their midst (see comments on chapter 7). Just as John had seen a vision of the sealing of God's people, so now he sees them being measured. They will once again be 'measured' when finally the people of God, the 'new Jerusalem', appear in glorious array at the Last Day and are forever protected against any penetration of the evil one or of sin (21:15-27).

ii) God's people will be trampled upon

The command to **exclude the outer court...because it has been given to the Gentiles** has again raised difficulties for understanding what John means. The original temple had a court of the Gentiles which was designed to be a reminder to Israel that always there was a place in God's plans for Gentiles who would turn to worship the one true God. Here, however, the picture has changed. Because of the coming of Christ and his death and resurrection, the temple curtain has been torn down (Matthew 27:51). The temple of the Old Testament no longer exists. Gentiles can and do come as close to God, through faith in Jesus Christ, as do any Jews who trust in him (Hebrews 10:19-22). So the original symbolism of the temple courts has come to fulfilment in Christ, to whom the whole cultic system ultimately pointed. Since John here refers to the **outer court** of the **Gentiles** (the nations), he is surely thus referring to those who now remain *outside* the temple to which all, Jew and Gentile, can come through faith in Christ.

In other words, it seems John is saying that those *outside* the temple, which is the people of God, do not need to be measured. They are not protected and do not come under the covenant protection of the Lord Jesus. This understanding of what is going on helps us with the next sentence as well. The **Gentiles** are now clearly defined as those who **will trample on the holy city**. Thus they cannot possibly be Gentiles looking for Christ, but rather those who are opposed to the people of God, to the **temple of God.**

However, the period in which God's people will be persecuted and trampled upon is limited by God who remains sovereign. It is to be **for 42 months.**[74] God is sovereign not just over his people, in that he seals them and measures them, but he is even sovereign, as we have seen many times before in this book, over the evil that is perpetrated upon his people. He controls it, for it is through this that ultimately unbelievers are judged and God's people are refined and saved.

'And I will give power to my two witnesses, and they will prophesy for 1,260 days, clothed in sackcloth.' These are the two olive trees and the two lampstands that stand before the Lord of the earth. If anyone tries to harm them, fire comes from their mouths and devours their enemies. This is how anyone who wants to harm them must die. These men have power to shut up the sky so that it will not rain during the time they are prophesying; and they have power to turn the waters into blood and to strike the earth with every kind of plague as often as they want (11:3-6).

During this time of being trampled upon (42 months = 1260 days), **two witnesses ... will prophesy for 1,260 days** (= 42 months).

Summary so far

God's people, the temple, have been measured for their protection against the attacks that come upon them as the Gentiles, the nations of unbelieving people, trample over them. The period of this suffering for the church is specifically limited by God. During that *same* period of time two witnesses will prophesy.

iii) Two witnesses

As we come to these two figures, we must keep in mind the background we have already noted that relates to witnessing and dying for the faith, for here lies a vital clue to the identification of **the two witnesses**. In 1:5 and 3:14 Jesus Christ was designated 'the faithful and true witness'. In 1:9 John himself has indicated that he is on Patmos precisely because of his 'witness' (NIV 'testimony'). In 2:10 the highly commended church at Smyrna is urged to 'be faithful even to the point of death'. In 2:13 in the letter to Pergamum, Antipas, a recent martyr for the faith is called by Christ 'my faithful witness'. In 6:9 the martyrs are described as having been 'slain because of the word of God and the witness (NIV 'testimony') they had maintained'.

Verse 3 begins with the word **and** indicating a direct link with the discussion of the persecution of the church in verse 2. We are now shown God's people have been 'measured' for their protection. They are to 'witness' even to the point of death. Thus it seems right to understand the two witnesses as standing symbolically for the truth of the witness of the church.

The mention of **two** witnesses probably arises from two ideas. First, two witnesses were required for truth to be established in biblical times (see Deuteronomy 17:6; John 8:17; and Mark 14:56-59). Secondly, the church models itself on Christ, who has already been called the 'Amen, the faithful and true witness' (3:14). True witness involves these two facets of faithfulness and truth.

iv) Witnessing by the power of the Spirit

The identification of these witnesses with the suffering church is reinforced by their being called **two lampstands,** a description that has only been given to the church in the book of Revelation. This description, as we saw in the opening chapters, describes the church's mission to witness as a light to the world, following Christ and speaking of him to unbelievers.[75] There is no doubt that this is a painful mission of prophecy that has been given to the church. This is reflected in the phrase **clothed in sackcloth**, a sign of mourning, for many will die in this service for their Lord. And yet the people of God are a beautiful people and here they are also called **two olive trees**. The value of the olive in terms of oil, food and as a source of light when put in lamps gave rise to Israel itself being called an 'olive tree'. For example, when Jeremiah (11:16) pleads with God's people to return to the Lord and become again the witness they should be, he says: 'The LORD called you a thriving olive tree with fruit beautiful in form.' John, in fact, is probably drawing on the prophet Zechariah. In Zechariah 4:1-6 the prophet has a vision which includes lampstands and olive trees. The lampstand represented the temple which, as we have seen, in the Christian era stands for Jesus and his people, the church. The olive trees provide the supply of oil for the lampstands of the temple. But Zechariah tells us more because, when the angel is asked about the olive trees, he is told: 'This is the word of the LORD to Zerubbabel: "Not by might nor by power, but by my Spirit," says the LORD Almighty' (verse 6).

What John sees therefore is a reminder of *how* God will give power to his church. The olive trees represent the work of the Holy Spirit in the church, just as Zechariah had been told all those years before. It is the Holy Spirit who will enable God's people to carry out their calling. This again adds to the amazing comfort for God's people that we experience in this vision. We may find the Christian life very hard to live. We or our friends may be persecuted. On top of that, we live in a world which continues to see all sorts of tragedies as the angels of God's judgment are released. Yet, through it all, we are kept as his people and, moreover, we are empowered to be his witnesses by his Holy Spirit. God's Spirit continues to provide the power for the light to the world, the lampstand; that is our calling.

These witnesses, though suffering and appearing at times to be defeated, are in fact the ones who **stand before the Lord of the earth**. Their persecutors will be amazed at the irony here as the unbeliever's question of 6:17 is answered. 'Who can stand?'

The prophecy the church will give[76] is really to be summed up in the gospel words of 'The Kingdom of God is near. Repent and believe the good news!' (Mark 1:15). Put another way, they are to tell the world of the need to repent before the great and mighty day of judgment comes. This will include telling people of all their sin and the effects even now of God's judgment upon them. Such a message will never be palatable to unbelievers in any generation. The two great prophets Moses and Elijah faced the same reaction to their message.

v) The fire of God's Word
Nevertheless, **if anyone tries to harm them** they are protected, for **fire comes from their mouths and devours their enemies**. The **fire** reminds us both of the fire of God's word of judgment (Jeremiah 5:14), and of the rejection of Elijah's word of prophecy when God sent fire from heaven in judgment upon the false prophets (1 Kings 18:24-39).[77] This should not be taken literally as if happening straightaway. Many Christians have already been harmed, are being harmed and will be harmed in bitter persecution. But they will be protected, as we have

151

repeatedly seen. More than that, though, the word of the gospel itself, as it is proclaimed in its fulness, will be a word of fire, for it tells people of the judgment to come if they do not repent. God will not simply let unbelievers get away with harming his people. Impending serious judgment is part of the witness of the church.

Elijah had the **power to shut up the sky** so it didn't rain for three years. Moses had the **power to turn the waters into blood** and to bring about the **plagues** of Egypt. Of course, both proclaimed the word given them by the Lord and it was by his power, the power of his Spirit, that fire and plagues came. And so it is true even for us in this age. We proclaim God's word and it will be for God to decide when judgment will come, but it will be as sure in coming as it was for the Egyptians and for those who followed Baal in Moses' and Elijah's day.

As we watch Satan seeming to exercise such power in the world and especially against God's people, we need to recall, says John, that we have the power of the Holy Spirit with us to continue to help us speak out (prophesy) for the Lord in our generation. Moreover, no spiritual harm will come to us even if we suffer and are put to death. Furthermore, God will bring justice, and those who have attacked his church will be judged as surely as others have been in the past.

3. The two witnesses are killed

There will come a time when Christians will have accomplished[78] their witness, **when they have finished their testimony**. They will have lived for Christ and proclaimed him to the world. We are reminded of those mentioned in 6:9-11 who have already died for the faith but who were told that the time would come when 'the number of their fellow servants and brothers who were to be killed as they had been was completed'. So now we hear how **the beast** attacks God's people and kills them.

Now when they have finished their testimony, the beast that comes up from the Abyss will attack them, and overpower and kill them. Their bodies will lie in the street of the great city, which is figuratively called Sodom and Egypt, where also their Lord was crucified. For three and a half days men from every people, tribe, language and nation will gaze on their bodies and refuse them burial. The inhabitants of the earth will gloat over them and will celebrate by sending each other gifts, because these two prophets had tormented those who live on the earth (11:7-10).

i) The beast

John draws on the prophet Daniel to explain what he sees in his continuing vision. We are introduced to a figure called **the beast**, of which we hear more in Revelation 13 and 17. We have already seen that the **Abyss** is the place where all Satan's forces are kept (see comments on chapter 9:1-2).

Does John now describe a specific event that happens at the end of the age just before Christ returns, or is it something that has already happened or continues to happen? We believe that John is still talking here about the experience of the church and the people of God on this earth. Note that John says the beast **comes up**. This is not something in the future but in the present, but it is also an appearance that seems to be ongoing. In other words it is 'a permanent cast of its character' that the beast continues to come forth from the Abyss.[79] As we shall see in a moment, the experiences being described here are very much the experience of the church through all ages.

In Daniel 7 four great beasts arise who represent kingdoms that have fought against God's people. But the *fourth beast* is described as the most awful, and it 'crushed and devoured its victims'. The beast had 'ten horns on its head' and 'was waging war against the saints and defeating them until the Ancient of Days came and pronounced judgment in favour of the saints of the Most High, and the time came when they possessed the kingdom' (Daniel 7:19-22). The horns represent kings who will come and go, and 'the saints will be handed over to him for a time, times and half a time' (Daniel 7:25). This seems to describe directly what John sees. A beast who has power for three and a half years, a limited time under God's sovereignty, will kill and defeat God's people until judgment is pronounced by God and his people possess the kingdom. The witnesses carry on doing their job under different rulers, kingdoms and peoples. And each one of these will think that they have finally got rid of the Christian witness for their country or their generation.

ii) The enemy wins

The victory will appear to go to the enemy and the witness of the gospel will seem to have died out in various places and various times throughout the history of the church. More than that: **the inhabitants of the earth**[80] **will gloat over** all that has happened and especially over those martyred, dying and suffering Christians. The reason these evil people will **gloat** is straightforward enough. The church, the **two witnesses**, has **tormented** them. In other words, the repeated witness of Christ's people to judgment and salvation, to sin and forgiveness, has deeply angered unbelievers, and so they are pleased now to have had their revenge, as they see it, in winning this battle.

This gloating will continue as the **bodies** of the witnesses lie out in the street **of the great city**. The **city** here is the place where the inhabitants of the earth (verse 10) live. In other words, it stands as a symbol for the place where 'Satan has his throne', like Pergamum (2:13). Specifically John calls it by three different names. First it is called **Sodom**. This city stands as a byword, among all who have ever heard the stories of Scripture, for all that is evil and immoral but also proud and arrogant against God. The people of Sodom refused to repent as Lot told them what was about to happen. Secondly, the city is called **Egypt.** The fact that Egypt is not a city should remind us here that the city referred to is not one literal city but a general description of the world where unbelievers and Satan hold sway. **Egypt** is an example for God's people of a place that arrogantly held out against the witness of Moses as he proclaimed God's word. We have seen how the ongoing judgments of the trumpets have been modelled on the plagues of Egypt. Finally, and rather more difficult to understand, the **city** is called the place **where also their Lord was crucified**. That, of course, is Jerusalem. Christ was actually crucified outside the city (Hebrews 13:12), but the key point is that this **city** is the 'city' which crucified Jesus. Thus **the great city** represents all the **inhabitants of earth** and is the place where they live, the place of immorality, greed and idolatry, the place that ultimately crucified Christ who was left a laughing stock for 'three days'. No wonder unbelievers gloat, for the battle has been theirs and the beast has won.

It is important to see that this part of John's vision, complicated though it is, applies to the seven churches addressed in chapters 2–3 and to Christians and churches down through the centuries. As Jesus said in Matthew 10:18: 'On my account you will be brought before governors and kings as witnesses to them and to the Gentiles.' Churches will suffer the persecution of seeing people like Antipas killed. There will be churches like Smyrna who are about to suffer 'even to the point of death' (2:10). Satan will win 'on the streets', as it were! Such a church needs to be reminded that in spite of this they will 'not be hurt at all by the second death' (the final judgment). There will be churches like the one in Pergamum which knows it exists in a city 'where Satan has his throne' and where Antipas and others will die as Satan, **the beast that comes up from the Abyss**, wins another battle.

But we shall see all this happen in our own generation as well. Some of us can remember the proclamation that was sent around the world from Shanghai when Madam Mao announced in that huge city that religion, and specifically Christianity, was dead. Many, many Christians had been put to death, others were to be publicly tried and executed, and others humiliated in re-indoctrination camps. Satan won a victory. Christians have been all but exterminated in area after area of our world in recent years, either being forced to flee or being put to death. The beast has surely **attacked** and **overpowered** and **killed them**. And people in nations around the world have spent time rejoicing at such events and often even a **burial** has been refused.

155

This is the age of the church. It was real for the churches in John's day and it is real for us today. But the time of such victory by the beast and such suffering by God's people remains, as we have seen, strictly limited under the sovereign purposes of God.

iii) The church follows Christ

The mention of the city as the place where Christ was crucified reminds us that what John describes for the church is the same as Christ himself experienced. Jesus witnessed (testified) before antagonistic leaders (John 8:13). His condemnation of the leaders, of the spiritual plight of Jerusalem and the work that was being done in the temple, all helped lead to his conviction. The beast comes up from the Abyss, to use John's words, and the leaders win a victory, and Christ died on the cross. The authorities provided no grave, and for three days they were relieved and 'the world' rejoiced (John 16:20). But the time was limited under the sovereign purposes of God. Christ was protected and sealed. There would be no 'second death' for him. This is the route the church must follow and it must expect to follow. But the church follows Christ beyond death as well.

4. The two witnesses are raised to life

But after the three and a half days a breath of life from God entered them, and they stood on their feet, and terror struck those who saw them. Then they heard a loud voice from heaven saying to them, 'Come up here.' And they went up to heaven in a cloud, while their enemies looked on. At that very hour there was a severe earthquake and a tenth of the city collapsed. Seven thousand people were killed in the earthquake, and the survivors were terrified and gave glory to the God of heaven (11:11-13).

After the God-limited time of **three and a half days**, an amazing event happens. If we have understood how the church follows Christ, then what happens next should not surprise us unduly. **A breath of life from God entered** the witnesses. Is it any wonder that **terror struck those who saw them**? Ezekiel 37:1-

14, which describes Ezekiel's vision of a valley of dead bones coming to life, provides the background here. Ezekiel prophesies about how God's people will be brought back from exile in Babylon to the land of Israel. John sees the fulfilment of this 'coming alive of God's people' as God raises them back to life in full view of **their enemies**. Another **loud voice from heaven** calls out to them, **Come up here**. And we see that **they went up to heaven in a cloud.** They go up to heaven in glory as God's protected people. The **cloud** is a symbol of that glory and protection as it had been in the wilderness for the Israelites and Moses (see Exodus 24:15-18).

Of course, ultimately, this will be fulfilled when Christ returns and at the day of judgment. At that time all God's people will be raised to life and taken to be with him. But is that what is at the front of John's mind? Probably not, for although this 'resurrection' is attached to a judgment, it is still only a partial judgment. The final day has not yet come. There was a **severe earthquake**, which we have noted before is often attached to times of judgment. But only **a tenth of the city collapsed**. A specific number of people **were killed**.[81] And there were **survivors**. So it is most unlikely that what John now sees is a vision of the last day with many individual Christians being raised from the dead. Certainly that is what all other resurrections are pointing towards, but what is in mind here?

i) Some give glory to God

Given that the vision thus far has been about the church of this age and the persecution it has faced and does face, then it seems reasonable to assume that the **breath of life** that comes into them, comes into them as a church. This would fit with Ezekiel's prophecy of the dry bones in which the 'new life' is not so much the final resurrection, though it is ultimately fulfilled at that time, but is the restoration to an active worshipping community of the people of God. We believe this makes best sense of the passage. Thus what John is seeing is this: however many times churches are destroyed and God's people martyred or exiled or persecuted, and however many celebrations there are of those events among the unbelievers across the world, God will continue always to raise up for himself his church. This will be a matter of **terror** for those who look on. For, if only they will look, they will see that something utterly supernatural is going on. They will see evidence that God is protecting not just individuals but his church as a community in this world. Indeed, quite marvellously there will be some who are not killed in the judgment that accompanies the resurrection of the two witnesses who will now give **glory to the God of heaven**. Here is another indication that we have not yet reached the time of the final judgment, for there is yet time to repent and at least some take advantage of God's grace (in that they did not die) and turn to him.

ii) The church continues to witness

Try as it might, the city of this world cannot eradicate God's church. No sooner does it think it has done so, than the church rises again. Here we are specially reminded of those martyrs like Stephen (Acts 7) who saw heaven opened and 'the glory of God'. As he does so, he is rushed upon and put to death. And yet standing there is Saul. Later, from the weakened church, persecuted vehemently by Saul and the others, arises a witness such as the world had not seen to that point. The apostle Paul witnessed around the known world and eventually even as far as Rome itself. Earlier we mentioned Madam Mao's pronounce-ments on the demise of the church in Shanghai. Who would have imagined that a few years later there would be over one million Christians in that city! As we think of the fall of communism and the numbers who have turned back to God in the former Soviet Union, we again see life being breathed into what had been perceived by the 'inhabitants of the earth' as dead. Truly we can say that the witnesses have been dead and yet come once again to the point when they **stood on their feet**.

iii) The church follows Christ

As in persecution and death, so now in resurrection, God's people follow their Lord Jesus. As Jesus was raised from the dead and witnessed on earth before ascending back to heaven, so the church continues to rise from the dead under God's sovereignty to witness again and again so that yet more may give glory to God. And it does so while persecution continues and while God's judgment comes upon the **inhabitants of this earth**. But it does so as a people who are protected by God, and it does so in anticipation all the time of the final judgment and the great resurrection of the dead that also happens then. Just as the provisional and partial judgments of the first six seals and first six trumpets have been a precursor to the final judgment unleashed in the seventh seal and seventh trumpet, so the resurrection of the witnesses is a precursor to the final great day of resurrection when God's people will indeed experience the new heavens and the new earth. In John 16:20 Jesus said: 'I tell you the truth, you will weep and mourn while the world rejoices. You will grieve, but your grief will turn to joy.' Here is the expectation of the witnesses even as they die for the faith.

The Seventh Trumpet

The second woe has passed; the third woe is coming soon. The seventh angel sounded his trumpet, and there were loud voices in heaven, which said: 'The kingdom of the world has become the kingdom of our Lord and of his Christ, and he will reign for ever and ever.' And the twenty-four elders, who were seated on their thrones before God, fell on their faces and worshipped God, saying: 'We give thanks to you, Lord God Almighty, the One who is and who was, because you have taken your great power and have begun to reign. The nations were angry; and your wrath has come. The time has come for judging the dead, and for rewarding your servants the prophets and your saints and those who reverence your name, both small and great – and for destroying those who destroy the earth' (11:14-18).

The interlude, which has talked of the church during the time of the first six trumpets and of its duty to witness in the midst of persecution and suffering, is now over. We pick up where we left off at the end of chapter 9. The sixth trumpet, or the **second woe** is over. The **third woe** is now coming as the **seventh angel sounded his trumpet**. This is accompanied by **loud voices in heaven** that proclaim the final day, the day when the **kingdom of the world** becomes Christ's **kingdom** over which he reigns **for ever and ever**. The event is so certain that the past tense is used. This last day has been so long awaited by the angelic hosts of heaven and also the people of God already with the Lord, that they sing a hymn of praise.

It is this that all God's servants, angelic and human alike, have been waiting for. It is the time when God's **wrath has come**. It is the time of **judging the dead** and of **rewarding** the Lord's **servants**, who include the **prophets** but also all **who reverence** the Lord's **name, both small and great**. This is the time for which you and I and all Christians throughout history have been waiting. God's kingdom (**the kingdom of our Lord**), which is also **Christ's**, has at last taken full control. It is noticeable that as the **elders,** who are reigning on their thrones as well, give praise, they do so to the **Lord God Almighty**. But he is now the **One who is and who was**, and they do not add the usual *and who is to come*, for he has now come. This again helps us to see that the vision has transported us right forward to the time when God in Christ has come in glory and rules.

John draws on Psalm 2, a psalm which had prophesied about these events. There we see the nations (verse 1) plotting against God's people, and the kings of the earth setting themselves up against his anointed. But now the **kingdom of the world** is replaced by the **kingdom of our Lord and of his Christ** (anointed one). John is not saying that God was not king before this time, for he is sovereign over the whole universe all through history, and he is the only Lord. Indeed that is what this whole book of Revelation has been at pains to emphasise for the sake of the suffering church. Never before, however, have the nations of the earth had to acknowledge that fact. They have deliberately rejected this truth. God has allowed Satan a certain but limited power, and he has been the lord of the 'inhabitants of the earth'. But now Satan is defeated and the nations of the world can no longer ignore the truth or refuse the true King. As Caird says: 'A king may be king *de jure*, but he is not king *de facto* until the trumpet which announces his accession is answered by the acclamations of a loyal and obedient people.' The faithful Christians through the ages and the believers of the Old Testament have always acknowledged that kingship. On the last day no one will be able to deny it and its power will be shown in full salvation and full and permanent judgment.

The king has begun to **reign** with **great power** and has brought with him judgment that carries wrath and rewards. The suffering elect, and especially the martyrs, will have nothing to fear, but much in which to rejoice. The unbelievers are judged, for the time of repentance is passed. It is the time **for destroying those who destroy the earth**.

Then God's temple in heaven was opened, and within his temple was seen the ark of his covenant. And there came flashes of lightning, rumblings, peals of thunder, an earthquake and a great hailstorm (11:19).

In this description of the last day, we are drawn back to the start of the seven trumpets, where we suggested the battle of Jericho and the Lord's judgment of people in that city provided some of the background.[82] Now the **ark of his covenant**, which had been taken round Jericho each day, and had been the symbol of God's presence with his people, is specifically mentioned. As **God's temple in heaven was opened** the ark is seen. All that the ark had for so long symbolised has come to fulfilment. It had stood for the presence of God with his people and also for his grace and love for them. But it had also stood, as it had for Jericho, as the sign of the presence of the God who judges all who are evil.

The description of the judgment that now appears is more intense than the description of the same event in 8:5. All the symbols of judgment that we have seen before are here put together, for the last day has come and God rules over all.

Revelation 12

1. A pregnant woman

The seven trumpets and the three woes are over. Twice now, John's visions have taken us through the time of the seven churches and of the age in which we live as far as the final judgment and rule of Christ. But his visions are not over. He will take us through all this yet again, giving us much more detail about the nature of the judgment and, praise God, about the nature of the reward for those who belong to him. But now a new series of visions begins and carries through until 15:4. Each of these has to do with the issues that the suffering church is facing. Here we are given a panoramic picture of the great fight through history between the people of God and Satan. We know what will happen in the future when Christ rules over all. But now we hear again about the present. While Satan has great powers that seem to do so much damage to believers, nevertheless Christ has already won the victory on the cross. Satan is not the victor at all. The church, and therefore we too, must take encouragement from what we read here, as we have from previous visions, where we see God protecting his people.

> A great and wondrous sign appeared in heaven: a woman clothed with the sun, with the moon under her feet and a crown of twelve stars on her head. She was pregnant and cried out in pain as she was about to give birth (12:1-2).

i) The woman's identity

The **pregnant woman** is not Mary about to give birth to Jesus, as some have suggested. There is a stark contrast between this woman and the 'great prostitute' we shall read about in chapter 17. The prostitute too is well dressed, in 'purple and scarlet', but she is **drunk with the blood of the saints** (17:6). That woman stands for Babylon, the people of this earth set against

162

God. Here in chapter 12, however, we have the opposite. Here we have a woman who stands for the people of God, the church. She is **clothed with the sun** and is thus a resplendent figure. This is a **wondrous sign** that appears **in heaven**, not because the church is already ascended with the Lord, but because it is from there that the true picture can be seen. What appears far from resplendent as she suffers here on earth has, in fact, a great glory of her own **and a crown of twelve stars on her head**. This picture probably recalls the twelve tribes of Israel (see Joseph's dream in Genesis 37:9), and the crown is the reward promised to the suffering church (Revelation 2:10; 3:11).

The woman **cried out in pain** as she prepared to give birth. The birth is surely the birth of the Messiah, but it should not surprise us that the woman refers not to Mary herself but to the nation of Israel. This picture of Israel as a woman struggling to give birth is found on a few occasions in the Old Testament,[83] but specially in Isaiah 66:7-10:

'Before she goes into labour, she gives birth; before the pains come upon her, she delivers a son. Who has ever heard of such a thing? Who has ever seen such things? Can a country be born in a day or a nation be brought forth in a moment? Yet no sooner is Zion in labour than she gives birth to her children. Do I bring to the moment of birth and not give delivery?' says the LORD. 'Do I close up the womb when I bring to delivery?' says your God. 'Rejoice with Jerusalem and be glad for her, all you who love her; rejoice greatly with her, all you who mourn over her.'

The faithful Old Testament people of God suffered before eventually God brought them to the point where the Messiah was born. But now that the birth has taken place, the woman (the people of God) is still attacked and still suffers for the sake of the child, for the sake of Jesus.

ii) The woman and her child under attack

Then another sign appeared in heaven: an enormous red dragon with seven heads and ten horns and seven crowns on his heads. His tail swept a third of the stars out of the sky and flung them to the earth. The dragon stood in front of the woman who was about to give birth, so that he might devour her child the moment it was born. She gave birth to a son, a male child, who will rule all the nations with an iron sceptre. And her child was snatched up to God and to his throne. The woman fled into the desert to a place prepared for her by God, where she might be taken care of for 1,260 days (12:3-6).

The vision now moves on and John sees a **dragon** waiting **to devour** the woman's **child the moment it was born.** We will learn more about where this dragon comes from in verses 9-13. But it is clear that here we are dealing with Satan himself. The vision stresses how fearful a creature this is. He is **enormous**. His **seven crowns** and his **seven heads** indicate his authority, and his **horns** his great power. The imagery that is used here to describe Satan is replete with allusions to the Old Testament. For example, in Psalm 74:13-14 Pharaoh is described as a sea monster (or dragon; see also Ezekiel 29:3). The fact that he has **seven heads** and **crowns** may indicate that part of his aim is to usurp the place of God and so to deceive people. One of his ways of doing this will be to become the evil angelic guide for corrupt kings, nations and kingdoms. So, for example, King Herod tried to have Jesus killed as a child (Matthew 2:13). Much as Christ represents all his people, the church, so the dragon is behind and represents evil people, kings, rulers and nations. This would include the Roman empire and its Caesars who wanted to be worshipped as God, as well as more modern examples that often come in the form of humanistic societies and governments who treat God and his Word and his people with disdain, and persecute them in more subtle ways.

When Satan was thrown from heaven (see verse 9) other angelic beings (for **stars** see comments on 1:16-20) were **swept** from heaven and **flung to the earth**. Satan's attacks on God were not limited to this earth, but he first sought power in heaven.[84] God refused him and those who fought with him (see verse 7).

The child to whom the woman gave birth was **male** and is

clearly identified as the Messiah, for he **will rule all the nations with an iron sceptre**. This is a quotation from Psalm 2:8, a psalm that speaks of those who have gathered against 'the Lord and his Anointed One'. But God's Messiah will rule even these rebellious nations. It is for this reason that the child so obviously becomes a target for Satan. He wants to stop Jesus assuming his full power, **his iron sceptre,** over **the nations.**

For a while it appeared that Satan had succeeded. Evil rulers both Jewish and Roman led the attack and had Jesus crucified, and yet Jesus was raised from the dead and **snatched up to God and to his throne** in the ascension. Meanwhile, with the Messiah seated in heaven, the church continues to live in this world. However, just as Israel was delivered from the evil dominion in Egypt by being taken into the wilderness (desert) across the Red Sea, so the woman also is being kept safe in the **desert**, which is a **place prepared for her by God**. In Exodus 19:1-4 God speaks to Moses of their rescue from Egypt and being taken into the wilderness and says, 'You yourselves have seen what I did to Egypt, and how I carried you on eagles' wings and brought you to myself.'

In other words, the church will **be taken care of** during this time of attack. The **desert** represents this world. It is not a comfortable place, but it is a place where God's people are protected. The word translated here as **taken care of** in fact means *fed.* In other words the picture is that just as Israel was cared for and *fed* during the time in the wilderness, so God's church will be fed and nourished during this time, no doubt by God's Holy Spirit and by his Word in Scripture. Of course, the time in the wilderness for the Israelites was a time of protection by God. But it was also a time of testing. The Israelites failed in this testing and had to wander for 40 years in the wilderness. For us, our period in the desert will be a time of testing but, in Christ, this will prove to be a period of refining of our faith and will not end in failure, for we are protected by God himself.

The time that this will last is the time we have now encountered on a number of occasions: **1,260 days.** This is the period specifically limited by God, that will come to an end with the return of Christ. In a most marvellous way, we can talk of a 'second exodus' of God's people that many passages of the New Testament point towards. For one day we too will be delivered from the wilderness and taken to the Promised Land. We are, as Peter puts it, 'aliens and strangers' in this land, but we shall be defended and protected and fed by God during this time (1 Peter 2:11; also Hebrews 11:13). Peter sums up what we see here in Revelation: 'And the God of all grace, who called you to his eternal glory in Christ, after you have suffered a little while, will himself restore you and make you strong, firm and steadfast' (1 Peter 5:10).

2. The dragon is hurled to earth

And there was war in heaven. Michael and his angels fought against the dragon, and the dragon and his angels fought back. But he was not strong enough, and they lost their place in heaven. The great dragon was hurled down – that ancient serpent called the devil, or Satan, who leads the whole world astray. He was hurled to the earth, and his angels with him (12:7-9).

The vision now steps back and gives us more detail of how Satan was thrown down from heaven. There was a **war in heaven**. **Michael**, an archangel, is mentioned as a leader of **angels** and heads God's forces. Satan and his followers fought back. Michael won and so **the dragon and his angels** were **hurled to the earth.** Here, lest there be any doubt, the **great dragon** is identified as **the devil** and also as the one who originally tempted Eve in the Garden of Eden, **that ancient serpent**.

Then I heard a loud voice in heaven say: 'Now have come the salvation and the power and the kingdom of our God, and the authority of his Christ. For the accuser of our brothers, who accuses them before our God day and night, has been hurled down. They overcame him by the blood of the Lamb and by the word of their testimony; they did not love their lives so much as to shrink from death. Therefore rejoice, you heavens and you who dwell in them! But woe to the earth and the sea, because the devil has gone down to you! He is filled with fury, because he knows that his time is short' (12:10-12).

There is great joy in heaven at this great exercise of God's **salvation** and **power** and rule. The hurling down of Satan has revealed, against what has appeared to be true, that Christ in fact has the **authority**. They **rejoice** because the one who has been **the accuser of our brothers before our God** has been done away with. Satan's position as accuser and deceiver was continually to question, slander and seek to undermine God's people even before God himself. This is what he tried to do with Job (Job 1:6-12).

Now we discover the basis of Michael's victory. **They overcame him by the blood of the Lamb**. The victory over Satan was achieved by Christ's death on the cross. The death of Christ was the only route to the defeat of Satan. Christ died as a sacrificial **lamb** for his people, in their place. This was **the word of** the angels' **testimony**, that Jesus has overcome death and sin. Satan had no response to this. He was defeated by Christ's death on the cross. As Jesus put it in Luke 10:18, 'I saw Satan fall like lightning from heaven.' From that point on, Satan's power was vastly limited, and his final end is assured, **he knows that his time is short**. But even more significantly, no accusation or slander will unseat any of God's people from their security in Christ.

i) No more accusation

It is good that we pause here to rejoice ourselves in the truths that this passage presents. The fact is that Satan was able to accuse all people before God because of their sin. He could well argue the case that no one deserved salvation and that their sin meant they belonged to him rather than God. Sin had created a great barrier between God and all people because all are sinful. Satan had brought about this sin in the first place by deceiving Eve, then Adam, and then men and women through the ages.

This gave him the possibility of continually presenting a person's sin before God, of pointing to it and thus seeking to get the person judged by God and condemned. Satan wanted to see God exact his judicial wrath on his own people. But God had always planned a people who would be for ever his own, and he had planned the means by which their sin would be dealt with. Once sin was dealt with, there would be no possibility of further accusation. His people would be justified, declared not guilty at the judgment day, for no evidence would be offered against them.

It was this that God achieved in Jesus Christ for his people, for all who have faith in Christ. This is why the figure of Christ as a Lamb in chapter 5 is so vital to the whole account of Revelation. For it was as a sacrificial Lamb that Jesus paid the penalty they deserved. The accusation was made against Christ. He died in their place. As a result, 'Therefore, there is now no condemnation for those who are in Christ Jesus (Romans 8:1). The church that has been urged to 'overcome' in the early chapters will overcome because of the blood of the Lamb. It is worth remembering how the apostle Paul centres in on this wonderful truth that Satan can no longer make accusations against God's people. In Romans 8:31-39 he says this:

> If God is for us, who can be against us? He who did not spare his own Son, but gave him up for us all – how will he not also, along with him, graciously give us all things? Who will bring any charge against those whom God has chosen? It is God who justifies. Who is he that condemns?... For I am convinced that neither death nor life, neither angels nor demons.... will be able to separate us from the love of God that is in Christ Jesus our Lord.

What more can God's people want? We too should join with the heavenly hosts we hear in these verses in Revelation and **rejoice.**

ii) Satan continues to pursue the woman

Nevertheless, Satan's fury is still there and he **pursued** (or persecuted[85]) **the woman**. He cannot win in heaven for he can no longer accuse God's people whose sin has been atoned for and who are already justified by grace through faith in Christ. But he can continue for a limited time ('three and a half years', see verse 14) to pursue the church.

> When the dragon saw that he had been hurled to the earth, he pursued the woman who had given birth to the male child. The woman was given the two wings of a great eagle, so that she might fly to the place prepared for her in the desert, where she would be taken care of for a time, times and half a time, out of the serpent's reach. Then from his mouth the serpent spewed water like a river, to overtake the woman and sweep her away with the torrent. But the earth helped the woman by opening its mouth and swallowing the river that the dragon had spewed out of his mouth. Then the dragon was enraged at the woman and went off to make war against the rest of her offspring – those who obey God's commandments and hold to the testimony of Jesus (12:13-17).

Once again we return to the fact that the church will **be taken care of** (see verse 6) in a place **prepared** for her in the **desert**, for the time during which she is persecuted. We have already referred to Exodus 19:4 in the comments on verse 6. God carried Israel 'on eagles' wings and brought' them to himself. In his great love for his people, God carries us beyond harm as he protects us from **the serpent's reach**. The fact that Satan **spewed water like a river, to overtake the woman and sweep her away** simply refers to Satan's intense pursuit of Christians. But it may look back to the way the **torrent** of the river Jordan in flood stood between the people of Israel coming out of the wilderness and their entry into the Promised Land. Of course, the torrent was no barrier for a people protected and led by God himself and they walked across unhurt on dry land (see Joshua 3:6-17).[86] Similarly in John's vision, the waters do not reach God's people to drown them, for the **earth** swallows up **the river**. It achieves nothing. This **enraged** the serpent still further who **went off to make war against the rest** of those who belong

169

to God and witness for Jesus. Why John sees the dragon moving, as it were, from attacking the church to attacking **the rest** who are obviously also the church is thoroughly unclear. Many suggestions have been made which can help explain what John saw here. Perhaps the first part of the church that is saved has now died and gone to the protection of heaven where Satan can't go, thus Satan turns his attention to the rest of Christians still left on this earth. However, what is clear is the most important thing, and that is that all God's people are protected from this ongoing vicious attack on them by the dragon.

Revelation 13

Two Beasts Appear

Satan's attack on the 'offspring' of the woman is the final desperate fling of a defeated being. The theme of chapter 12 now continues as we see how the beast seeks to win people over to his side. As believers we are all to take careful note of this and beware lest we should fall for his deception.

> And the dragon stood on the shore of the sea. And I saw a beast coming out of the sea. He had ten horns and seven heads, with ten crowns on his horns, and on each head a blasphemous name. The beast I saw resembled a leopard, but had feet like those of a bear and a mouth like that of a lion. The dragon gave the beast his power and his throne and great authority. One of the heads of the beast seemed to have had a fatal wound, but the fatal wound had been healed. The whole world was astonished and followed the beast. Men worshipped the dragon because he had given authority to the beast, and they also worshipped the beast and asked, 'Who is like the beast? Who can make war against him?' The beast was given a mouth to utter proud words and blasphemies and to exercise his authority for forty-two months. He opened his mouth to blaspheme God, and to slander his name and his dwelling-place and those who live in heaven. He was given power to make war against the saints and to conquer them. And he was given authority over every tribe, people, language and nation. All inhabitants of the earth will worship the beast – all whose names have not been written in the book of life belonging to the Lamb that was slain from the creation of the world (13:1-8).

1. The first beast

The **dragon** stands where he can summon his minions to work for him. **On the shore of the sea** reminds us of 12:12 where a 'woe' was pronounced on earth and sea because the devil, having been thrown out of heaven, is now at work there. It suggests he is about to do things which will affect the whole world. The first evil being to make an appearance is **the beast** that we have seen back in 11:7. (See comments there on 'the beast'.) This time it comes **out of the sea**. Once again it is Daniel 7 that provides the background for this vision. The beast John sees seems to epitomise all the horrors of the four beasts mentioned in Daniel 7:3-8. For example, he is described as a **leopard**, which is Daniel's description of his third beast. In Revelation 14, when John moves on to looking at how the saints will survive, he returns again to Daniel 7 and the victory that comes with the son of man (Revelation 14:14; Daniel 7:13). In Daniel the fourth beast has **ten horns** that indicate ten kings, and his work is 'to speak against the Most High and oppress his saints' (Daniel 7:25). This is clearly the work of the beast that John sees.

i) The beast persecutes the church
He works against God and so has **on each head a blasphemous name**. The **crowns** remind us that he has power as he rules. If we allow Daniel to help us understand this vision, then it seems that the beast is the satanic force that lies behind the evil kings and rulers and nations of this world. The dragon gives them **his power and his throne and great authority**.[87]

What John now describes, therefore, is the way Satan uses unbelieving humanity, and specifically its leaders and government structures to further the persecution of the church. That **one of the heads** of this beast seemed to **have a fatal wound** that **had been healed** reminds us that these are, in fact, the last struggles of Satan and his evil followers before God finally puts an end to it all. But for the time being it seems that that fatal wound has been healed. The beast seems to be fully alive and fully powerful. This is like a perverse parody of Christ's resurrection. Yet appearances are not everything as Christians should know. God's judgment on Satan as it appears in Genesis 3:15 still stands as true and has been confirmed by the work of Christ on the cross: 'I will put enmity between you and the woman, and between your offspring and hers; he will crush your head, and you will strike his heel.' The **mortal**

wound shows that Satan has been defeated, and yet he is permitted by God to live on for a while. The curse of Satan in the Garden of Eden is finally coming to fulfilment. Satan will not be able to do anything more than 'bruise the heel' of God's people. His head has already been crushed. The wound is actually **fatal**, though for a while it does not seem that way.

ii) The beast seduces unbelievers

As the vision continues we see just how easily unbelievers across the world fall for his seduction. They are particularly drawn to his power and authority, saying, **Who is like the beast?** This question itself again indicates how people have been taken in by his parody of Christ and of God. Even as a question it is blasphemous, for time and again in the Old Testament the same question is asked of the true God, as people behold his glory and power and dominion. For example, in Exodus 15:11 as praises are sung to God who has defeated the Egyptians, we read: 'Who among the gods is like you, O LORD? Who is like you – majestic in holiness, awesome in glory, working wonders?'[88]

They continue, **Who can make war against him?** They end up worshipping him and thus also worshipping the one who lies behind it all, **the dragon,** who **had given authority to the beast**. Here we receive a salutary reminder that allegiance and subservience to evil leaders and powers is in fact ultimately worship of the dragon himself, for all the beast's evil and power is derived from Satan himself. Working on behalf of Satan, the beast continues to exercise his power for the 42 months (three and a half years) which is the time during which the church has to be protected (see 12:14). The beast does everything he can to undermine God and all that is associated with him and his people and his heavenly dwelling. He sets out to **blaspheme** and to **slander**.

In summary, the beast **makes war against the saints...to conquer** (overcome) **them**. Using every method of temptation and seduction and every bit of power and authority still available

173

to him, the beast's aim is **to conquer** God's people, **the saints**. It is this **war** against them that the churches of John's day were experiencing. This is why John, on a number of occasions (see comments on 2:7), urges them to *overcome* (the same word in Greek as is translated here 'to conquer'). Through perseverance and with the Spirit's help and with the guarantee of their names in the book of life, they will overcome and Satan will not.

The beast rules in every nation and **all inhabitants of the earth will worship the beast**. They, the unbelievers, **whose names have not been written in the book of life**,[89] are the ones who worship this deceitful being. The 'book of life' belongs to the **Lamb**. We are reminded that the people included in that book are part of God's plans from the very beginning to save a people for himself, for the Lamb **was slain from the creation of the world.** Whatever power and authority the beast appears to wield, whatever damage the beast seems to do as he wars against the saints, the Lamb is still there and he has won the victory, and it is impossible for those who belong to him to be removed from this book of life. Indeed they will not worship the beast as the rest of the world does.

If it were not for the fact that we are utterly secure with our names in the Lamb's book of life, 'measured' and protected, then we too would find ourselves worshipping the beast. Let's be aware of how real the temptations are. There is a price to be paid for resisting these temptations and taking our stand against the beast. This is the point of the next two verses.

iii) Christians must persevere

He who has an ear, let him hear. If anyone is to go into captivity, into captivity he will go. If anyone is to be killed with the sword, with the sword he will be killed. This calls for patient endurance and faithfulness on the part of the saints (13:9-10).

There were areas in the life of those early churches where the stand against the beast was weakening. So also there are in our churches today. Thus the challenge we saw after each of the seven letters in chapters 2–3 is repeated here ... **let him hear** (see comments on 2:6.)

Christians may well **go into captivity** as a result of the work of the beast, probably because anti-Christian laws have been passed. And some **will be killed**. As Christians we are therefore called, as were those seven early churches, to have **patient endurance** and to remember to be **faithful** to our Lord and Saviour and to the one true God.

iv) A parody of Christ

Everything about this beast, his assumed authority, his crowns and even his apparent resurrection, is a parody of Christ. The beast is not simply Nero, as some people have suggested (see Introduction), nor is he only a symbol of some great manifestation of the antichrist at the very end of time. Nero, Rome, Nazi Germany, the governments of Iraq or Sudan, and so on, are all continuing examples of this work of the beast. As men and women abuse power and government and assume to themselves rights that belong only to God, so the monster in fact becomes the state or society generally – given over entirely to the power of Satan. Institutionalised persecution of Christians becomes the norm. Nevertheless, it is interesting how easy we find it to see the beast elsewhere! In this passage, John sees him present in every nation and tribe. Those of us who live in so-called 'free' societies also should be aware that the beast is with us right now. Humanism has virtually complete control in our society. Humanity has set up its own structures and laws. This usurping of God's position and his laws is blasphemy. The beast is alive and kicking and waging war in all our countries. As John says in 1 John 2:18: 'Dear children, this is the last hour; and as you have heard that the antichrist is coming, even now many antichrists have come. This is how we know it is the last hour.' John is concerned that we realise the antichrist, Satan, appears in many forms and at many times, and the antichrists are among us now as they were present in John's world of the late first century.

175

2. The second beast

Then I saw another beast, coming out of the earth. He had two horns like a lamb, but he spoke like a dragon. He exercised all the authority of the first beast on his behalf, and made the earth and its inhabitants worship the first beast, whose fatal wound had been healed. And he performed great and miraculous signs, even causing fire to come down from heaven to earth in full view of men. Because of the signs he was given power to do on behalf of the first beast, he deceived the inhabitants of the earth. He ordered them to set up an image in honour of the beast who was wounded by the sword and yet lived. He was given power to give breath to the image of the first beast, so that it could speak and cause all who refused to worship the image to be killed (13:11-15).

i) A false prophet

John now saw a second beast come out **of the earth.** He is to be identified with a **false prophet** (see 16:13; 19:20; 20:10). His job was to be a prophet and point the way to the beast and encourage unbelievers (**inhabitants** of **the earth**) to **worship the first beast**. As we have seen, this involves worshipping all the sinful powers of the day that can be represented by societies and by governments, such as the Roman one in John's day or others in our own. This beast too appears as a parody of Christ. Where Christ is the 'faithful and true witness', this beast is false. While *the* Lamb appears with seven horns in 5:6, this beast looks **like a lamb**, though with only **two horns**. The two horns remind us of one of the evil beasts who appeared in Daniel's vision (8:3). Of course he spoke **like a dragon** because he too received his power and words from Satan. He worked on behalf of the beast as the beast's messenger. And again he **exercised all the authority** that was delegated to him by the first beast. Like the beast, he **deceived** people into thinking that he was something that he wasn't, for he **performed great and miraculous signs**. He was even able to do what the prophets of Baal at the time of Elijah were unable to do and to cause **fire to come down from heaven** (see 1 Kings 18:24-29). It is not much wonder that people were thus led astray.

ii) The beast targets the church

If the first beast lies behind secular powers who strive to overthrow all that is Christian, the second beast comes as a prophet drawing people towards **worship**. In other words, this beast targets people within the church itself. Many passages in the New Testament warn about the rise of false prophets within the church and the demonic source of all their work. He will do things among God's people that they have come to think of as things only God himself does, for example, bringing fire down from heaven. He will do great signs such as Moses and Elijah and the apostles did, and his ability and power to deceive is very great. Here is the one behind the false prophets who come like 'sheep', of whom Jesus said, 'Watch out for false prophets. They come to you in sheep's clothing, but inwardly they are ferocious wolves' (Matthew 7:15). Later in Matthew 24:24 he says, 'For false Christs and false prophets will appear and perform great signs and miracles to deceive even the elect – if that were possible.' We praise God that we know that, as Jesus indicates and John has repeatedly shown, it is not possible ultimately to deceive the elect. It is only those who are in fact unbelievers, yet within the church, who will follow the beast.

No doubt the particular form of temptation will differ from age to age, but it will focus on compromise with the state and the consensus of society, behind which lies the first beast. So deceitful is the second beast's **power** that sinful humanity sets **up an image in honour of the** (first) **beast**. He leads people to worship human leaders or societies and their values, norms, powers and influences. He persuades people that what is on offer is not much different to the Christian faith. It may even look very similar with its ethics and laws and so on, yet at its heart is humanity rather than God, and behind this human-centred institution and power lies, in fact, the evil being of Satan himself. In whatever way and whatever form people have been deceived, they will be idolatrous and worshipping the parody rather than the true God. Jesus is replaced by that which represents Satan himself. In many western cultures this is exactly what humanism is all about. Man replaces God and Christ with himself, and in doing so succumbs to the full deception of the beast. For in setting himself up in the place of God, man in fact sets up an image of the one who drives him forward and stands behind all such actions, Satan himself.

The fact that the second beast was **given power to give breath to the image of the first beast** suggests that at each turn, the second beast will seek to persuade people that what they are giving themselves to in worship will live for ever. The power of deception here is that Satan's **mortal wound** is hidden completely. At every point, the first beast is shown by the second to be alive and well and eternal, again parodying Christ who lives forever. If the first beast represents human institutions, empires and world leaders who set themselves up in the place of God, it is easy to see how this delusion of permanence could be very persuasive in leading people away from a suffering and dying church. If this beast was able also to **cause all who refused to worship the image to be killed**, then the deception is dramatic. 'Life' now lies in the hands of the beast, therefore he should be worshipped. On the other hand, the way of the church and of the Christian faith is 'death'. So the beast's offer to those who follow him sounds like this: 'worship the one you can see and thus live and enjoy life. Or don't worship the beast and see that your life will be impermanent and you are heading for suffering and death.'

The church must be aware that the first beast is at work 'out there' behind the authorities and powers of this world, but the second beast is a false prophet who comes again and again in each generation right into the church. He comes in a deceitful way. Christ has warned us. The apostles Paul and Peter warned us[90], and now John warns us through his vision.

> He also forced everyone, small and great, rich and poor, free and slave, to receive a mark on his right hand or on his forehead, so that no one could buy or sell unless he had the mark, which is the name of the beast or the number of his name (13:16-17).

iii) The mark of the beast

These evil forces control the powers of government and state. Thus people can be required to 'toe the line' with this worship of all that is evil. Whatever status in society a person may have, no matter how lowly or how exalted, all will find they have to identify with the beast. They will find that, if they do not, then they will not even be able to take part in the normal activities of human society like buying and selling. They will need something that will identify them as followers of the beast if they are even to get enough to eat. We have seen already in 2:9 that this was going on in John's day. This is a further parody of Christ's work. Christians are 'sealed' by Christ. Here evil governments and leaders do their own form of 'sealing'. It is most unlikely that this will be a literal mark on a **right hand** or a **forehead**. It is simply a picture taken out of the world of slavery, where slaves were branded. The question will be for all, however, 'Are you owned by the beast?' If the answer is 'no', then they will be barred from activities such as buying and selling. John's vision does not envisage that all Christians will always be faced with such awful situations, but rather he prepares each generation for such fearful manifestations of the grip of power that the beast has over the evil rulers and kingdoms of the world.

iv) The number of the beast

John has one thing more to say in this vision about **the number of the beast**.

> This calls for wisdom. If anyone has insight, let him calculate the number of the beast, for it is man's number. His number is 666 (13:18).

This enigmatic number has given rise to so much speculation we cannot possibly deal with it all here. Clearly, if it is to be taken literally, then it is not a visible mark on the followers of Satan at present. But we have argued that these numbers are not literal and that this work of the beast continues throughout the period of the church. We can certainly dispose of some of

179

the wilder ideas of some popular films or even some preachers. For example, it does not refer to the sort of tattoo-figure seen on evil people in modern occult-type films, nor does it refer to the ubiquitous numbers found on credit cards (as I was once told by a well-meaning pastor)! It is just possible that the numbers are equal to a name, since numbers can occasionally stand for letters. Thus some say it may stand for 'Nero Caesar'. However, the explanation is better understood symbolically. We know that seven is the number of fullness or perfection, and it is a divine number usually associated with God. Perhaps therefore we may see **666, man's number**, as never perfect but always imperfect, symbolising evil and the falling short of God's standards.

Revelation 14

The Redeemed

We are now well used to the way John's vision moves between the realities of suffering and judgment and evil, and the joy of Christian security guaranteed by Christ. His vision now once again turns to see how God protects and secures his people, and he immediately sees again **the Lamb** (5:6-14). Here is the true Lamb, unlike the false lamb of 13:11, to whom genuine allegiance and worship must be given. He is **on Mount Zion**, indicating that he is indeed the Messiah and King of all, who saves and who judges. He is the one whom the Father has 'installed' on the throne and who should make 'the kings of the earth' who follow the beast 'tremble'. [91]

> Then I looked, and there before me was the Lamb, standing on Mount Zion, and with him 144,000 who had his name and his Father's name written on their foreheads. And I heard a sound from heaven like the roar of rushing waters and like a loud peal of thunder. The sound I heard was like that of harpists playing their harps. And they sang a new song before the throne and before the four living creatures and the elders. No one could learn the song except the 144,000 who had been redeemed from the earth. These are those who did not defile themselves with women, for they kept themselves pure. They follow the Lamb wherever he goes. They were purchased from among men and offered as firstfruits to God and the Lamb. No lie was found in their mouths; they are blameless (14:1-5).

In chapter 13 the triumph of the beasts and dragon seems almost complete. They have been allowed to 'conquer', that is, to put to death, the saints (13:7, 15). And yet the period of the dragon's power is limited (12:12) to the symbolic three and a half years ('forty-two months' 13:5). This is the time during which the woman (the church) is 'taken care of' in 'the desert' (12:6, 14).

So now John receives another vision of great encouragement that builds on these facts. This vision can be seen as a leap into the future, reminding us of the realities that will be as Christ saves those who are his and judges those who follow the beast. Certainly the vision moves again towards that final judgment as we come to the end of this chapter and into chapter 15. But the vision at this point mainly portrays the real *current* position of the Lamb who has been exalted by the Father to his right hand of ruling power. This is still part of the present context of the appeal for 'patient endurance and faithfulness on the part of the saints' (13:10), as we will see below in 14:12. The attacks of the beasts are in the present world, and the messages of the angels (14:6-20) are for this world. So also this vision is for Christians in this world.

1. 144,000
The figure of 144,000, as we saw back in 7:4, represents the complete number of the **redeemed from the earth**. These are the ones who **were purchased from among men** by Christ's death on the cross. Figuratively, therefore, the number represents the total number of the elect of all ages. There is an obvious contrast here between those who have the beast's mark on them and the elect who have the **Father's name written on their foreheads.** God's people, who are suffering so terribly in a world that seems to be overcome by the beasts, belong to and are protected and empowered by Christ himself (see comments on 7:1-3 and the 'sealing').

i) Their new song
As John continues, we are reminded further of images that have already been seen in this book. The sound of **rushing waters** (1:15) and of **thunder** (4:5; 11:19) tell us clearly that we are in the presence of God and of Christ. But the noise that John hears is of **harps** and singing. Here are God's people singing **a new song before the throne.** The **new song** is the song of those who know that Christ has 'purchased' his people 'for God'.[92]

In 15:2 we shall see that **harps** are held by those who now stand in God's presence having 'been victorious', in other words, in the future. But what of the present? Is it possible really to suggest that John sees the same persecuted people we have heard of in chapter 13 with the Lamb and before his throne *even* while they are being persecuted?

Certainly this is possible. The apostle Paul speaks like this in Ephesians 2:6: 'And God raised us up with Christ and seated us with him in the heavenly realms in Christ Jesus.' Even now, Paul is saying, Christians share in the rule of Christ, for they are *in Christ*. John knows that God's people already sing a 'new song' even in the midst of tribulation and suffering and persecution, for they sing the song of the redeemed. They sing of their salvation in Christ and, along with those already before the throne, their praises join together with the people of God from all ages. It is therefore clear that only the redeemed **learn the song**. Only they understand the profound reality that Christ has already overcome sin and Satan and that this will truly be manifest at the end of the age.

ii) Their purity

Interestingly John further describes the redeemed as those who **did not defile themselves with women** and who were **pure**.[93] This description has certainly caused some interpreters real problems![94] However, we need to remember that ideas of adultery and prostitution are typical metaphorical biblical language for going after other gods (see, for example, Ezekiel 16:15-22; 1 Chronicles 5:25). The redeemed are those who have not worshipped the beast, but who are betrothed to the Lamb (2 Corinthians 11:2). In other words, they are those who have not committed spiritual and religious adultery. Indeed, as John goes on to say, **they follow the Lamb wherever he goes**.

Special lessons for today

There have always been two great temptations for the church. *First, we are tempted to compromise with the world.* We have noted this on several occasions already. However, the description of the two beasts, and particularly the second that comes as a false prophet, reminds us just how seductive the values and gods of the world around us really are. Many are asked to wear the 'mark of the beast' in various ways. The temptation to compromise the faith and God's truth is already a day-to-day issue for many Christians in the workplace. Christians are asked to tell lies about what they sell, exaggerate accounts or turn a blind eye to dishonesty and theft. Refusing to go along with this leads to loss of promotion and, increasingly, loss of jobs. Even in our Western countries, many in the church are feeling the power of the beast already. In many other countries the impact is, of course, far more noticeable. In some Islamic countries food aid has only been made available to those who identify as Islamic. Certainly the mark of the beast – an enforced compromise with the gods of this world – is a reality even today for many Christians.

Secondly, Christians can easily be tempted to become overly pietistic and opt out of the world, simply waiting and suffering until Christ returns to the rescue. John has already shown that compromise is wrong. The second option is now also seen to be wrong. The church is not called to suffer passively, but to preach the gospel extrovertly and directly and to keep the commandments of God and follow Christ **wherever he goes**. The church is involved in warfare with the dragon who wants everything to obey him. *We* must seek to bring *every* area of life in this world into obedience to Christ, keeping the new song of the redeemed of God always on our lips, keeping ourselves pure and free from compromise, and always telling the truth, especially about Christ, rather than promoting the lies of the beast. John now speaks of gospel proclamation which is an essential part of the work of the church in this age.

2. The gospel proclaimed

> Then I saw another angel flying in mid-air, and he had the eternal gospel to proclaim to those who live on the earth – to every nation, tribe, language and people. He said in a loud voice, 'Fear God and give him glory, because the hour of his judgment has come. Worship him who made the heavens, the earth, the sea and the springs of water' (14:6-7).

John has seen how believers are protected and belong to the Lord, but now he sees an angel who goes out to those who do not believe (note again **those who live on the earth**, 3:10; 11:10). He proclaims **the eternal gospel**. Here is an angelic figure who does what the church is also called to do. In the very midst of persecution and the sufferings of the last days, still the gospel must be proclaimed. The message shows us again the grace of God in all its magnificence. Just when the beast and Satan are seen to be at the height of their authority and the church apparently at its weakest point, God still ensures that the gospel is heard in the world. The angel proclaims, as it were, the last clarion call to **Fear God and give him glory**, for the time for **judgment has come**. The call urges that people worship the great Creator.

Nevertheless, the emphasis of the message is actually on the arrival of judgment, for it contains the news of Jesus' kingship and of his return to judge and to save. As this angel flies out from the presence of God, it is clear that the time for grace has all but disappeared. In fact, it is this message that will, for the most part, confirm unbelievers in their sin. It will lead to more Christians being put to death and to still further rebellion, but in God's great plan it must be proclaimed to the very end of time. The gospel looks forward to that time when God's final sovereign power will be seen and when the suffering church will be vindicated. But it is also the time when Satan will finally be completely defeated and sin eradicated. Thus, even the judgment side of the gospel is 'good news' for God's people, as it tells them of the time when they and their Lord will be vindicated and they will be saved. In all God's dealings with men and women, even back in the Old Testament covenants, two alternatives lie before them: blessing or curse. People may be recipients of God's grace or, if they deliberately rebel and turn against him, they will be recipients of his judgment. **Babylon**, that is, the evil world set against God, *will* fall as the next angel now makes clear, for time moves on.

Babylon Falls

A second angel followed and said, 'Fallen! Fallen is Babylon the Great, which made all the nations drink the maddening wine of her adulteries.' A third angel followed them and said in a loud voice: 'If anyone worships the beast and his image and receives his mark on the forehead or on the hand, he, too, will drink of the wine of God's fury, which has been poured full strength into the cup of his wrath. He will be tormented with burning sulphur in the presence of the holy angels and of the Lamb' (14:8-10).

The state and institutions of the world that have followed Satan, those who have obliged people to join in the blasphemous and anti-God lies they have lived (**adulteries**), have **fallen**. The vision looks to the time of the final judgment and beyond. Those who thought they were victorious have again heard the gospel but still refused it and have shown their rebellion as they continue to **worship the beast and his image**.

1. Babylon's identity
Here is the first mention of **Babylon** in the Revelation.[95] The people of the seven churches would probably have seen Babylon in terms of Rome and the pagan empire (see comments on the 'seven hills', 17:4-9). But the reason for using this nation and city as a symbol of all that is evil and judged by God comes from the Old Testament. Babylon was the city and nation state to which the Israelites were taken in captivity. Babylon conquered God's people, destroyed their temple, and took them away. Many Israelites, like Daniel and Ezekiel, did not compromise with the Babylonians nor did they give way in the

times when their captors sought to enforce worship of their gods or their ruler, Nebuchadnezzar. But when the Israelite believers did not compromise, they suffered greatly at the hands of their oppressors. For example, Daniel was thrown into the lions' den and his friends into a fiery furnace. In these cases God protected them through their sufferings as they stood for him. But Babylon understandably thus became a symbol for a world and its rulers and people who are set against God. These people try again and again to conquer God's people and force them into compromise. Babylon is also, of course, the very city in which God's people find themselves protected by God. Eventually, God himself brings judgment upon this Babylon, as surely as he finally brought destruction upon the Babylonian empire.

2. She receives fearful judgment

It is this message of judgment and destruction that the **second** and third **angels** now pronounce so clearly. Babylon has **fallen**, and those who have followed her and worshipped **the beast**, and who have received **his mark**, will encounter **God's fury** and face **the cup of his wrath**. Drawing on Jeremiah 51:7-8,[96] John shows us how **all the nations** have been drawn into her seduction. They **drink** of her sin. So, in a careful play on words, we read that in the judgment they will **drink of the wine of God's fury** which will be at **full strength**. The picture, again coming from the Old Testament, is that God's wrath will not be like watered-down wine, but full strength. This is the end of the time of grace for Babylon and her people. Being **tormented with burning sulphur** is a different picture to describe the same reality of the horror and reality of this judgment. The judgment takes place in the presence of the Lamb. Jesus is judge. They will not remain in his presence because their final destination involves 'everlasting destruction' and being 'shut out from the presence of the Lord' (2 Thessalonians 1:9). The **burning sulphur** reminds us that this is the same end as came upon Sodom and Gomorrah (see comments on 9:17-18). This leads straight into the next description of their end.

187

'And the smoke of their torment rises for ever and ever. There is no rest day or night for those who worship the beast and his image, or for anyone who receives the mark of his name' (14:11).

The final end of all unbelievers, of Babylon, is the doom of Sodom. Here is the completion of the prophecy of Isaiah 13:19: 'Babylon, the jewel of kingdoms, the glory of the Babylonians' pride, will be overthrown by God like Sodom and Gomorrah.' Just as eternal life is continuous for ever, so here **their torment** is for ever. The lack of **rest** refers to the fact that they will never enjoy the 'rest' that belongs to the people of God. For them there is no eternal Sabbath of rest in the Lord's presence (Hebrews 4:3-11), but the opposite: an eternity without him, in which the people suffer the permanent and ongoing fate of Satan, their leader (20:10).

3. Further encouragement to the faithful

This calls for patient endurance on the part of the saints who obey God's commandments and remain faithful to Jesus. Then I heard a voice from heaven say, 'Write: Blessed are the dead who die in the Lord from now on.' 'Yes,' says the Spirit, 'they will rest from their labour, for their deeds will follow them' (14:12-13).

Once again in the midst of talk of the punishment facing those who will not worship Christ, Christians receive encouragement. These are the ones who **obey** God and **remain faithful to Jesus.** They are **blessed** and so will receive all the inheritance promised in God's covenants with his people. It is truly remarkable to realise that the death of believers (those **in the Lord**) that may come in a suffering world and at the hands of persecutors is the path to glory and God's blessings. As it was with Christ in his death and resurrection, so it will be for us. The Holy **Spirit** himself guarantees that we **will rest** from our **labour** (troubles) in an eternity with our Saviour. Our **deeds** provide evidence in the Christian life of that inward faith that has trusted entirely upon God's gracious salvation.

4. Judgment like a harvest

John has heard the proclamation of the gospel. He has heard
the descriptions of judgment on Babylon. He has once again
turned to see how God's people are dealt with during all this,
but now the vision moves back to judgment, which is described
as like a **harvest**. A **sickle** is used to cut the harvest of grapes.

> I looked, and there before me was a white cloud, and seated on the cloud
> was one 'like a son of man' with a crown of gold on his head and a sharp
> sickle in his hand. Then another angel came out of the temple and called
> in a loud voice to him who was sitting on the cloud, 'Take your sickle
> and reap, because the time to reap has come, for the harvest of the earth
> is ripe.' So he who was seated on the cloud swung his sickle over the
> earth, and the earth was harvested. Another angel came out of the temple
> in heaven, and he too had a sharp sickle. Still another angel, who had
> charge of the fire, came from the altar and called in a loud voice to him
> who had the sharp sickle, 'Take your sharp sickle and gather the clusters
> of grapes from the earth's vine, because its grapes are ripe.' The angel
> swung his sickle on the earth, gathered its grapes and threw them into
> the great winepress of God's wrath. They were trampled in the winepress
> outside the city, and blood flowed out of the press, rising as high as the
> horses' bridles for a distance of 1,600 stadia (14:14-20).

The picture provided by these verses is sadly all too clear. The
decision that the harvest is ready to be cut down is taken by
Christ himself. The **white cloud** reminds us that this scene takes
place in the presence of God in all his glory. King Jesus wearing
a crown of gold holds the **sickle** in his own hand. An **angel**
calls on the Lord to begin the work of **harvest**, and so it begins
and **the earth was harvested**. The angels mentioned in the
verses which follow carry out this work for the Lord. This is
the earth's vine, not the vine of God's people. In this awesome
picture, all that is harvested faces **God's wrath**. The vivid
picture reminds us that in the old days wine was made by people
treading on the grapes. As this crop is dealt with by being
trampled upon, so the picture switches from grape juice pouring
out to **blood**. The amount of blood provides another fearsome
picture of the full horror of the wrath of God against those who
have consistently rebelled against him and continuously rejected

his gracious presentation of the gospel.

The picture needs nothing adding to it here, except to say that its violence is deliberately designed to be breathtaking. While it is a picture, and not a literal description, of the final judgment, we must never undo its force. To be judged by the Almighty God and to be without rest for ever is a worse fate than we can imagine, and we are to be warned and to warn others. In contrast with this, how glorious is the rest and joy and blessedness of those who die in the Lord.

Special lessons for today

First, we must understand the relationship between the call for perseverance and our deeds. We have seen on many occasions how John calls Christians to 'overcome' and to 'persevere'. This is an emphasis on what Christians must *do* and how they are to *live* and *behave*. On the other hand, we have also repeatedly seen that, in his grace, God has 'sealed' us as his people and promised to protect us and keep us through the onslaughts of Satan and the forces of darkness. We must insist, therefore, that our works and deeds neither save us *nor* do they maintain us as members of God's people. Salvation and perseverance are a work of Christ and are ours entirely by grace. Nevertheless, those who belong to the Lord will be seen to persevere and to be faithful to Christ in all they say and do. Their actions will not deny their 'sealing' by Christ. Indeed when Christians die, their deeds do indeed follow them (14:12-13). These are the deeds of those who have known the grace of God in their lives. The challenge to us in the midst of a sinful world is to see that we never compromise with the world and that we follow Christ everywhere. When we fail we must repent. Let us make sure we ask ourselves whether we have succumbed to the seduction of the second beast.

Secondly, we must see damnation for what it really is. Nowadays, there seems to be an increasing tendency to downplay or ignore the full horror of God's final damnation of all who have set their minds, hearts and actions against him. To see damnation as it really is, in the passage we have just examined and in the chapters to come, should give us a great incentive to speak of Christ to friends and contacts before it is too late.

Thirdly, we need to say something about the nature of damnation, since this is much debated these days. Are people condemned to eternal torture going on for ever? Will there be eternal conscious physical and spiritual torment? Will the eternal torment be largely of the 'spiritual' kind?

Some propose a view of damnation that is referred to as 'conditional immortality'. This view suggests that souls are not inherently immortal, but become immortal when God justifies the sinner. Thus, the unsaved will cease to exist. Not dissimilar to this is the view that is sometimes called 'annihilationism'. This suggests that damnation is experienced by Satan's followers, but they are headed for complete annihilation and will not live forever in torment.

We believe that some form of the traditional view of hell more accurately reflects the biblical material both in Revelation and in Scripture generally. However, we need to be careful to let the Bible speak for itself. So often Christians let descriptions of Dante's *Inferno*, or of medieval art, describe for them a hell which they can then reject in favour of some form of 'conditional immortality'. One of the best ways of approaching the subject is by way of *contrast*. We know the righteous and the unrighteous (the justified and the unforgiven) will be raised bodily for the final judgment. We know that those who are judged righteous (justified by faith and redeemed by the blood of Christ) will then live for ever, perfected and holy, in the presence of God whom they will see. This contrasts with those who reject Christ. The biblical evidence suggests they will see their 'lord', Satan, and be in his presence for ever. There is surely no doubt that this will lead to spiritual torment for ever. They will never find the promises of God coming true for them. There will be no fulfilment of covenant promises, no 'rest', no 'peace', no viewing of the glory of God – the goal for which

191

people were created. More than that, they will not be living in the recreated 'new' heavens and earth. The results of the fall, pain and struggle in all things, will not be removed.

As we shall see later in this book of Revelation, there is a very real sense in which those who have followed Satan in this life are, most justly, given by God exactly what they have always wanted. It is neither unjust, nor in conflict with God's love for his creation and his people, that life in 'hell' should also last for ever. Since Satan suffers eternal torment (20:10), the ungodly suffer the same.

However, to become too specific about the nature of such judgment is dangerous. It is one thing to say it is a just judgment lasting for ever, and altogether another to talk of people having bodies that will always burn (literally) and yet never die or be consumed. Different metaphors are used, even by Jesus, which, if taken literally, are self-contradictory. 'Burning flames' and 'sulphur smoke' are hardly visible in 'outer darkness'.

What I believe we must do is to recognise the nature of these metaphors. Each is describing something so awful, so much without God, that current human language can no more accurately describe it, than it can accurately describe the joy and light and glory and surrounding habitation to be experienced by those who will be forever in the Lord's presence.

Revelation 15

Another Vision of the Throne Room of God

The following four verses bring to an end the series of visions which started back in 12:1 as well as providing a backdrop for what is yet to come. Each of the visions since 12:1 has had to do with the issues that the suffering church is facing. While Satan's great powers that seem to do so much damage to believers have been acknowledged, nevertheless we have seen that Christ has already won the victory on the cross. Satan is not actually the victor at all. John's vision is now about to move on and introduce us to yet another series of seven judgments, this time judgments seen in 'bowls of wrath'. Verse 1 shows that these will bring it all to an end and **God's wrath** will be **completed**. But just as this next series is about to be introduced, verses 2-4 again remind us of the glorious outcome of history for all who believe in Jesus Christ.

I saw in heaven another great and marvellous sign: seven angels with the seven last plagues – last, because with them God's wrath is completed. And I saw what looked like a sea of glass mixed with fire and, standing beside the sea, those who had been victorious over the beast and his image and over the number of his name. They held harps given them by God and sang the song of Moses the servant of God and the song of the Lamb:
　'Great and marvellous are your deeds,
　　　Lord God Almighty.
　Just and true are your ways,
　　　King of the ages.
　Who will not fear you, O Lord,
　　　and bring glory to your name?
　For you alone are holy.
　All nations will come
　　　and worship before you,
　for your righteous acts have been revealed' (15:1-4).

Verse 1 introduces the **seven last plagues** or the **bowls of wrath** and we return to these in verses 5-7. Meanwhile we see again into the throne room of God, which continues to provide the great backdrop to all that is happening. Notice that a description of this throne room has preceded both of the series of judgments John has already described. In 4:1–5:14 the description preceded the opening of the seven seals, and in 8:1-5 the description preceded the judgments of the seven trumpets. The vision helps us see once again, first, God's great holiness and, secondly, the time when all praise and glory will be given to God for finally having dealt with Satan and **the beast and his image**.

1. God alone is holy

We have already met the **sea of glass** in 4:6. It serves to separate God in his great holiness from sin and evil. It is a vivid symbolic reminder that sin and sinful people cannot come right into God's presence. In this sense it is also **mixed with fire**, for it points to judgment for those who might want to cross it and yet have not been cleansed of their sin. But John sees **those who had been victorious over the beast and his image and over the number of his name** standing right there beside the sea. The picture draws on the Old Testament and indicates that these people have, as it were, crossed the Red Sea into the Promised Land. That which separated them from enjoying the fulness of God's presence has been 'overcome'. Those who appeared to be on the losing side are seen in fact to have been victorious and they sing a victory **song.** This is, of course, not yet the end. Rather it serves as a reminder of what happens to those who die in the fierce tribulation and persecution the saints face. Note the future tense in verse 4 when **all nations will come ...** This has yet to happen. Indeed the time will come when there will be 'no longer any sea' (21:1). But for now, those who have overcome and are already with the Lord praise him as they see his justice being poured out across the earth and recognise that victory is already theirs. They are confirmed in their holiness and are now with

God. They have entered the holy presence of God himself, hence their song, **for you alone are holy**.

2. Praise in heaven for God's justice

Such a glorious inheritance causes God's people of all ages to be filled with songs of praise. The song specifically acknowledges God's **just and true ways**. The people of God have seen him vindicate them and vindicate his name. It is worth pausing to think about the way they describe God here: **Lord God Almighty** and **King of the ages.** His sovereignty and supremacy in all things have enabled his justice to triumph. Two songs here are merged into one. Here the faithful of the Old Testament era (**the song of Moses**) are joining with the faithful of this age (**the song of the Lamb**). This was what all God's people had been awaiting. Moses' song of victory as the Israelites finished crossing the Red Sea is found in Exodus 15. Another of his songs is found in Deuteronomy 32. These are great songs of praise to God, who had delivered his people from the persecution of Egypt and brought them through the plagues and Red Sea into the Promised Land. They are also songs that praise God for his justice in judging Pharaoh and the Egyptians. The song of the Lamb reminds us that, through faith in the finished work of Christ on the cross, the current tribulation, suffering and persecution also gives way in a new Exodus to an eternity in the presence of our Holy and Almighty God.[97]

As they sing to God of his **great and marvellous deeds**, so they look forward to the time when **all nations will come and worship** him. The time is coming when even God's enemies will (grudgingly) have to bow the knee to God (see Philippians 2:10). But for now we must return yet again to the harsh realities of a world facing the wrath of God, of judgment on Satan and his followers, and of salvation (but also suffering) for God's people. The final series of God's judgments is now described.

> After this I looked and in heaven the temple, that is, the tabernacle of the Testimony, was opened. Out of the temple came the seven angels with

the seven plagues. They were dressed in clean, shining linen and wore golden sashes round their chests. Then one of the four living creatures gave to the seven angels seven golden bowls filled with the wrath of God, who lives for ever and ever. And the temple was filled with smoke from the glory of God and from his power, and no one could enter the temple until the seven plagues of the seven angels were completed (15:5-8).

3. God's power in judgment

John sees **the tabernacle of the Testimony** which has been **opened** in **heaven.** Both the Tabernacle and the Temple were places where God's presence was made known for the Israelites. In the Tabernacle was the ark of the covenant, which we have seen before in 11:19. This contained the testimony of the Lord, the Ten Commandments, which summarised for all God's people the holiness and godliness that God expects of them. The fact that John now sees all this as **opened** indicates that God is now holding people accountable to his revealed word.

The agents whom God has commissioned to carry out this accounting and judgment are **the seven angels with the seven plagues.** While we have seen that the number seven indicates God's fulfilment and completion of his will, the idea of **seven plagues** also draws upon Leviticus 26:18, 21, 24 and 28. In that chapter God lays out the judgment that will come even upon Israel if they refuse to listen to him and obey him. Four times God repeats that he will judge the sinful *seven times over*, and with each statement the judgments are intensified. In just the same manner, as the seven bowls of wrath are revealed we shall see a greater and greater intensification until the final judgment itself is revealed.

In that one of the **living creatures** (see comments on 4:6) hands the angels **seven golden bowls filled with the wrath of God** we see clearly again that God is in control of what is now about to happen. Here once more we see that the prayers of the saints in 5:8 are indeed being answered, for God's justice is being revealed – 'the four living creatures and the twenty-four elders fell down before the Lamb. Each one had a harp and they were holding **golden bowls** full of incense, which are the prayers of the saints.'

So awful is God's justice and judgment that **no one could enter the temple**. No one can turn God's hand, for this is the **God who lives for ever and ever.** Here is God in all his **glory**. The **smoke** may be a reminder of the cloud that symbolises that glory elsewhere in Scripture. Here, though, it probably indicates the all-pervasive power of his judgment.[98]

Revelation 16

The Bowls of God's Wrath

This chapter breaks down into seven sections reflecting the pouring out of the seven bowls of God's wrath. The similarities between the judgment effected by the outpouring of these bowls and the blowing of the trumpets indicates that here again we are re-visiting the judgment of God that goes on throughout history and ends with the final judgment. We have briefly looked at a comparison of the judgments of the seals, trumpets and bowls back in the comments on 8:6-13, and it will help to have a look at the introductory comments on 8:6 once again.

When we looked at the trumpets, we saw that the first six described the ongoing judgment of God in the time between the resurrection and exaltation of Christ and his second coming. The seventh described the final judgment at Christ's coming. The bowls do much the same thing, except that the sixth bowl seems to concentrate more deeply on the state of the world at the point of Christ's return. The description of the judgment of the 'bowls' is less figurative and more immediate and direct than what we have heard before. In this sense, the 'trumpet visions may be compared to incomplete snapshots and the bowls to more detailed pictures.'[99] Yet even these vivid descriptions will be elaborated and expanded upon further in chapters 17 and 18, as the judgment on the harlot and on Babylon is described.

> Then I heard a loud voice from the temple saying to the seven angels, 'Go, pour out the seven bowls of God's wrath on the earth' (16:1).

The first thing John hears is a command that comes from God. The angels must begin their work. The picture of **bowls of God's wrath** comes once more from Ezekiel. There we often

198

find the prophet talking of the wrath of God being 'poured out'. For example, in Ezekiel 7:6-8 we read: 'The end has come! The end has come!... Doom has come upon you... I am about to pour out my wrath on you and spend my anger against you; I will judge you according to your conduct and repay you for all your detestable practices.'

We are again reminded that continued sin and rebellion has brought about the judgment being witnessed in the world and soon to be seen in its awful finality. God will not allow men and women to continue in sin for ever. The pictures that now follow again reflect, at least in part, the judgments that came upon the Egyptians in the plagues. And here it is worth remembering that, just as eternal salvation and the promise of a homeland for ever in the presence of God is prefigured in the way God saved his people from the Egyptians and brought them to the Promised Land, so the judgment that came on a continually rebelling pagan Egyptian people prefigured the way God would deal with those who continue to live in sin and rebellion. Thus, as we see parallels between the trumpet judgments and now the bowl judgments and the plagues of Egypt, John is reminding us in a vivid way of what we must expect – salvation or judgment.

1. The first bowl

> The first angel went and poured out his bowl on the land, and ugly and painful sores broke out on the people who had the mark of the beast and worshipped his image (16:2).

Resembling the plague of boils that God sent on the Egyptians (Exodus 9:8-12), this represents some form of suffering which will be suffered by those who are not Christians, by those who **worshipped** the **beast**. The **ugly sores** match the ugly and evil **mark** that identifies these people. In the way to which we have now become accustomed, John is speaking in picture language and so we do not need to expect literal sores and boils. But we do recognise that the punishment God metes out on this earth in people's lives is a 'punishment that fits the crime'.

199

Metaphorically they suffer marks on their bodies because they are *marked*. In the midst of their sin they find consequences that indicate an appropriate judgment from God. This ought to lead to repentance as people see that what they are doing is having consequences that are painful and ugly in their lives. Some do indeed repent, but many do not. The Egyptians had multiple opportunities to repent but sadly, to our knowledge, most did not.

2. The second bowl

> The second angel poured out his bowl on the sea, and it turned into blood like that of a dead man, and every living thing in the sea died (16:3).

This second **bowl** of wrath is not unlike the second trumpet (see comments on 8:8). It also resembles the plague in Exodus 7:17-18 where the Nile was turned to blood. The economic consequences of sin may be in mind here, as people depended on the sea for their transport, fish and so on. As people come to depend on materialism and comfort, while turning away from God, so the Creator will take away that comfort and the source of that materialism, for the Creator God is able to do this at his will. Whereas only part of the earth is affected by this action in the second trumpet blast, here the whole world witnesses the wrath of God. It is worth remembering that at times we shall see God bringing judgment on the world at large as well as on parts of it. For example, we may see wars between nations and we may see world wars. We may see economic depression in some countries or we may see a worldwide depression as in the 1930s. These events, John is telling us, are signs of God's judgment. While the judgment reminds Christians of their dependence upon God alone and their need to trust him, so it may lead to some who have the mark of the beast repenting and turning to the Lord. On the other hand, many will not repent and will find that these judgments confirm them in their sin and rebellion.

3. The third bowl

> The third angel poured out his bowl on the rivers and springs of water, and they became blood. Then I heard the angel in charge of the waters say: 'You are just in these judgments, you who are and who were, the Holy One, because you have so judged; for they have shed the blood of your saints and prophets, and you have given them blood to drink as they deserve.' And I heard the altar respond: 'Yes, Lord God Almighty, true and just are your judgments' (16:4-7).

This third **bowl** is also very like the plague just mentioned that made the Nile turn to blood, and also like the third trumpet in 8:10-11. The emphasis on blood indicates that these people are suffering and even dying. Their means of life has been taken away from them. As we see in more detail in chapter 18:11, 'the merchants of the earth will weep and mourn.' Meanwhile the **angel in charge of the waters** leads God's people in praise to God for his justice.

In an age that often sneers at the thought of righteous or fair justice, it is vital that we all hear what the angel says at this point. What is going on is indeed fearful, for people are suffering and even dying. But for those seated in heaven, who are able to see the whole picture, this is God being **just in these judgments**. This judgment is inherently *fair*. It is fair and righteous for a variety of reasons, many of which have already been spelled out in John's visions. But here the angel emphasises that the spilling of blood by God in judgment is fair and **just** because these people have **shed the blood** of God's people and even of his **prophets**. They receive the judgment **as they deserve.** Here again is the answer to the prayer of the martyrs in 6:10: 'How long, Sovereign Lord, holy and true, until you judge the inhabitants of the earth and avenge our blood?'

Now they can see what is happening, and so they join with the angels in praising the Lord whose **judgments** are **true and just.**

4. The fourth bowl

The fourth angel poured out his bowl on the sun, and the sun was given power to scorch people with fire. They were seared by the intense heat and they cursed the name of God, who had control over these plagues, but they refused to repent and glorify him (16:8-9).

We would surely imagine, with all that is happening around them, that those who are in rebellion against God would turn to him in repentance and seek his forgiveness and salvation from his judgment. All John sees here, however, are people who **refused to repent and glorify him**. Even after yet more judgment is poured out in the fourth bowl, still they continue to refuse God. Furthermore, as this **intense heat** (perhaps of economic disaster or 'natural' catastrophes) burns them, instead of crying out to God in sorrow **they cursed the name of God.**

Lest anyone should ask whether the problem lies in the fact that they don't know God is behind all this and have been unable to learn the lesson, we see that they *do* know and that is precisely why they curse God! Even as God judges, so those being judged themselves confirm the righteousness of God as they rail against him to the very last minute of their lives. There is no need to take the idea of heat and fire literally any more than we have taken the sea of blood literally. John continues to use the language of metaphor and vision, and yet what he describes is real enough. However we seek to describe an eternity separated for ever from the presence of God, we will never convey the full horror. If John's pictures here seem awful to our ears, let us remember that the reality is even worse.

5. The fifth bowl

The fifth angel poured out his bowl on the throne of the beast, and his kingdom was plunged into darkness. Men gnawed their tongues in agony and cursed the God of heaven because of their pains and their sores, but they refused to repent of what they had done (16:10-11)

As the **fifth angel** pours out his **bowl on the throne of the beast**,[100] so God judges the seats of authority held by the world leaders who are set against him. As Satan uses the leaders and structures of nations for his purposes, so God's judgment is poured out on the source of power. Those who have brought darkness to this world find God plunging the whole of their rule into **darkness**. This resembles the ninth plague that came upon the Egyptians, the plague of darkness (Exodus 10:21-23). The Christians of Pergamum (2:12-13) knew all about living 'where Satan has his throne'. It was indeed a place of great darkness, and one of their number, Antipas, had already given his life for Christ. We know all too well that, even in our own Western societies, the further people turn from God the further they fall into a great and deep spiritual darkness. Sin and evil behaviour don't just become commonplace, but are actually regarded as 'good'. The world is blinded by God as he condemns it to the darkness it deserves and which it has, in fact, sought. The apostle Paul reminded Christians in Ephesus of how the people around them were caught up in darkness while they, through faith in Christ, had been brought into the kingdom of light (Ephesians 4:17-5:2). In Ephesians 5:8-11 Paul says to Christians: 'For you were once darkness, but now you are light in the Lord. Live as children of light (for the fruit of the light consists in all goodness, righteousness and truth) and find out what pleases the Lord. Have nothing to do with the fruitless deeds of darkness, but rather expose them.'

Yet again we see the justice of what is happening as we read that **they refused to repent of what they had done** in spite even of the darkness that God sends on them and the pain it brings. As we have seen, these on-going judgments of God provide the opportunity for repentance. Paul in Ephesians was talking to those who had seized the offer of Christ as light of the world, but those John now sees have rejected the light. They have on them the mark of the beast whom they worship (verse 2). This vision is now taking us on towards the final great day of judgment when Christ returns, and as that time looms on the horizon the beast's followers become even more firmly his subjects, refusing **to repent**.

6. The sixth bowl

The sixth angel poured out his bowl on the great river Euphrates, and its water was dried up to prepare the way for the kings from the East. Then I saw three evil spirits that looked like frogs; they came out of the mouth of the dragon, out of the mouth of the beast and out of the mouth of the false prophet. They are spirits of demons performing miraculous signs, and they go out to the kings of the whole world, to gather them for the battle on the great day of God Almighty.

'Behold, I come like a thief! Blessed is he who stays awake and keeps his clothes with him, so that he may not go naked and be shamefully exposed.'

Then they gathered the kings together to the place that in Hebrew is called Armageddon (16:12-16).

The starkness of the description that is now given reminds us that it is Satan himself and his forces, including the evil spirits who do his work, who have taken people in with their lies and blasphemies.

i) The Euphrates

The drying up of **the great river Euphrates** reminds us of the Red Sea which dried up only to be unleashed in all its force to bring final destruction upon the Egyptians (Exodus 14:21-22, 27-28). The **frogs** remind us of the plague of frogs in Exodus 8:1-4. It is interesting to remember that the Egyptian magicians were also able to summon up frogs. It is not much wonder that **evil spirits** are described as looking **like frogs**. But while the judgment on Egypt is still in mind, God's judgment on the Babylonian empire also provides a clear picture for John to draw upon. **The great river Euphrates** was the river of Babylon where the Israelites were taken in captivity. So crucial to the prosperity of that empire was the great river that both Isaiah and Jeremiah prophesy that it would one day dry up as part of God's judgment.[101] Just as Egypt and Babylon were destroyed for having set their faces against God, so the same is about to happen to all the world that is in darkness. What has happened in the past becomes the best picture for John to use about what is happening, and will happen on a much larger scale in the future, as the world experiences the bowls of God's wrath.

The **kings from the East**, like Cyrus of Persia, came and conquered the Babylonian empire. One regime of darkness conquered another regime of darkness, and over it all God was sovereign. Even as this happened, we remember that God protected his people and even used Cyrus to bring his people back to the Promised Land. But here we see the name Babylon being used for all the world authorities, states and structures that are set against God and his people. John sees a picture of the forces of Satan, **the spirits of demons,** gathering **the kings of the whole world** together **for the battle**. These demonic spirits come **out of the mouth of the dragon**. They are sent out directly by Satan himself and from the **false prophet** whom we have seen described in chapter 13:11-18. Like that false prophet, they deceive the leaders and governments of the world by **performing miraculous signs**. The world order confirms its commitment to worshipping Satan as it is taken in by the demonic spirits, and follows the call to come together **for the battle** at a place **called Armageddon.**

ii) Armageddon

This symbolic name for the place of the final battle in which God's enemies are destroyed may be based on Megiddo in Israel where many important battles have taken place in the past. Some have suggested that there will be a literal battle as ungodly kings come from the East. But, as we have seen, the East came to be a symbol for the source of evil, since it was from there that the Persians came to destroy the Babylonians but, more than that, it was from the East that the Assyrians, Babylonians and others had come to fight against Israel and against the people of God in Old Testament times.

iii) The great day of God Almighty

As this bowl of God's wrath is poured out so, in his sovereign plan, the demonic spirits do his work as they draw all these people together to face the **great day of God Almighty**. This gathering for the great battle is further described in 19:19 and 20:8, where we see just how clearly God is behind all this. The authorities will come together and even end up fighting amongst and destroying themselves! They are gathering for God's full and final justice. What John sees here follows closely what Jesus prophesied in Matthew 24 (and Mark 13). In Matthew 24:11 and 24 Jesus warns that false prophets will deceive many people as wickedness increases in the world. They 'will appear and deceive many people'. Just as John has seen in 14:6-20, Jesus tells us the 'gospel of the kingdom will be preached in the whole world as a testimony to all nations, and then the end will come' (Matthew 24:14). In John's vision this has happened. The time for repentance has passed.

iv) Stay awake!

John reminds believers of more of Jesus' message: 'Therefore keep watch, because you do not know on what day your Lord will come. But understand this: If the owner of the house had known at what time of night the thief was coming, he would have kept watch and would not have let his house be broken into. So you also must be ready, because the Son of Man will come at an hour when you do not expect him' (Matthew 24:42-44).

Blessed is he who stays awake reminds us that while we have been told much about the end times in which we live, we have not been told the actual time at which the seventh bowl and the great day of the Lord will actually come. We must remain constantly vigilant, never allowing ourselves to be sucked into the world of darkness, and never being conned by the deceit of Satan and his minions. The picture of keeping our **clothes** on is most vivid. God's people are to go on a journey on that last day into the very presence of the Lord himself. We are reminded of the night of judgment in Egypt when the Israelites kept their travelling clothes on, waiting for their journey to the Promised Land, while the 'destroying angel' 'passed over' them and brought judgment on the Egyptians (Exodus 12:11). As unbelievers are judged, God's own people will be gathered from the ends of the earth to be with him. We are to make sure our clothes are in order. Like the people of Sardis (3:4) who have not soiled their clothes, we are to ensure we keep ourselves pure and do not fall into idolatry. We must accept the challenge to Laodicea and come to Christ to 'buy white clothes to wear', so that we can cover our 'shameful nakedness' (3:18).

7. The seventh bowl

The seventh angel poured out his bowl into the air, and out of the temple came a loud voice from the throne, saying, 'It is done!' Then there came flashes of lightning, rumblings, peals of thunder and a severe earthquake. No earthquake like it has ever occurred since man has been on earth, so tremendous was the quake. The great city split into three parts, and the cities of the nations collapsed. God remembered Babylon the Great and gave her the cup filled with the wine of the fury of his wrath. Every island fled away and the mountains could not be found. From the sky huge hailstones of about a hundred pounds each fell upon men. And they cursed God on account of the plague of hail, because the plague was so terrible (16:17-21).

Finally, we come to **the seventh angel** and final **bowl.** The proclamation now comes from God himself (**out of the temple**), that **'It is done!'** The work of final judgment is now announced. The time has come and it cannot be undone. With this pronouncement come all the signs of God's holy presence and power and majesty that we have already noted on a number of occasions in John's vision. All the temporary and partial judgments that have been going on throughout history have been pointing forward to this final great day. But now some of those same judgments come in a previously unequalled fury (**No earthquake like it has ever occurred**). This is **the cup filled with the wine of the fury of his wrath** that is now poured out on the whole world order opposed to God, on **Babylon the Great**. This causes **the cities of the nations** to collapse. Here at last is the final fulfilment of all the prophecies of all the ages, as **hailstones** bigger even than those that fell on Egypt (Exodus 9:18-19) now destroy the world and its people. Even the world itself is being destroyed as **the mountains could not be found**.

Staggering as it may seem, on this final day of judgment and battle, God's great justice is seen as his enemies, even at this last minute facing the full onslaught of God's judgment and judicial wrath, **cursed God**.

Special lessons for today

In John's day they may have identified Babylon with Rome. In the last century, the evil empires of Hitler and Nazism or Russia and communism were also seen as 'Babylon'. However, we need to recognize that Babylon is both them and more than them, for it is the world set against God, and our liberal Western democracies, nice as they seem, tolerant as they seem, are themselves set against anything that they see as challenging to their new ethics and new religion. This new order says above all that there are no absolutes. For the time being, Christianity is more or less tolerated within the Western democracies, but we must realise that they too are part of 'Babylon'. Just because these societies had roots established by our Christian forebears does not mean that we live in 'Christian' societies. The modern democracies are the very structures that are increasingly standing against those who would promote gospel values. They often pass laws that Christians find at best of dubious value and at worst in direct conflict with Biblical teaching. The time is coming very rapidly when Christians will find themselves hated within these democracies because they proclaim the one thing which is unacceptable in a society that tolerates almost every viewpoint. Christians say there is just *one* way to God, through faith in Jesus Christ. We need to heed what is being said in these chapters. Those of us who live in the so-called 'free' countries must recognise that we are not to rely on them to preserve us and protect us. We must be prepared for anything Satan can hurl at us, and it may come sooner rather than later.

In this passage about the bowls of the wrath of God we continue to learn about matters of eternity that we must apply to ourselves:

(a) The time for repentance will come to an end. There is no half-way house. Whose mark do we have?

(b) Are we awake, ready dressed, or are we like Laodicea (3:17)?

(c) Let us praise God that his justice is already being seen and will be seen in how he protects us, his people, and how he judges evil.

Revelation 17

God's Judgment falls on Babylon and the Beast

In chapter 16 we saw the seventh bowl of God's wrath, the final judgment, come upon Babylon (the evil world that is set against God). Chapters 17, 18 and part of 19 now give us a great panoramic overview of this judgment. Here we see how closely related the beast is to all that goes under the name of Babylon. Satan and his forces have been driving all the evil of this world's authorities, powers, peoples and nations.

We have already seen some of the background to this use of 'Babylon' as a symbol for the world set against God.[102] A number of commentators and Bible teachers throughout history understood Babylon as a reference to Rome. As we discussed in some detail when looking at chapters 2 and 3, the Roman empire was persecuting Christians and even causing its emperors to be worshipped. Undoubtedly the talk of 'seven hills' in 17:9, together with the evil nature of the empire and its great power around the world, would have encouraged such an identification in John's own day. We must not suggest that they were wrong in making that identification, for what we have found in reading through this book is that each age can and should learn from John's vision. Indeed other place names, such as Sodom and Egypt (see 11:8), are also used to describe the world in opposition to God. This means we must be very careful *never* to say, 'This does not apply to us!' Babylon is assuredly with us today as it was for God's people who lived under the dominion of Egypt or in the midst of the sin and corruption of Sodom.

In what follows, we quickly realise that 'Babylon' and the 'harlot' refer to the same thing. As the chapter opens, the evil world is seen to have a glory of its own. As we read this, it is worth remembering the woman described in 12:1-2 as being clothed with the sun and having a crown of twelve stars. We commented there that she provided a picture of the beauty of God's people seeking to serve him and bring glory to him. What a contrast between her and the one here who, though evidencing great wealth and pomp in her dress is, in fact, a *harlot*. Once again the sexual imagery comes from the Old Testament prophetic pictures of people who forsake the true God who made a covenant with them, and go after other gods.

1. The great prostitute's punishment

One of the seven angels who had the seven bowls came and said to me, 'Come, I will show you the punishment of the great prostitute, who sits on many waters. With her the kings of the earth committed adultery and the inhabitants of the earth were intoxicated with the wine of her adulteries' (17:1-2).

John is now invited by one of the **seven angels** to see the **punishment** of the **great prostitute**. As we see clearly in verse 5 below, this prostitute is Babylon. The picture of the prostitute is sad but very apt. Just as a prostitute sells her body to another person to be used as he or she wants, so the world that has turned against God has sold itself to Satan to do as he pleases. We shall see later in this passage that what Satan does with her is to bring her death and destruction.

The **many waters** refer to the peoples of the whole world, as verse 15 makes clear. The prostitute **sits** on them, in the sense that she is present throughout this world exercising her seductive powers and thus gaining authority over the nations. Everyone who is not following Christ (i.e. **the inhabitants of the earth**[103]), together with all their **kings** and leaders have been seduced into following her and finding their pleasure in her. Indeed, they are dominated by her, as the sexual imagery of her 'sitting' on them makes clear.

Then the angel carried me away in the Spirit into a desert. There I saw a woman sitting on a scarlet beast that was covered with blasphemous names and had seven heads and ten horns. The woman was dressed in purple and scarlet, and was glittering with gold, precious stones and pearls. She held a golden cup in her hand, filled with abominable things and the filth of her adulteries (17:3-4).

John, led by the Holy **Spirit**, is now taken **into a desert**. We saw earlier that the desert or wilderness represents this world. It has not been a comfortable experience for God's people but, while there, they have been protected by God (12:3-6). Now, though, the desert, this world, has become the place of judgment and John is allowed to witness that final judgment. As he watches he sees the prostitute in all her perverse glory. In 12:1 we have seen the glorious woman (the church) dressed in all her finery. She had been protected by God while in the desert and while being attacked and tormented by an 'enormous red dragon with seven heads and ten horns and seven crowns' (12:3). What John sees now is a stark contrast with that protected woman. This prostitute is **sitting on a scarlet beast**. Earlier, in 13:1, we saw that the beast is the satanic force that lies behind the evil kings and rulers and nations of this world. The **blasphemous names** with which the beast is **covered** show that this satanic force is completely set against God in all that he does. The woman relies upon this emissary of Satan to give her some temporary glory. **Purple** was a fine and pompous colour on expensive cloth. Her dress glitters with **gold, precious stones and pearls**. There is no doubt that the world that follows the beast can receive real economic gain. We must recognise that temporary economic prosperity is just one of the ways of 'this world' that Satan, and hence the evil authorities of this world, uses to keep people under his control. The source of her apparent prosperity is ultimately Satan himself, and it comes together with all her **abominable things**. These things will include her persecution and killing of God's people, her rejection of all that is godly, her commitment to evil and dark spiritual forces.

This title was written on her forehead: MYSTERY BABYLON THE GREAT THE MOTHER OF PROSTITUTES AND OF THE ABOMINATIONS OF THE EARTH. I saw that the woman was drunk with the blood of the saints, the blood of those who bore testimony to Jesus. When I saw her, I was greatly astonished (17:5-6).

The woman's true character is revealed in the name on her forehead. She is the mother of, or representative of, all who follow Satan and of all who enjoy the **abominations** to which she has introduced them. The **mystery** refers to the fact that this title reveals who she really is. Her true character has often been hidden through history, but as we come to the last day her character will be revealed to all through God's judgment on her. Once again, at the heart of her character, reflecting the nature of Satan himself, is her absolute hatred of all those people who do not follow her but rather look to Christ for life and joy. As we have seen on a number of occasions before, the final judgment brings an answer to the cry of the martyrs in 6:10: 'How long, Sovereign Lord, holy and true, until you judge the inhabitants of the earth and avenge our **blood**?'

2. Symbols explained

Then the angel said to me: 'Why are you astonished? I will explain to you the mystery of the woman and of the beast she rides, which has the seven heads and ten horns. The beast, which you saw, once was, now is not, and will come up out of the Abyss and go to his destruction. The inhabitants of the earth whose names have not been written in the book of life from the creation of the world will be astonished when they see the beast, because he once was, now is not, and yet will come' (17:7-8).

On seeing this woman and the beast, John **was greatly astonished** and so the angel now gives some further explanation, a 'revelation' of the **mystery**. Some have said that this explanation from the angel helps us identify times and rulers to which the book of Revelation refers. So, for example, some have counted seven Roman emperors and then taken the passage to refer to a myth that Nero would return from the dead ('now is not, and will come'). But even if some of the early churches thought of this myth as they read the passage, this cannot exhaust the meaning here. The angel is describing not so much *who* the **beast** is, but his nature or character, and it is clearly intended to contrast dramatically with Christ who came from God, who lived and died and rose from the dead to victory and exaltation.

i) The beast

The **beast**, on the other hand, comes from the abode of Satan, the **Abyss** (see 9:1-11; 11:7). And there is no doubt that in this judgment from God he will **go to his destruction**. As John looks into the future and sees this final judgment day, he sees the beast revealed. The beast has appeared from time to time. This is part of his character. His presence is always felt in this fallen world, but he is not always seen. Satan can appear as an angel of light. It is part of the nature of the beast he sends forth that, at times, he will be seen by the people of the world and at other times he will not be seen. His whole nature is to lead people through deception. **The inhabitants of the earth** (those who are not Christ's) **will be astonished** when they see him because they have not realised who stands behind their life of rebellion against God. They have not always seen who 'pulls their strings'. On the last day they and all creation will see the beast coming **out of the Abyss.** Furthermore, the scene will cause astonishment because the beast does seem to 'rise from the dead'. He had been defeated by Christ's death on the cross, but here he is *alive*! No doubt those who belong to him will think that they have won and that Christ's work on the cross has not been successful in defeating Satan and the beast. What they will shortly see, though, is that he has **come up** only in order to **go to his destruction**. Christ's work is complete: he has conquered.

John describes these people as those **whose names have not been written in the book of life from the creation of the world**. We have already encountered the 'book of life' and have discussed it in the comments on 3:4-6. In that passage John drew attention to the book by way of encouragement for

Christians. Its existence provides them with great assurance of their ultimate salvation when they are in the midst of persecution. To know that God knows us and has chosen us to be with him for ever in this way is a great joy. Here, the contrast could not be greater. These people are without hope in their rebellion against God as they face the final judgment *without* having their names in this book. Once more we are reminded that in God's extraordinary sovereignty, the protection afforded to those who are his has been secured from the very **creation of the world**. For others, God's sovereign purposes over history are seen in their exclusion from that book.

Excursus: sovereignty and responsibility

The exclusion of these people from the book of life makes us ask all sorts of questions about God's justice and 'fairness' and the relationship between human responsibility and God's sovereignty. This side of eternity we shall no doubt continue to wonder at these teachings and to sense that we simply cannot adequately understand the relationship between these doctrines. However, a few thoughts that we have discovered in this book of Revelation provide a context for our thinking about these matters.

First, we have seen that God is indeed utterly sovereign, and we must not diminish that active sovereignty just because we do not fully understand his purposes. We have seen that his sovereignty is not just one of *foreknowledge* about the way events will go, but that he actually *determines* those events. If this were not so, we could not be sure of anything that this book has been teaching us about the demise of Satan, the final judgment, or the vindication of God's people.

Secondly, we have seen that men and women are called to repentance and are held responsible for their sin. On several occasions in this book, we have read statements that people 'still did not repent' (9:20-21), or 'refused to repent' (16:9-11).

Thirdly, Revelation has consistently shown God's judgment to be, above all, *just* and *deserved*. People actually receive what they have asked for, as God allows them to receive the consequences of their choice to follow the woman and beast.

Fourthly, for the most part, the doctrine of divine sovereignty in this book, and in the rest of Scripture, is concerned above all to provide security and assurance for those who believe. Revelation is written to encourage Christians who are living in this world with all its suffering, persecution, pain and death. It calls upon us to remain faithful *because* God is sovereign and the future certain.

Much more could be said on this matter, but it is wise always to remember that Scripture clearly calls upon those who do not know and love the Lord to turn to him in repentance and faith. For those of us who have done so, Scripture reminds us that our salvation is not, praise God, dependent upon our fickle and sinful decisions, but is entirely of grace. Our eternal security is assured, for our names are in 'the Lamb's book of life'.

ii) The seven heads

> This calls for a mind with wisdom. The seven heads are seven hills on which the woman sits. They are also seven kings. Five have fallen, one is, the other has not yet come; but when he does come, he must remain for a little while. The beast who once was, and now is not, is an eighth king. He belongs to the seven and is going to his destruction (17:9-11).

As the angel continues with his explanation he talks of **a mind with wisdom**. This describes the mind of the Christian, which is not taken in by the deception of the beast's re-appearance. It does not mean that the Christian understands everything, but that he or she does understand the flow of history that the angel previously has described and is about to describe further. We have seen that some understand the **seven hills** to refer to the seven hills on which Rome is built. But that is unlikely. The **hills** are **also seven kings**. This suggests that the picture describes the authorities and rulers of this world who follow Satan. Some have tried to identify the specific kings with particular empires, for example, Egypt, Assyria, Babylon, Persia,

Greece and then Rome (**one is**), and a future one coming at the end of time. Again such identification makes little sense. Many great evil world dominions have come and gone since the Roman empire. The fact that the figure **seven** is used suggests that the scene being described is symbolic of God's sovereignty over history. The world is still ruled by evil. The woman still **sits** in authority. Those who are against Christ seem to dominate. The one who **has not yet come** is probably the **beast** who is also called **an eighth king** yet **he belongs to the seven**. There is no doubt this is difficult symbolism, but perhaps it is designed to show that, although the beast will make this special appearance at the final judgment day when people will be 'astonished', he is nevertheless, as we have seen, part and parcel of what is going on right now as well. He may not be seen, but his influence is felt everywhere among the evil empires and rulers of our age, for he **belongs to the seven**. Nevertheless, we are again reminded that he **is going to his destruction**.

Let's remember as we see that final phrase that though the woman, representing all who are set against Christ, seems to have so much authority at the moment, Christians know how it will all end. They know God is sovereign. They know that while one woman, representing the church (all God's people), will be protected and saved, the other, representing those at war with Christ, will not go on for ever.

iii) The ten horns

'The ten horns you saw are ten kings who have not yet received a kingdom, but who for one hour will receive authority as kings along with the beast. They have one purpose and will give their power and authority to the beast. They will make war against the Lamb, but the Lamb will overcome them because he is Lord of lords and King of kings – and with him will be his called, chosen and faithful followers' (17:12-14).

The symbolic description of the authorities of this age and this world continues. Much of the imagery continues to be drawn from Daniel 7:4-8.

The **ten kings** represent the world rulers who are given their authority and lay this at the feet of the beast. But the length of their rule is limited by God. **One hour** is an indication of just how brief will be this final time when they draw together for war against the Lamb. God's judgment will be fast. Here is a further fulfilment of Jesus' words in Matthew 24:22: 'If those days had not been cut short, no one would survive, but for the sake of the elect those days will be shortened.'

The beast and the rulers of this world meanwhile rely upon each other. The beast drives them forward in evil, and so the kings use their power for the beast's purposes. This is their **one purpose**. Together with the beast **they will make war against the Lamb.** There is a great irony here. The kings of this world and the beast, who have continued throughout their time of **authority** to attack Christians and Jesus Christ, come together for what they see as the final battle against God and his people. They expect to win. They still have not grasped that they are up against the sovereign Lord, the one who is **Lord of lords and King of kings**. He is **Lord** over them and **King** over them, for he is Lord of all lords and King over all kings. Christ, the one who has seemed so weak, whose death on the cross seemed to achieve so little in the eyes of the world, is the Lamb on the throne who has been given full and final authority (see chapter 5).

The rulers of the world may have taken the battle to Christ and his followers throughout history, but that time has been limited and now, on the last day, it is not they who in fact are forcing this battle, but Christ himself. Accompanying Christ will be those whose names are in the Lamb's book of life, those who are his **faithful followers**.[104] These are the ones who have stood firm and 'overcome' in the face of the persecution of the beast and the authorities and 'inhabitants of this earth'. They are his **called** because they responded to his call to follow him. This means they are also his **chosen** and their future is certain.

iv) The waters

> Then the angel said to me, 'The waters you saw, where the prostitute sits, are peoples, multitudes, nations and languages' (17:15).

We have said that the woman, the prostitute, represents people around the world who are set against God. Here the angel confirms this understanding of her significance. She spreads herself across the world and draws them together. The powers of this world thus feel secure and safe in their numbers.

v) The defeated woman

> 'The beast and the ten horns you saw will hate the prostitute. They will bring her to ruin and leave her naked; they will eat her flesh and burn her with fire. For God has put it into their hearts to accomplish his purpose by agreeing to give the beast their power to rule, until God's words are fulfilled. The woman you saw is the great city that rules over the kings of the earth' (17:16-18).

The irony now continues. While **the prostitute** has drawn her authority from the beast, it is now the authorities of the world, the **ten horns** (**ten kings**, verse 12), who turn against her. This is certainly a *mystery*! How unexpected is God's way of dealing with evil. It is as though the last day will see a great civil war. **God has put it into their hearts** to bring about **his purpose.** His promise of judgment will be **fulfilled.** That will happen even as the prostitute is brought to ruin by the **beast.** We have seen a precursor to this so often through history. Leaders and people alike follow the path of evil and decadence. Empires grow and prosper for a while. They derive their authority and apparent comfort from the power of the beast. But eventually people turn against the leaders and the leaders against the people. Civil war may be the result, or civilisations may simply disappear. It happened with the great splendour of the Babylonian, Persian and Greek empires. In John's day it was no doubt good to look forward to the time when Rome would turn against itself and the people end up destroying its power.

In the mid-twentieth century we saw it happen with the Nazi dream of world domination, and in the latter part of the twentieth century we saw it happen with Communism in the Soviet-controlled world. We have yet to see it happen with the materialistic capitalism, which is the basis of much of today's world. But as Christians, persecuted for standing for the faith, we may be assured that all such structures have within themselves the seeds of their own demise, for God **has put it into their hearts to accomplish his purpose**, and that purpose is that those who do not put Christ first will turn against themselves, and their whole prosperity and way of life will cave in.

The **woman** has been highly regarded by the **kings of the earth**. The people set against God have had the leaders they want, but now they are set against each other. The woman's doom is certain. The kings too are condemned. As chapter 18 now makes clear, prosperity is brought to ruin, civilisations crumble, and world order as we know it ceases.

Special lessons for today

The seductive qualities of the harlot are not to be underestimated, so John is taken by the Spirit to the wilderness to observe her, for there he is safe and protected by God (12:6, 14). We Christians are often tempted to underestimate the seductiveness of the world, but when we do, the dragon is almost in sight of victory. We are sinners saved by grace, not perfect and unassailable automatons. Let us remember that even in the vision it seems that John himself would have been seduced by what he saw, had he not been under the direct protection of God. The wealth and splendour of our age draws many away from the Lord. Where do we stand?

Revelation 18

This chapter continues to describe the horror of what happens to Babylon as God brings about 'the punishment of the great prostitute' (17:1). Here more detail is added to the brief description of Babylon's ruin in 17:16. The account is interspersed with two appeals to God's people. The first appeal is to those Christians living at the moment (verses 4-5) who are urged that they not take part in Babylon's sin and so suffer the same end. The second is to all in heaven who, witnessing the events of this final day, are urged to rejoice as they see judgment coming upon those who have so mercilessly persecuted the followers of Christ.

3. An angel pronounces judgment

> After this I saw another angel coming down from heaven. He had great authority, and the earth was illuminated by his splendour. With a mighty voice he shouted: 'Fallen! Fallen is Babylon the Great! She has become a home for demons and a haunt for every evil spirit, a haunt for every unclean and detestable bird. For all the nations have drunk the maddening wine of her adulteries. The kings of the earth committed adultery with her, and the merchants of the earth grew rich from her excessive luxuries' (18:1-3).

The next thing that John sees (**after this**) is another angel who proclaims judgment on Babylon. This angel comes from the presence of God with God's pronouncement. Coming **from heaven** with **great authority** and illuminating the earth with **his splendour** ('glory' in Greek) all point to his being sent from the presence of God and specifically from Christ's presence, the Light of the World. Some have even suggested that this is Christ making the announcement, but it is enough to recognise that it is Christ who stands behind the announcement and on whose behalf the proclamation is made.

As we hear the words, **Fallen! Fallen is Babylon the Great!**, it is good to remember again that these visions that John writes down are for us who follow Christ. The voice is, above all, for God's people to hear. We have heard such proclamations a few times before, starting with the second angel in 14:8. Here the past tense is used. More literally we might translate this as 'It has fallen! Babylon the Great has fallen!' So certain is this judgment that is yet to happen, that when it is presently being described the completed past tense can be used.

John draws on Isaiah 21:9: 'Babylon has fallen, has fallen! All the images of its gods lie shattered on the ground!' Here John says she **has become** the **home** of **demons** and **evil spirits**. The pronouncement reminds us that as Babylon is judged so the spiritual forces who have led her astray and to which she has given a home are themselves judged. These evil spirits have been behind her worldwide influence as **all the nations** have participated in her evil, drinking the **maddening wine of her adulteries.** Many all around the world have followed her in her rejection of the true God and in following after other religions and idolatry. Humanly speaking, that route has not seemed so bad. Just as Babylon is arrayed in garments of great wealth, so here we read **the merchants of the earth grew rich from her excessive luxuries.** Satan, the beast and Babylon the Great have been able to make people feel comfortable in their life of idolatry, just as people today so often feel comfortable in their modern forms of idolatry. God's judgment will reveal the shallowness of such comfort as he removes it all in a very short space of time.

This too is a reminder for those who are suffering as Christians, many of whom are poor because of their faith,[105] that there should be no envy of those who seem to have so much in this world, for it will all eventually be taken away from them. The cry of most Christians at some point in their life is reflected in the words of Jeremiah when he says: 'You are always righteous, O LORD, when I bring a case before you. Yet I would speak with you about your justice: Why does the way of the wicked prosper? Why do all the faithless live at ease?' (Jeremiah 12:1).

The answer in this passage is much the same as was given to Jeremiah. All is not what it seems. Final judgment is certain. John is given a vision of it all happening, and the way of ease and prosperity will not last. But before we hear more of that, John hears **another voice**.

4. An angel calls on God's people

> Then I heard another voice from heaven say: 'Come out of her, my people, so that you will not share in her sins, so that you will not receive any of her plagues; for her sins are piled up to heaven, and God has remembered her crimes' (18:4-5).

This voice specifically addresses God's people, and we are back into the present day. John sees what happens at the last day, but the message is for Christians in this world *today*. It is a message of encouragement that ultimately the wicked receive true justice from God himself, but it also is a message that carries with it the challenge to remain faithful and to 'overcome'. This was the great common theme of the letters to the seven churches in chapters 2–3. The believers need to persevere and to overcome. Christ himself is with his people to empower them to do this. But as John sees the reason for the final judgment and its full horror, it provides another occasion of challenge to God's people. They must not be seduced by the prostitute. They must not be drawn into the ways of the demons and evil spirits. They must not **share in her sins**. Babylon's **plagues** are, as we have seen so many times before, the judgments that God brings upon her. God **has remembered her crimes**. No one can hope that God has not seen her sin or that somehow he will forget it. Christians must stand apart from this world and be holy and thus avoid the judgment inflicted upon Babylon.

5. Background in Jeremiah 51

Jeremiah's words, concerning the first Babylon coming under God's judgment, provide the background here. In Jeremiah 51:1-9 we read: 'This is what the LORD says: "See, I will stir up the spirit of a destroyer against Babylon... " ' Israel and Judah are thus urged: 'Flee from Babylon! Run for your lives! Do not be destroyed because of her sins. It is time for the LORD's vengeance; he will pay her what she deserves. Babylon was a gold cup in the LORD's hand; she made the whole earth drunk. The nations drank her wine; therefore they have now gone mad.' In language similar to John's description of **her sins...piled up to heaven**, Jeremiah says, 'let us leave her and each go to his own land, for her judgment reaches to the skies, it rises as high as the clouds.' When we look at verse 18 below we shall see that Jeremiah 51 also lies behind the call for God's people to rejoice at Babylon's destruction.

6. Judgment to fit the crime

> Give back to her as she has given; pay her back double for what she has done. Mix her a double portion from her own cup. Give her as much torture and grief as the glory and luxury she gave herself. In her heart she boasts, 'I sit as queen; I am not a widow, and I will never mourn.' Therefore in one day her plagues will overtake her: death, mourning and famine. She will be consumed by fire, for mighty is the Lord God who judges her (18:6-8)

Whether the same angel continues to speak here or whether another angel provides John with a commentary on what he witnesses is unclear. Jeremiah said of old Babylon that she gets *what she deserves*. This is the point of these two verses. In his judgment God is to **Give back to her as she has given.** Mention here of a **double portion** seems to suggest that her punishment is greater than her crime, but the Greek is best understood as meaning 'an exact equivalent'.[106] Her judgment is the precise **double** of her crime. This is then restated again as she is to receive **torture and grief** in proportion to the **glory and luxury**

she gave herself, at the expense, of course, of those Christians to whom she doled out torture and grief.

Arrogance and pride is at the heart of all sin, just as it is part of the nature of Satan, who lies behind all that is evil. Babylon, the **queen**, has boasted that she will go on and on. She is **not a widow** and **will never mourn**. Here is the ultimate arrogance of the world set against God, that puts itself in the place of God. Like despotic leaders of the past who assumed their empires would continue for a thousand years or more, she assumes she cannot be defeated and will always be wealthy and living in luxury. But it will take just **one day** for all this to be reversed as God brings **plagues** (judgment) upon her. The reference to **plagues** as a symbol for judgment is one we have encountered many times, but it always reminds us of how God judged the Egyptians. When God finally brought death on the firstborn sons of Egypt it took just one night. The **one day** here simply reminds us that God will come like a thief in the night (3:3; 16:15) and his justice will be extraordinarily swift.

In verse 8 the 'punishment to fit the crime' is described in vivid picture language. She thought she would live for ever, but **death** will come. She thought she was **not a widow**, but **mourning** will be her lot. She thought she had great **luxury**, but she will encounter **famine**. But this is not like former plagues that were designed to remind people of God's presence and, if possible, to bring repentance. This is the final judgment and the last sentence reminds us of this as it summarises what now happens to Babylon. She is judged by the **mighty Lord God** and is **consumed by fire**. In God's purposes we have already seen in 17:16 how this fire will in fact be brought upon her by her own former allies. However, the picture of **fire** reminds us of Sodom's end, which came about with a judgment of fire, and its destruction was permanent. Whether the final judgment will involve a literal fire, as happened with Sodom, is not clear. The point of the statement is its finality. Babylon as we know it, the state, structures and people set against God, will be destroyed as certainly and as finally as Sodom was destroyed.

225

7. Mourning over Babylon's destruction

When the kings of the earth who committed adultery with her and shared her luxury see the smoke of her burning, they will weep and mourn over her. Terrified at her torment, they will stand far off and cry: 'Woe! Woe, O great city, O Babylon, city of power! In one hour your doom has come!' The merchants of the earth will weep and mourn over her because no one buys their cargoes any more – cargoes of gold, silver, precious stones and pearls; fine linen, purple, silk and scarlet cloth; every sort of citron wood, and articles of every kind made of ivory, costly wood, bronze, iron and marble; cargoes of cinnamon and spice, of incense, myrrh and frankincense, of wine and olive oil, of fine flour and wheat; cattle and sheep; horses and carriages; and bodies and souls of men. They will say, 'The fruit you longed for is gone from you. All your riches and splendour have vanished, never to be recovered.' The merchants who sold these things and gained their wealth from her will stand far off, terrified at her torment. They will weep and mourn and cry out: 'Woe! Woe, O great city, dressed in fine linen, purple and scarlet, and glittering with gold, precious stones and pearls!' (18:9-16)

Even though **the kings of the earth** and **Babylon** have been fighting against each other, all who enjoyed sharing in her ill-gotten luxury will be appalled at what happens to her and the speed of it all. Those who thought in their arrogance that they would not mourn now **weep and mourn**. In the face of the Almighty God who moves swiftly to bring this judgment, they are **terrified at her torment**. The impact of what is happening to her is all too clear to them, hence the cry of **Woe!** We can barely imagine the horror with which all those who have fed off Babylon's deceptive wealth and luxury now view her demise. All they have ever **longed for is gone.** Everything they have ever counted dear goes up in smoke and once again the emphasis is on the speed of it all ... **in one hour your doom has come**.

We have friends whose house burned down in a major fire and catastrophe. Because the husband worked from home, most of his livelihood disappeared in a matter of a couple of hours. The enormity of such a tragedy can hardly be guessed at by those of us who have never experienced something like this. The picture John gives us is one that affects every unbeliever in the world in this way, but there are no insurance policies to help pick up the pieces later, for this is the final catastrophe to fall upon those who have continued to resist God and his call.

It is clear that Satan's deception of kings, peoples and nations has centred on offering them financial comfort and ease. The weeping and mourning of **the merchants of the earth** pivots on the fact that, as they watch Babylon being destroyed, they see their whole livelihood and purpose for living disappearing before their eyes. All that they have counted valuable is gone. The list of their **cargoes** is a list of all that the world of John's day counted valuable. Some of the commodities remain valuable in our time, for example, **gold, silver and precious stones**. Other commodities such as foodstuffs were and remain essential for normal life: **spice, fine flour and wheat**. If all this happened in our generation, then no doubt we would say that people mourn as they see their stocks and shares burned up as fast as paper burns. The city of the world was, humanly speaking, a **great city**. But that was always its deception, for it was founded upon the beast who comes up from the Abyss, and to the Abyss and to destruction he will return (17:8; 20:3).

As John finishes listing the products and trade of the world that have provided security for the merchants of Babylon, he describes their terror. They are **terrified at her torment**. The cry is repeated again: **Woe! Woe, O great city**.

> In one hour such great wealth has been brought to ruin! Every sea captain, and all who travel by ship, the sailors, and all who earn their living from the sea, will stand far off. When they see the smoke of her burning, they will exclaim, 'Was there ever a city like this great city?' They will throw dust on their heads, and with weeping and mourning cry out: 'Woe! Woe, O great city, where all who had ships on the sea became rich through her wealth! In one hour she has been brought to ruin!' (18:17-19)

In one hour it has been destroyed. John now turns to those who work internationally, and speaks of **every sea captain**, and those who earn their living by transporting the goods of Babylon. Those who **had ships** and had become **rich** on the back of Babylon's wealth and trade find their whole way of life is destroyed.

John's picture implies that these merchants and sea captains and sailors are, as it were, able to stand back and see what is happening to Babylon as **they see the smoke of her burning**. But we must remember this is all figurative language. In reality, John is describing that **one hour** of judgment. His description shows how it leaves no one untouched. All who have been committed to Babylon rather than Christ are caught up in this. None is spared.

John's emphasis that the luxurious lifestyle and wealth of the world has gone is a sober reminder to us of what drives so many people who do not follow Christ. It is their own comfort and desire for the so-called 'good things of life' that become their gods. This is not to say that unbelievers cannot have other motivations, but underneath it all is a desire to be one's own god, to have control and to enjoy prosperity. Remove the prosperity, and the world of so many comes tumbling down around them. The portrayal of the fall of Babylon is therefore one which all generations can understand. Even those who have no money and none of these luxuries can understand the horror of this, for such luxurious prosperity is still their envy. Satan has bought the people of the world with a bribe that proves not to be able to withstand God's judgment even for an hour! The cries of **Woe! Woe, O great city** have now been repeated three times (verses 10, 16 and 19).

8. Rejoicing over Babylon's destruction

The angel now turns again to God's people, who watch on as these tragic events unfurl. His words can sound strange to our ears.

> Rejoice over her, O heaven! Rejoice, saints and apostles and prophets! God has judged her for the way she treated you (18:20)

The idea of rejoicing over Babylon's judgment is not one that may immediately appeal to us, and yet this verse introduces us to an important theme that is developed in 19:1-6. In Jeremiah 51, which we have already seen provides a background to the description of judgment on Babylon, we read in verses 47-49: 'For the time will surely come when I will punish the idols of Babylon; her whole land will be disgraced and her slain will all lie fallen within her. Then heaven and earth and all that is in them will shout for joy over Babylon.... "Babylon must fall because of Israel's slain...." '

As God's people, we are to **rejoice over** Babylon's destruction, not because of some perverted desire to see people suffering, but because the Lord is carrying out his promises. Ever since the expulsion from the Garden of Eden, God's faithful people have been asking, 'How long, O Lord?' They have longed for that day when the damage Satan did to this world and to all creation would be judged and things restored to God's perfect will. The destruction of Babylon is warranted on many grounds but, as Jeremiah points out, her persecution of Israel (God's people) is one of the most important. God has always said to his people, 'It is mine to avenge; I will repay' (Deuteronomy 32:35; Romans 12:19). Faithful people throughout the centuries have held on to this great fact and have not sought their own vengeance when mistreated or abused or persecuted for their faith. So, for example, we read of Saul's persecution of David. There, given the opportunity, David does not kill Saul, rather he says: 'may the LORD avenge the wrongs you have done to me, but my hand will not touch you' (1 Samuel 24:12). More than this, however, the Scriptures have urged God's people to recognise and take note of the times when God does move to avenge his people. When they see this happening, they are to rejoice in God's action, for it is the action they have waited for with patience. It is the action in which God vindicates his name and shows his glory, power and sovereignty, and it is the action in which he moves to show the world that his people really are his. Thus, returning to Jeremiah 51, we read in verse 6: 'It is time for the LORD's vengeance; he will pay her what she deserves.'

As they see this judgment in the context of God's great sovereign work to avenge all the blasphemy and hideous works of darkness in history, his people will inevitably rejoice. They are thrilled that no longer will Babylon be able to go on resisting God and killing his people, and no longer will other gods seem to hold sway on earth. As the angel says, **God has judged her for the way she treated** his people, and this is to give cause for rejoicing to all. Notice that all believers are included in this command to rejoice: **saints and apostles and prophets**. So, as we shall see further in chapter 19, our rejoicing centres on God's 'true and just judgments' and his 'salvation' and his 'glory'.

9. A mighty angel describes Babylon's fall

> Then a mighty angel picked up a boulder the size of a large millstone and threw it into the sea, and said: 'With such violence the great city of Babylon will be thrown down, never to be found again. The music of harpists and musicians, flute players and trumpeters, will never be heard in you again. No workman of any trade will ever be found in you again. The sound of a millstone will never be heard in you again. The light of a lamp will never shine in you again. The voice of bridegroom and bride will never be heard in you again. Your merchants were the world's great men. By your magic spell all the nations were led astray. In her was found the blood of prophets and of the saints, and of all who have been killed on the earth' (18:21-24).

Jeremiah wrote his prophecy about the destruction of the first Babylon on a scroll. He then told his secretary to read the words aloud before tying a stone to the scroll and throwing it in the Euphrates river. The sinking of the scroll was to be a picture of Babylon: 'So will Babylon sink to rise no more because of the disaster' that God would bring upon her (Jeremiah 51:61-64). Now, in John's vision, another **mighty angel**, using different words, restates the suddenness and horror of Babylon's destruction and looks back to that prophecy of Jeremiah. The disturbance caused by water dropping a large rock into it is obvious for all to see. The rock itself disappears completely from sight. And this is how Babylon **will be thrown down,**

never to be found again. It will be like the rock lost at the bottom of the deepest sea.

If the previous description centred upon the destruction of the economic system of Babylon's world order, now we see how every other area of life is destroyed in just the same way. People involved in cultural and artistic activities such as **flute players and trumpeters** are gone forever. Tradesmen and artisans who helped create the comfortable way of life people enjoy are gone. Even personal relations are brought into this, as **the voice of bridegroom and bride** are never again heard. Every area of life in Babylon had been captivated under her **magic spell**. All who followed her had been led as the Pied Piper led his children, captivated by his spellbinding tune. But they had been led **astray**. And now, as she is destroyed, we find again the justice of God's action, for in this city **was found the blood of prophets and of the saints**. Not only has she been the source of persecution of Christians and the one who has made them martyrs but, ultimately, she is responsible for **all who have been killed on the earth**. All the massacres, murders and bloodshed of which we are only too well aware in our own day and age are part of the activities of the prostitute, Babylon. No wonder God's people rejoice as they see him moving in on her to judge and destroy her forever.

Finally, in this chapter, it is worth seeing the great God-ordained irony of some of what happens here. How ironic that the ones whose blood is now found in her streets are among those who, as God's **saints**, rejoice from their place in heaven at her demise! How ironic that just as Babylon had withdrawn food and trading rights from God's people in her implacable opposition and persecution of them, so now all food provision and all trade ceases in the city! How ironic that she who gathered the world together to destroy God's people is watched by those people as God destroys her.

Special lessons for today

We have talked of the dangers of being seduced ourselves by the 'harlot'. So here we need to recognise the comfort of Babylon. We must certainly not assume that people in Babylon are desperate and therefore just waiting to hear the gospel. Satan deceives by making them feel comfortable. As far as they are concerned, they lack nothing.

From the church's point of view, the church in Laodicea was beginning to succumb to the temptation of Babylon, to trust in her own wealth. Every congregation can face this temptation. We are being warned.

Finally, we need to note how much our thinking about these awesome matters of God's judgment can be distorted by the values of the harlot and Babylon. It is interesting that, in the modern church, people often find it more disturbing that God should judge a church for compromise with the world than that the church should compromise in the first place. We should be deeply disturbed by the ease with which the church seems to give in to the thinking and ways of the modern world. This passage has called for holiness and demanded that we should not be 'sharing in her sins'.

10. The rejoicing in heaven

As we begin chapter 19, we need to remember that, as with the visions of this book, the description of the final judgment that we have just considered is given for the encouragement of believers. However much we may be appalled at what will happen to those who resist God to the end, we who believe and trust in him are to give him praise and glory for vindicating his name and bringing us to victory through Jesus Christ our Lord. Thus, what was presaged in 18:20 is now seen in all its glory. The wailing of the kings of the earth and the merchants of the earth gives way to a vision of heaven where God is being praised by all the heavenly multitudes.

> After this I heard what sounded like the roar of a great multitude in heaven shouting: 'Hallelujah! Salvation and glory and power belong to our God, for true and just are his judgments. He has condemned the great prostitute who corrupted the earth by her adulteries. He has avenged on her the blood of his servants' (19:1-2).

Following on from John's description of the judgment day, he now hears a great **shouting** going on in heaven. It is an overwhelming noise that, as he describes it, sounds almost intimidating. But then he hears the words that are being shouted and they reflect the great praise of heaven to Almighty God who has finally **condemned** Babylon, **the great prostitute**.

Hallelujah! is a transliteration of a Hebrew word meaning 'Praise Yahweh'. It is found nowhere else in the New Testament, but is used several times in the Psalms.[107] In many places through this book we have seen the praises of God that are going on in heaven, but here they reach a great climax. This is the end of history as we know it. Judgment has taken place, and the whole of heaven is seen to participate in a great shout of praise. The praises centre around four main points to do with who God *is* and what he has *done*.

i) God is glorious and powerful

Time and again we have heard in this book of God's **glory and power**. Although the context for this was set for us back in chapter 1, we especially noticed it as we saw God on the throne in chapter 4. God's **glory** describes something of *who* he is. For us, glory carries connotations of great light and brilliance, but God's glory is much more than that. To talk of God's 'glory' is to summarise all of God's character and being. He is like none other. It is part of his 'glory' that he is Light, that he is self-existent, and that all **power** belongs to him. It is also part of his glory that he brings salvation and that he does conquer all that is evil and set against him. God's **power** enables him to do all that he promises and to ensure that his purposes come to fulfilment. Thus, as the final judgment takes place, his power is clearly revealed.

ii) God's judgments are true and just

Throughout Scripture God is portrayed as one who is always **true and just**. God cannot be 'bought off' by anyone. Unlike humans, he cannot be 'tempted' to sin or to veer from his foreordained purposes. Above all, because he is holy and all knowing and all-seeing, every judgment he makes is righteous. Here God is praised because he is the perfect judge and has proved utterly trustworthy in his judgment upon Babylon. More than that, his judgments are true and just because he has saved his people.

iii) God saves

Salvation belongs to God, they shout. This saving of his people is part of his justice and his trustworthiness. How we rejoice that God in all his glory still condescends to remain true and just and to bring salvation for all to whom he has promised it. He will not let his people down on that last day. We experienced 'salvation' when we became Christians, and continue to experience it through this life, for we know that through faith we are among those whom Christ has redeemed. But, wonderful as this assurance is right now on earth, nothing can compare with the glory of that final day when the whole world will see that God is a *saving* God. No wonder they shout praise to God for his salvation.

iv) God condemns and avenges

Part and parcel of God's truth and justice is that he also condemns unbelievers and avenges his people. We have seen how throughout history God has continued to promise his people that the time will come when no more opportunity for repentance will be afforded to their oppressors and he will avenge his people (see comments on 6:9-11 and 18:20). The heavenly hosts praise God that this has now happened in the final judgment. History has been brought to this awful and yet glorious climax. Those who have not followed the Lord and have been *untrue and unjust* in persecuting and killing the Lord's people are now condemned. God's word is fulfilled and his power is shown. The whole of heaven praises *Yahweh*, the covenant God who always promised that this is how it would be.

> And again they shouted: 'Hallelujah! The smoke from her goes up for ever and ever.' The twenty-four elders and the four living creatures fell down and worshipped God, who was seated on the throne. And they cried: 'Amen, Hallelujah!' Then a voice came from the throne, saying: 'Praise our God, all you his servants, you who fear him, both small and great!' (19:3-5)

In Isaiah 34 the prophet prophesies that God will judge all the nations as he comes to the defence of and salvation of Zion (his people): 'For the LORD has a day of vengeance, a year of retribution, to uphold Zion's cause' (verse 8). As Isaiah goes on to speak specifically against Edom he says: 'Edom's ... land will become blazing pitch! It will not be quenched night and day; its smoke will rise for ever' (verses 9-10). It is this prophecy particularly, but also the judgment on Sodom and Gomorrah (Genesis 19:28), that lies behind the words chosen here as the heavenly host praise God. Prophecies which had a partial fulfilment with the destruction of Sodom and of Edom have now been completed. God is to be praised for keeping his word.

The idea of praising God for the smoke that rises from judgment is such a difficult concept for us. We have discussed the general issues we face in the comments on 18:20. This passage does not focus on the **smoke**, rather the smoke points towards God who has remained faithful to his word and who is now making all things perfect. Thus we read of the great hosts of heaven headed by **the twenty-four elders and the four living creatures** falling down and worshipping God. Once again we are in the throne room so vividly described to us in chapter 4. God is **seated on the throne**. He rules over all and is to be worshipped. The words of praise are then overtaken by a great command, possibly from Christ himself, that comes from the throne. Now all God's people, not just the angelic hosts, not just those who have represented God's people before the throne, but **all his servants**, that is all **who fear him**, are called upon to give praise. No one is excluded from this summons to **praise our God**. On that great day, not one of us who are his people will be left out, whether **small** or **great**, we shall all fall down and worship and praise *our* God, and we shall be praising God along with those who have given their lives for Christ throughout history. The picture is one of wonder and delight.

The Marriage of the Lamb

Then I heard what sounded like a great multitude, like the roar of rushing waters and like loud peals of thunder, shouting: 'Hallelujah! For our Lord God Almighty reigns' (19:6).

As all people and all of the heavenly host join in praise the noise is overwhelming, like **rushing waters** and **peals of thunder**. We have seen both these descriptions being used before as indications of being in the presence of God himself. Now the praises reveal the heart of it all. The **Lord God Almighty reigns**. We are reminded of the earlier description of final judgment made by the seventh trumpet.[108] There we read: 'We give thanks to you, Lord God Almighty, the One who is and who was, because you have taken your great power and have begun to reign' (11:17). The Lord Almighty has always been king and always reigned, but that has not always been seen. Specifically, it has not been acknowledged by, and only rarely witnessed in, Babylon. Now his rule is seen to be what it always has been, absolute.[109]

> 'Let us rejoice and be glad and give him glory! For the wedding of the Lamb has come, and his bride has made herself ready. Fine linen, bright and clean, was given her to wear.' (Fine linen stands for the righteous acts of the saints.) Then the angel said to me, 'Write: "Blessed are those who are invited to the wedding supper of the Lamb!" ' And he added, 'These are the true words of God' (19:7-9).

We now come to the concluding verses of the vision that began back in 18:1. The verses speak of the praise of God's people as they now look ahead to what lies in store for them after the judgment of Babylon. They also introduce us to one of the more beautiful pictures of the relationship between God's people and the Lord Jesus Christ, their Saviour. Here is the joy of a wedding ceremony. John sees the church as the bride of Christ.

1. The bride's dress

How the end of this vision contrasts with what we read earlier in 18:23! There will be no more marriages and happiness in Babylon. But here is a wedding more glorious than anything the human institution of marriage could ever properly prefigure. It is a picture that will be developed in more detail in chapter 21. Here we see God's overarching work in preparing the church to be a suitable bride, for he is the one who gave her **fine linen** to wear, he has issued the invitation, and he is the one who has so **blessed** his people. But we also see that the saints themselves have produced **righteous acts** and thus the **bride has made herself ready** for the marriage.

We are reminded here of the believers in Sardis 'who have

not soiled their clothes' and who 'will walk' with Christ 'dressed in white' (3:4). In 7:9 we have also read of God's people dressed in a way that is acceptable to God and 7:14 went on to explain how this happens: 'they have washed their robes and made them white in the blood of the Lamb.' The great righteous act of all time was the death of Christ on the cross. The acts of God's people start at that point, trusting in and relying upon the sacrifice of Christ. This is what they do to wash their robes and make them white, the colour of a bride's gown. Of course, God's people are to go on to live lives that are honouring to God and so continue to reflect righteous acts, including leading a life of perseverance in the faith. But the whole of this life is dependent on grace, on the work of Christ who achieved our righteousness by his substitutionary death on the cross. This starting point in God's grace continues for the believer with an ongoing out-pouring of grace through the work of the Holy Spirit, enabling the believer to become more and more conformed to Christ.

What joy there will be when we arrive at that time of meeting Christ face to face. The apostle Paul refers to this in 1 Corinthians 13:12. As the church, the bride, we currently see 'but a poor reflection as in a mirror; then we shall see face to face.' He says, 'Now I know in part; then I shall know fully, even as I am fully known.' This is the way marriage works, isn't it? Bride and groom only fully and intimately come to know each other after the wedding itself. As the angel shows John this amazing picture of the culmination of history for God's people, he confirms the message with the words, **These are the true words of God.** What more could we want? God has said this is how it will be. We await the great marriage supper with the deep longing of the bride who wants to be united with her husband fully and completely for all eternity more than she wants anything else.

2. Marriage as a picture of God's love for his people
The image of marriage between God and his people has its roots in the Old Testament. Traditionally, many Christian teachers

have assumed that when God was seeking a way of describing the depths of his love for human beings, he latched on to the human institution that reflects the deepest qualities of human love. Effectively, their view is this: God was saying, 'Your practice of marriage is like what I have in store for you in the future. Your love for each other in marriage is similar to my love for you.' But this is not really the picture we get in Scripture. Rather we discover that marriage itself is instituted by God right from the beginning, from the creation of Adam and Eve. As we read on in Scripture, we find that far from God choosing marriage as a useful picture of his love for us, God actually instituted marriage itself in order to let us know something of the depths of his love for us! Viewed this way round, marriage and the sexual relationship between husband and wife are even more remarkable. God has built into our very make up and way of behaviour a foretaste and picture of the depths of his love for us as his people, his bride.

The God-given institution of marriage is a God-given picture for all people in all societies for all of history of how wonderful is God's love for us. This is why the Bible insists on fidelity in marriage, because our marriage is a picture of God's love for us, and God is always faithful to us. This is why adultery is wrong, for God does not go in search of another bride. This is why sexual perversion of any sort is wrong, because God created sexual joy to be at the heart of marriage and so reflect the joy of his relationship with us. It is thus this picture that God picks up again and again through his prophets and in the words of Jesus himself and the apostles. As Hosea shows so clearly,[110] God continues to be faithful to his wife, his people, even when she is tempted to go after other 'men' (gods). God woos his wife, even though she is so unattractive, as Ezekiel 16:8-14 demonstrates in vivid detail. God cares for his wife even in providing her clothing (as here in John's vision). Isaiah 61:10 describes it this way: 'My soul rejoices in my God. For he has clothed me with garments of salvation and arrayed me in a robe of righteousness, as a bridegroom adorns his head like a priest, and as a bride adorns herself with her jewels.'

In the New Testament Jesus also picks up this imagery. In Matthew 22:2 the kingdom of heaven, says Jesus, 'is like a king who prepared a wedding banquet for his son'. In the parable of the wise and foolish virgins in Matthew 25, the issue with which Jesus confronts us is whether we are ready for the wedding itself, Christ's return. The apostles also develop the theme. For example, in Ephesians 5:21-33 we see how human marriage follows God's love for his people and is to imitate that love, rather than simply that (imperfect) human marriage has become a picture of God's love. Here the behaviour of husbands and wives in marriage is to be modelled on the *prior* marriage. Husbands are to love their wives *as* Christ loved the church and even died for her. Wives are to submit to husbands even *as the church submits to Christ*. In verses 5:31-32 Paul even goes so far as to say that as the two *become one flesh* (i.e. as they enjoy the intimacy of a sexual relationship), so even in that deepest of all human expressions of love, it is possible to see the reflection of the perfect giving from Christ to the church.

The whole picture of marriage and God's love is also seen negatively throughout Scripture, and we have seen this already in Revelation. There is not the time to trace this here, but we must remember that the prostitute Babylon is the reverse of this picture. She is the one who has sold herself in unfaithfulness. She has served other gods (husbands). She has committed adultery with other gods, and so on.

So as we return to Revelation and later look at this picture again in chapter 21, we need to realise the depths of God's love that the picture reveals. It speaks of how he sought us out, how he gave his life for us, how he has adorned us with clothes that are white, clothes of righteousness, and how now at the end of time this relationship is to be consummated as we see our husband, Saviour and Redeemer, 'face to face' (1 Corinthians 13:12).

3. John's mistake

> At this I fell at his feet to worship him. But he said to me, 'Do not do it! I am a fellow servant with you and with your brothers who hold to the testimony of Jesus. Worship God! For the testimony of Jesus is the spirit of prophecy' (19:10).

John is clearly overwhelmed by the beauty and joy of this occasion and correctly responds with worship. But it is strange that he should be tempted to worship one who is not God. The angel has to remind John to look in the right direction. Only God is to be worshipped. This angel is a **fellow servant**. He carries the message which is ultimately from Jesus himself: **the testimony of Jesus**. In 22:8-9 we again see John worshipping an angel who then rebukes him. There is no doubt that it is always easy to be tempted into worshipping the messenger or some greater being rather than God himself. Even overwhelming spiritual experiences can draw us into this temptation. How often do we hear Christians testifying to great spiritual experiences rather than focusing on **the testimony of Jesus**. Here is a clear warning to us all. If even the apostle John fell into such a sin at such a time of majestic revelation, how much more may we be tempted! The postmodern age in which we live has once again seen a great rise of interest in angelic beings both within and outside Christian circles. Let us be aware that such interest, if it is not focused on their role in communicating the testimony of Jesus, may be deeply unhelpful and may lead us into worshipping the creature rather than the creator. Colossians 2:18-19 summarises the warning for us: 'Do not let anyone who delights in false humility and the worship of angels disqualify you for the prize. Such a person goes into great detail about what he has seen, and his unspiritual mind puffs him up with idle notions. He has lost connection with the Head ...'

The Battle is Joined

In the vision that now follows, John sees in even more detail Christ's 'second coming' and particularly his conquest of Satan on that final judgment day. Whereas previous descriptions of the judgment have focused on God's judgment and what happens to Babylon, and on the protection and eventual consummation of the relationship between God and Christ and his people, the church, this vision takes us to the heart of this holy war. Here we see not just the destruction of Babylon, but specifically we see Christ's final conquest of Satan, the one whose evil lies behind Babylon and the beast and all unbelieving people who have resisted Christ's rule.

I saw heaven standing open and there before me was a white horse, whose rider is called Faithful and True. With justice he judges and makes war. His eyes are like blazing fire, and on his head are many crowns. He has a name written on him that no one knows but he himself. He is dressed in a robe dipped in blood, and his name is the Word of God (19:11-13).

1. Jesus is King

As John describes it, we see yet another magnificent and majestic picture. A king, whose authority is stressed by his **many crowns**, is seated on a **white horse**. Here is one who is ready to make war. His **blazing** eyes **like fire** remind us of God's judicial wrath and the coming of the Son of man in glory (see comments on 1:12-16 where the same expression is used). Here is one who in his perfect **justice** comes to judge and war against all that is evil. On the day that John now describes, the whole world will finally recognise Jesus' kingly rule, his kingdom. No doubt under duress, all the world will finally acknowledge him as King (Philippians 2:10). In verse 16 we see his title written both on his thigh and on his robe, both places that would be highly visible on anyone seated on horseback: 'King of Kings and Lord of Lords.' Jesus is the one who rides out to battle.

2. Jesus is called Faithful and True

The rider is also called **Faithful and True**. The name recalls the title used by Jesus as he addressed the Laodiceans (3:14). He is faithful to all the covenant promises to save and to judge. All through history, ever since Genesis 3 and the Fall, God had promised that Satan would be crushed and defeated.[111] God had promised that as Satan and his forces waged war on God, so God would meet them and defeat them in battle (e.g. Isaiah 41:12-16). Christ is unswerving in his commitment to uphold the promises to save his people and condemn all that is evil. He is **true** in his judgments and the way he carries them out.

3. Jesus is the Word of God

Now we are told that his name is **the Word of God**. This title reminds us that Jesus is the definitive revelation of God in words and deeds. He not only reveals the will and purposes of God to the world, but he is also the one who brings about that will. The Word of God is not just passive. It doesn't just remain in the realm of good ideas or of theory, but rather the Word of God always carries through what has been spoken, and this is who Jesus is. He reveals the will of God for us and for Satan and for the end of this world and he puts that plan into effect. Thus, we read in Hebrews 4:12 that 'the word of God is living and active. Sharper than any double-edged sword, it penetrates even to dividing soul and spirit, joints and marrow; it judges the thoughts and attitudes of the heart.' The author there speaks of the proclaimed message of the gospel, but the content of that message is Jesus himself, who is the one who is alive and active. He judges even the thoughts of the heart and he wields the dividing sword, as we see here in Revelation. It is through Jesus, the Word, that the will of God in salvation is brought about, but even God's will in creation is also spoken and effected by Jesus (Colossians 1:15-16). Here in verse 13, it is this active work of God in judgment that is in mind as Jesus is called the Word of God. Jesus is ready for war both as he pronounces the final judgment and as he puts it into effect.

4. Jesus' unknown Name

We have just seen that Jesus is King and is known as 'Faithful and True' as well as 'the Word of God', so it seems strange that we should also be told that he **has a name written on him that no one knows but he himself**. It is an especially peculiar statement given that his title 'King of Kings' is in fact written on his thigh and his robe. It may be that in saying this, John recognises that exactly how Jesus is King, Faithful and True, and the Word of God, etc., is never fully revealed to believers or unbelievers. The 'name' of Jesus, like the 'name of God', could simply stand for the whole character and nature of Jesus. This indeed remains hidden in its detail. On the other hand, it may be that the name that he only knows himself is in fact the coming together of the three names we have seen above, along with the many other names and titles that have been given to him in this book. While we may understand something of these names and titles as we see Christ in action and read the word of Scripture, we do not and cannot ever grasp the totality of his kingship, sonship, faithfulness and so on, for we are not God. Christ alone knows the whole of who he is. He alone has been found able to open the seals of God's will and purposes and he alone can put it all into effect. Only he has a full understanding of his nature.

If this is the right way to understand this expression that no one knows the name **but he himself**, then it serves as a great reminder to each of us, even if we understand his kingship, even if we begin to understand what it means that he is the Word of God and even if we recognise that he is Faithful and True, to remain truly humble before the one who is God himself. As created beings we shall never, even in all eternity, know all that God knows, for he is God and we are still the creature.

5. Jesus the Judge

The armies of heaven were following him, riding on white horses and dressed in fine linen, white and clean. Out of his mouth comes a sharp sword with which to strike down the nations. 'He will rule them with an iron sceptre.' He treads the winepress of the fury of the wrath of God Almighty. On his robe and on his thigh he has this name written: KING OF KINGS AND LORD OF LORDS (19:14-16).

Christ rides out **dressed in a robe dipped in blood**. Even as he rides to victory at the head of his forces, we are still reminded constantly that his victory and his kingship have come through his suffering and death on the cross. The blood on his robe will always be a reminder of where the victory was actually won, on the cross. Those who ride with him do so, like him, on white horses. Although some have thought that these forces must be angelic, the stress on their wearing **fine linen** and that it is **clean** suggests they are probably the saints themselves, the redeemed. (Note the repetition of words from verse 8 above.) This would also link up with 17:14 where we have seen that Christ, as King of kings, makes war against the evil kings of this world and 'with him will be his called, chosen and faithful followers'.

We need to remember that we are here looking right forward into the time of the final judgment of the beast and Satan's followers. Revelation 17:12-14 drew on Daniel 7. In Daniel 7 the time was prophesied when the evil kings and last evil king would be overcome by God: 'The Ancient of Days... pronounced judgment in favour of the saints of the Most High, and the time came when they possessed the kingdom' (verse 22). Then in Daniel 7:27 we read: 'Then the sovereignty, power and greatness of the kingdoms under the whole heaven will be handed over to the saints, the people of the Most High. His kingdom will be an everlasting kingdom, and all rulers will worship and obey him.' It seems most likely, therefore, that John sees God's people, all the redeemed of all the ages, riding forth with Jesus. They are the saints who follow Christ the King wherever he goes. In fulfilment of the Word of God in prophecy, they ride forth with their Lord to rule with him.

As Jesus leads his people forward, **a sharp sword** that will destroy the nations comes **out of his mouth**. We are reminded that Jesus is called the **Word of the God**, for this is the picture here. Jesus speaks the command to fight against these evil beings and they are defeated. His word is God's word and it is *active*. Thus the sword comes from his mouth. He only has to speak the word and his full kingly **rule** is seen. The quotation comes from the famous messianic Psalm 2. There we read in verses 7-10: ' "You are my Son; today I have become your Father. Ask of me, and I will make the nations your inheritance.... You will rule them with an iron sceptre; you will dash them to pieces like pottery." Therefore, you kings, be wise; be warned, you rulers of the earth.'

The kings of the earth have not heeded the warning and the end has come. They thought they were gathering for a final war in which they would defeat all God's people on earth, but this is not what happens, for Christ has returned to lead his people in this great battle. The Son of God, Jesus the King, now fulfils prophecy as he comes to rule with an iron sceptre, one that judges and destroys everything that stands against him. He does indeed **strike down the nations** as he **treads the winepress of the fury of the wrath of God Almighty.** The speed with which this is carried out and the power that is shown simply reinforces his claim to the title that is written on his robe and his thigh. He is indeed **King of kings and Lord of lords.**

As he rides forth with his people for the great battle, another angel emphasises the totality of the judgment that will come as Christ and his saints win the battle.

> And I saw an angel standing in the sun, who cried in a loud voice to all the birds flying in mid-air, 'Come, gather together for the great supper of God, so that you may eat the flesh of kings, generals, and mighty men, of horses and their riders, and the flesh of all people, free and slave, small and great' (19:17-18).

The imagery is of the sort we met in chapters 17 and 18. It is vivid and clear and horrific. It is a picture of birds being summoned to eat the carcasses of those who die in battle.[112] On that battlefield it will not just be the troops (**free and slave, small and great**) who lie dead, but all their leaders, **the kings, generals, and mighty men**, also die. No one escapes.

6. The demise of the beast and the false prophet

> Then I saw the beast and the kings of the earth and their armies gathered together to make war against the rider on the horse and his army. But the beast was captured, and with him the false prophet who had performed the miraculous signs on his behalf. With these signs he had deluded those who had received the mark of the beast and worshipped his image. The two of them were thrown alive into the fiery lake of burning sulphur. The rest of them were killed with the sword that came out of the mouth of the rider on the horse, and all the birds gorged themselves on their flesh (19:19-21).

There have been two distinct episodes in this final judgment. Babylon has already been destroyed under God's sovereign plans, but the evil kings of the earth have carried out the destruction. That judgment and destruction was announced at the start of chapter 18 by an angel with great authority (18:1-2). Now, in the second and final episode, Christ comes to finish the job and this too has been announced by an angel with great authority, **standing in the sun** (19:17). **The kings of the earth and their armies** must be destroyed in this battle for which they have gathered and which, no doubt, they think they can win. They have come to fight Christ, **the rider**, and his people, the **army**. In this battle, the kings are destroyed and the **beast** and **false prophet** are also **captured**.

We encountered the false prophet in chapter 13.[113] There we saw how the **beast** seemed to lie behind all the secular powers on earth that are set against Christ, while the **false prophet** had targeted people in the church itself, seeking to get them to worship the beast rather than the true God. He did this through every form of deception including performing **miraculous signs** on the beast's behalf. In fact, the elect had not been led astray for they had been protected, but those **who had received the mark of the beast** were led deeper into their sinful worship of the beast. But now the one who is *True* captures both the beast and the false prophet and they receive their reward for all their evil as they are thrown into **the fiery lake of burning sulphur**. These two, who have set themselves up in the place of God and

247

deceived so many, are now judged by the one true God. In 20:10, when we see Satan himself also cast into this lake, we are told that this is the place where 'they will be tormented day and night for ever and ever'. All whom the figures of the beast and false prophet represent are judged in this way. The fact that John emphasises that they **were thrown alive** into the fiery lake, and that (20:10) the torment continues for ever, is evidence enough that 'hell' continues for ever as a place of punishment.

The armies that ride out behind the beast and the false prophet are put to death by the **sword**. Although this may be a literal death in battle, it is more likely to refer back to the sword that comes from the mouth of Jesus. He pronounces the penalty that has long been decreed for sin, namely, death. That death, also called the 'second death' (2:11; 20:14), is an everlasting spiritual death when they are all 'thrown into the lake of fire' (20:15). It is interesting to see that Jesus had specifically said that his word (the gospel message) would itself become the judge of all who rejected him: 'I have come into the world as a light, so that no one who believes in me should stay in darkness. As for the person who hears my words but does not keep them, I do not judge him. For I did not come to judge the world, but to save it. There is a judge for the one who rejects me and does not accept my words; that very word which I spoke will condemn him at the last day' (John 12:46-48).

The **fiery lake** is a metaphor for total, eternal and irrevocable judgment. Other terms, equally horrific, describe this punishment elsewhere in the New Testament (for example, Matthew 25:30). As we saw earlier, in suggesting that such descriptions are metaphorical let us be extremely careful not to mitigate the nature of this eternal punishment. The fact of the matter is that hell is so dreadful and final that only metaphorical language can communicate anything of its nature.

The greatest of all days has been described, but the description has not been altogether pleasant. Let us be thankful that if we know and love the Lord, if we believe that he has shed his blood for us (verse 13), then we have been sealed with his mark and will be vindicated on that day. Let us be encouraged also to use the time that remains before Christ's return to tell others of the light of the world and of the salvation to be found in King Jesus.

Revelation 20

A Vision of the Millennium

And I saw … (20:1)

John does not place this next vision of chapter 20 in a time relationship with chapter 19. He simply says, **And I saw**…. What he sees begins with an angel who appears with a great chain and with a key indicating his control of the Abyss (see comments on 8:10 and 9:1-2). This is where we have seen that Satan has been bound. But here we read that he captured Satan and bound him 'for a thousand years'. We have suggested earlier that Jesus bound Satan when he won the victory through his death and resurrection (see comments on 8:10; 9:1-2; and 12:7-17). Can it be that this vision now turns the clock right back in time to describe Jesus' victory on the cross? If that is the case, verses 1-6 here would be describing the time between Jesus' first coming and his second coming when Satan emerges for the final battle. The **thousand years** would then be a *symbol* for the time that stands between Christ's work on the cross and his return in glory. This is indeed the view that we believe makes the most sense of the passage and which we take in the commentary below.

1. The millennium question

However, it will be immediately obvious that the precise interpretation of these verses gives rise to what we might call the 'millennium question'. To get a brief overview of the different positions people have held regarding the 1000 years mentioned in 20:3, it would be good to return to the introduction to this commentary (see pages 12-16). Each position on this matter seeks to be faithful to Scripture as God's word, but each view also clearly has its merits and its problems. The passage thus serves as a good reminder to us all that, while God's Word is infallible, our understanding and interpretation of his Word must always be put forward with humility and a recognition that we may be wrong. As we read Scripture and believe we understand it, we must always remain open to others convincing us *from Scripture* that what we have previously understood may need to be modified or changed. It is a sad fact that Christians have often divided acrimoniously over these issues that should be matters of the greatest rejoicing for all of us. Whatever position we take, we should always bear in mind that the *function* of John's message here is, as we have repeatedly seen, to continue to give joy and comfort to Christians in the midst of their present suffering and persecution. John's message functions to provide a context for the present church and to help that church persevere in its faithfulness to the testimony of Christ.

The three basic positions on this chapter can be summarised in this way:[114]

i) Pre-millennialism

Though there are many variants of this general approach to the Book of Revelation, it is insisted that chapter 20 follows chapter 19 in *history*. Christ returns (chapter 19), the righteous dead are raised and rule with him for a specific period of 1000 years (20:1-6), before the rest, who do not belong to Christ, are raised for the final judgment (20:7-15). Christ returns, therefore, *before* (pre) his Millennium rule which will show him to be King Jesus. It will also show that sin lies within the heart of men and women as some continue to reject him even while Satan is bound. Meanwhile, the world will see that people ruled by Christ will face no threat even from a 'loosed' Satan.[115] Some pre-millennialists prefer to see the '1000' as a symbol describing the fulness of time of Christ's actual rule of peace here on earth. Some see this time of rule entirely in terms of a restored *national* Israel with Christ at its head. The common understanding within this view is that Christ actually rules for a specific period of time here on earth during history as we know it and before the final judgment.

ii) Post-millennialism

This view suggests that chapter 19 does not actually describe the second coming, but rather is symbolic of the way the church, under Christ's Lordship, gradually regains control of the world and leads it into a time of peace towards the end of this age. In this manner, the church prepares the way for Christ's return. At his return, *after* (post) the millennium, a set period of time, he will raise the dead for judgment and bind Satan and his followers. Thereafter, heaven and earth are re-created for Christ and his people.

iii) Amillennialism

This tends to see most of chapter 20 as a recapitulation of all that has gone so far. The millennium is thus regarded symbolically as the period of time between Christ's exaltation to the right hand of the Father (the start of his rule) through to the end of this age when he returns in glory. This is the understanding of the text that we believe makes most sense of the book as a whole and so is laid out below.

2. Satan bound for a thousand years

> And I saw an angel coming down out of heaven, having the key to the Abyss and holding in his hand a great chain. He seized the dragon, that ancient serpent, who is the devil, or Satan, and bound him for a thousand years. He threw him into the Abyss, and locked and sealed it over him, to keep him from deceiving the nations any more until the thousand years were ended. After that, he must be set free for a short time (20:1-3).

An angel of great authority and power comes from **heaven** and seizes Satan and casts him into the Abyss for a set period of time, **a thousand years**. We understand this to be a symbol for a perfect and complete period of history ordained by God. Here ten to the power of three (1000) indicates God's perfection in setting and also in limiting that time.

i) Other related passages of Scripture

Earlier, in Revelation 12, we have encountered Satan being called the **dragon**, **serpent** and **devil**. And that passage can help us understand the sequence of events here. There we saw that it was 'by the blood of the Lamb' (the death and resurrection of Christ) that Michael and his angelic forces were able to throw Satan down from heaven. His power to accuse believers before God was taken from him as he was 'hurled down' and all his other powers dramatically reduced. Other passages also talk of Satan being 'bound' and being 'thrown down'. Each one of these indicates that the time of that binding is to be linked directly to Christ's victory on the cross.

Jesus' own words are particularly instructive in this. In John 12:31-33, he speaks of the time of his death as the 'hour' for which he has come into this world. A voice from heaven confirms Jesus in his mission to bring glory to the Father. Then Jesus says: 'Now is the time for judgment on this world; now the prince of this world will be driven out. But I, when I am lifted up from the earth, will draw all men to myself.' John informs us that Jesus 'said this to show the kind of death he was going to die'.

In Mark 3:27-28, Jesus speaks of his authority over Satan: 'In fact, no one can enter a strong man's house and carry off his possessions unless he first ties up the strong man. Then he can rob his house. I tell you the truth, all the sins and blasphemies of men will be forgiven them.'

The apostle Paul and the writer to the Hebrews both pick up on the conquest of Christ gained at his victory on the cross: 'And having disarmed the powers and authorities, he made a public spectacle of them, triumphing over them by the cross' (Colossians 2:15); 'Since the children have flesh and blood, he too shared in their humanity so that by his death he might destroy him who holds the power of death – that is, the devil – and free those who all their lives were held in slavery by their fear of death' (Hebrews 2:14-15).

Satan is variously described in these verses as being 'driven out', 'tied up', as being 'disarmed' and 'destroyed' through the death of Christ on the cross. In chapter 12 we saw how Satan's powers were severely limited at that time. This all fits well with 20:1-3 except that, like Hebrews 2, the destruction or binding seems to leave no room at all for Satan's continued manoeuvring, and we know only too well from the rest of Revelation that Satan's forces and minions do indeed continue to work even after Christ's death. Can it really be said that he has, since then, been **locked** and **sealed** to keep him from **deceiving the nations any more until the thousand years were ended**?

ii) The effect of Satan's 'binding'

In 12:9 Satan was described as the one 'who leads the whole world astray'. Two points in translation are worth considering here to help us understand the verse. First, the Greek word in 12:9 ('leads astray') is the same as here in 20:3 where it is translated as 'deceiving'. Secondly, the word for 'nations' is the one that is usually used in the New Testament to describe those nations who are not part of Israel, that is, the rest of the world, or the Gentiles.[116] With these two points in mind, we can help explain this verse with a slightly different translation: *to keep him from still (anymore) deceiving or leading astray the Gentiles until the thousand years were ended.*

In other words, we suggest that this passage is not necessarily saying that Satan is bound and locked in every way so that he has no impact whatsoever on this world, but that his power specifically to rule the Gentiles has been utterly broken, and he is sealed and locked out of being able to pretend and deceive the nations of the world that he alone is *their* 'lord'. He is locked out of being able to lead those nations in a final war against God's people, the church. This view of the verse makes sense in the light of much else that is said in the New Testament.

The coming of Christ and his death and resurrection changes things on earth in a most dramatic way. John 1:5 reminds us that Jesus has come 'as a light shining in the darkness'. Luke 2:32 tells us that Jesus has come as 'a light for revelation to the *nations* (Gentiles)'. The extraordinary prophecy given us in Isaiah 9:2 says as much: 'the people walking in darkness have seen a great light; on those living in the land of the shadow of death (i.e. not in Israel) a light has dawned.'

Of course this does not mean that Satan is without his followers in the world. The book of Revelation has done nothing if it has not told us how evil the world remains. Just as Israel with its special light from God went astray and many did not believe, so it is in the world at large, in spite of the light of the gospel and of Jesus. People continue to follow the one whose power is contained by the sovereign God. But during this age of the Christian church, the time between Christ's exaltation and his second coming, the light goes out into the darkness and Satan is bound in such a way that the light makes real progress and extends throughout the world, bringing people into the community of faith and the glory of Christ's kingdom. This is the time in which God's mercy and grace is offered to all. Satan is so bound that he cannot lead the final battle against the church and against Christ until God himself allows it.

In Acts 14, the apostle Paul also takes this view of the effect of Christ's incarnation. As he preaches he says, 'In the past, he let all *nations* go their own way' (verse 16), but now Christ has changed things. In Ephesians 2:11-13 Paul makes the same point about the Gentiles to whom he writes: 'But now in Christ Jesus you who were once far away have been brought near through the blood of Christ.'

The death of Christ (and his resurrection and exaltation) constitute the great climactic event of history so far. In Jesus' work on the cross Satan was defeated and 'bound'. As Jesus said in Luke 10:18, 'I saw Satan fall like lightning from heaven.' In fact, it could be said that the cross actually confirmed the conquering power of Christ over Satan that had already been demonstrated during Jesus' life. One of the most significant events in Jesus' life occurred right at the start of his ministry when he was taken by the Spirit into the wilderness and was tempted by Satan. There Jesus demonstrated where the real power lay. Here was one who would not succumb to Satan's enticements. Here was one who behaved as Adam and Eve should have behaved. Here was one who stood in the wilderness where Israel had once stood and who withstood the temptations to which Israel had succumbed.

So, through the blood of Jesus, Satan was bound. He is bound for a set period of time, a time in which the church can take the light of the gospel out into the darkness of the nations, to those who have never before heard or seen the light of Christ. However, the day will come for the final judgment when the final conquest of Satan by Jesus must be *seen* to be completed. It is thus in God's plan that Satan be allowed his freedom again in order that Jesus may overcome him in the battle of the last day in such a way that the whole world can see what is happening. That is why we read **he must be set free.** This is God's will: that the world that has continued in sin and refused the light of the gospel may see their leader finally overcome. But this release of Satan is only **for a short time.** From our perspective we cannot know what this **short time** really means. In fact, it may be that it is literally for a very short time indeed, simply for the battle in which he arises to lead his forces. This would fit with Jesus' statement that 'for the sake of the elect those days will be shortened' (Matthew 24:22).

Summary so far
John's vision thus takes us back to the time of Christ's death and exaltation. As a result of his work on the cross and his conquering of Satan, Satan is bound with a **great chain for a thousand years**, that is, until Christ returns to judge. During that time Satan is **sealed** in **the Abyss** (the spiritual realm of darkness) specifically **to keep him from deceiving the nations** until that time is ended. This enables the gospel to be heard and the light of Christ to be seen all around the world and not just in the nation of Israel. The work of Christ is for people from all over the world, and the binding of Satan allows this to be preached to all. Of course, during this time, Satan's emissaries

continue to work against the gospel. The beast, the false prophet, and Babylon are all doing Satan's work, and Satan still stands behind all their work and influences them and leads them. But he will not be seen until he is 'unbound' and allowed, by God, to lead his forces against Christ and his church. Once again Satan will deceive all those from the nations of the earth who have not received the gospel and will lead them out to their judgment in that final battle. We shall see this happening in verses 7-10 below. This release will be for a very short time. As we saw in chapter 18 and 19, the speed of Jesus' conquest is phenomenal.[117]

3. The saints reign with Christ for a thousand years

John now moves on to talk of the place of Christ's people during this same period of Satan's binding.

> I saw thrones on which were seated those who had been given authority to judge. And I saw the souls of those who had been beheaded because of their testimony for Jesus and because of the word of God. They had not worshipped the beast or his image and had not received his mark on their foreheads or their hands. They came to life and reigned with Christ a thousand years. (The rest of the dead did not come to life until the thousand years were ended.) This is the first resurrection. Blessed and holy are those who have part in the first resurrection. The second death has no power over them, but they will be priests of God and of Christ and will reign with him for a thousand years (20:4-6).

John now sees **thrones**, which are the seats of authority, power and judgment. The picture is a glorious one and it is the one to which we have returned many times in this book. The church is preserved by God through this thousand years. Satan is bound and cannot destroy God's people.

However, many Christians have died during this time. For some, their death has been the death of martyrdom and they have even been **beheaded** for proclaiming the gospel and standing for and living by God's Word. These people are Christ's followers and they have **not worshipped the beast** nor have they taken his **mark** on them, even when it has meant starvation and further persecution. So what has happened to them? Has Satan after all had some sort of victory over them? Not at all! For **they came to life and reigned with Christ a thousand years.**

God's faithful people do not cease to have a meaningful existence when they die. Far from it! They are alive and even **reign with Christ**. The saints who have been urged repeatedly in chapters 2 and 3[118] to *overcome* are now seen to have overcome! Here we see the fulfilment of the promise to the Laodicean church in 3:21: 'To him who overcomes, I will give the right to sit with me on my throne, just as I overcame and sat down with my Father on his throne.' Those who die in the faith of Christ go straight to be with him. Their bodies may have been destroyed on earth but their **souls** are now seen by John ruling with Christ in heaven. They are **blessed and holy**, for they have enjoyed the privilege of being part of the **first resurrection**. On the other hand, those who have not died in the faith (**the rest of the dead**) do not **come to life** until Christ returns.

The idea of a first and **second death** is quite straightforward. The first death is the one we all go through on this earth (unless Christ returns first). The second death which **has no power over** Christians is the death of the final judgment, after the resurrection, that John is in the process of describing and will return to in verses 7-10. That second death is reserved for all who follow Satan. For Christians there is no second death, rather it describes what happens to those who die as unbelievers.

Reference to the first resurrection is, however, a little more difficult to understand. Most likely it refers to people first becoming Christians. From that time forwards they belong to Christ and have eternal life. They have been 'raised' from the death of sin to eternal life. Also from that time forwards they reign with Christ in the sense that he represents all his people as he sits in glory on his throne in heaven. The apostle Paul says as much in Ephesians 2:6. Talking of conversion, he says, 'God raised us up with Christ.' Indeed, he goes further and says, 'and seated us with him in the heavenly realms in Christ Jesus'. Paul, of course, was very much alive when he wrote this and yet he uses the past tense. Because we are 'in Christ' we are represented by him in heaven and when we die we, our souls, join him there. What is true of our King is thus true of us. He reigns and so those whom he represents also reign *with him*. Jesus has been raised from the dead and so those whom he represents are even now *raised*. More than that, when Christians die, their souls go immediately to be with the Lord in heaven. They may not yet be raised *bodily* but they are still alive and are seen to reign with him in heaven.

Of course, Christians look forward to what for them is the second resurrection when they will be raised *bodily* from the dead and enjoy the new heavens and the new earth. Unbelievers, on the other hand, have no first resurrection of this sort because they do not enjoy eternal life; they are not converted and have not come to life in Christ. And yet they will indeed be raised *bodily* on that last day for judgment, before going to the *second death* which is the death of eternity away from God.

How **blessed** Christians are that **they have a part in the first resurrection**. This is a privilege that does not belong to others and it is part of the great inheritance that is ours through faith in Jesus Christ. How blessed, as well, that the **second death** has no power over them. Just as God's people are protected in this life, and at death their souls go to be with the Lord where they continue to be protected by him, so at the last judgment day when they are raised bodily from the dead, they are raised never to die again.

Special lessons for today

Sometimes people ask, 'What happens to me when I die?' While we cannot be sure how things will look in heaven, surely this passage comes as a wonderful reminder to all people of faith in Christ, that when we die our souls immediately go into the presence of the Lord. We are in 'heaven', that spiritual place where Christ and the Father are enthroned, and where we too find we are part of Christ's ruling multitude. Of course, going to be with Christ when we die is not the end of all that we look forward to. Wonderful as that is, we still look forward to the great resurrection of our *bodies* and to participating in the new heavens and the new earth which will be talked of in chapter 21. This is what we call the 'general resurrection' or the 'second resurrection' (for believers). In Acts 24:15 we read, 'there will be a resurrection of both the righteous and the wicked'.

Though Christians will still usually find physical death painful, frightening and even fearful as a process through which we will all have to pass, nevertheless, this is to be the limit of our fear. In Christ we know that death has no ultimate fear but rather leads to eternal joy in Christ's presence. Unlike believers, those who have rejected Christ and followed the beast face two 'deaths'. The first is the one we all face, the second is the spiritual death they face when, having been raised bodily from the dead, they face their judge and are condemned to eternal death. They go to that place where the life of Christ is never experienced, that place that is the abode of Satan and all who have followed him.

The Final Judgment

When the thousand years are over, Satan will be released from his prison and will go out to deceive the nations in the four corners of the earth – Gog and Magog – to gather them for battle. In number they are like the sand on the seashore. They marched across the breadth of the earth and surrounded the camp of God's people, the city he loves. But fire came down from heaven and devoured them. And the devil, who deceived them, was thrown into the lake of burning sulphur, where the beast and the false prophet had been thrown. They will be tormented day and night for ever and ever (20:7-10).

The thousand years are over at the end of this church age when Christ returns. At that time, as we have seen in 20:3, Satan will be released **for a short time**. And this is now developed here in verse 7. He is released in order **to go out to deceive the**

nations.[119] We have seen that Satan has indeed been bound from stopping the nations hearing and receiving the gospel of Christ. That gospel has been preached around the world as Christ commanded, and now the end has come. The time for repentance is at an end, and so, probably as Christ returns, or just before, Satan is allowed to come to those who have never accepted the gospel and he draws them all together for a battle against God's people. At last he is freed by God to do what he has always wanted to do, to wage war on Christ and his followers. In New Testament terms, the people of God, Israel, now include people of all nations and nationalities. The *nations* here that Satan goes out to deceive are those who are *not* the people of God. They are ready now to follow Satan where he will lead and so he gathers them together **for battle**. Sadly they are very great in number and they come from all over **the breadth of the earth**.

The picture that John uses to describe Christ's final conquest of Satan and his followers is of those evil forces surrounding **the camp of God's people**. We are reminded of the camp of the Israelites in the wilderness as God protected them when they were surrounded by hostile enemies.[120] But John has another picture in mind as well as he calls these people **the city he** [God] **loves.** How different this city is from the city of the 'inhabitants of this earth', the city of Babylon. In every way Jerusalem stands as a contrast with Babylon. As Babylon is described as a prostitute and the church as the bride of Christ, here Jerusalem is the city God loves and stands in contrast with Babylon that has just been destroyed by God.

This 'city' of course speaks to us of Jerusalem where God particularly showed his love for his people. This was the place where his glory came down on the temple. This was the city where his people met with their God. So the people of God are here referred to as both **the camp** and **the city**. We are reminded of Jesus' words to the church at Philadelphia (3:12): 'Him who overcomes I will make a pillar in the temple of my God. Never again will he leave it. I will write on him the name of my God and the name of the city of my God, the new Jerusalem, which

261

is coming down out of heaven from my God; and I will also write on him my new name.' Once again this is wonderful picture language that will be developed in the last two chapters. It is of course the people who are important here rather than the literal Israelite camp in the wilderness or the literal city of Jerusalem.

Meanwhile Satan, in his last desperate attack, seems to surround God's people, Jerusalem, to wipe them out. In fact the people of God, so long persecuted, so long suffering in this world, are led into battle by Jesus, the one whom we have seen rides the 'white horse' and who is 'King of kings and Lord of lords'. They are led and protected by the one who now, in a matter of moments throws **the devil ... into the lake of burning sulphur**. This is where the beast and the false prophet have already been thrown. In this place he and they will find eternal punishment.

The general resurrection
The last five verses of this chapter now change the picture in order to show us what happens to the people who have followed Satan. We have heard the fate of the false prophet, beast and Satan, but we need to hear of the fate of **each person** who was prepared to follow him and seek to destroy the *city of God*. While Christians enjoy a 'second' resurrection, unbelievers face a 'second death' as they are judged for their sin. But before this, all people, good and evil, are raised bodily to life.[121]

> Then I saw a great white throne and him who was seated on it. Earth and sky fled from his presence, and there was no place for them. And I saw the dead, great and small, standing before the throne, and books were opened. Another book was opened, which is the book of life. The dead were judged according to what they had done as recorded in the books. The sea gave up the dead that were in it, and death and Hades gave up the dead that were in them, and each person was judged according to what he had done. Then death and Hades were thrown into the lake of fire. The lake of fire is the second death. If anyone's name was not found written in the book of life, he was thrown into the lake of fire (20:11-15).

When we looked at Revelation 1:13 and then later at 4:3 we saw how the descriptions of God on his throne often drew upon Daniel 7. This is true here in 20:11 as well. As that chapter spoke of God on his throne ready to judge, so John now describes God seated on an enormous **white throne**. The purity of God and his righteousness and justice as he comes to judge is stressed by the emphasis on whiteness (see Daniel 7:9). The universal impact of his appearance in glory and his judgment is made vivid with a picture of even **earth** and **sky** running away from him. We shall see in 21:1 that they 'pass away' as the 'new heaven and a new earth' appear.

Those who have rejected Christ will do their best to flee this moment. As in 6:16, they will cry out to the rocks, 'Fall on us and hide us from the face of him who sits on the throne and from the wrath of the Lamb!' But it will be to no avail, for the **dead** are now **standing**. They are raised for judgment. All are raised. The **sea** gives up those who have died, and even those who have gone to **Hades** (the place of departed spirits who have not gone to be with the Lord) are **judged.** Again like Daniel's vision, the **books were opened**. The dead who are now standing are faced with one book, but there is another book as well and that is **the book of life**. We have looked at the meaning of this in the comments on 3:4-6 and 13:8.

Judgment according to what people have done will serve to demonstrate God's absolute justice. As we saw earlier, this is not a matter of 'good works' saving people and 'bad works' condemning people. Rather it is that the works indicate which master people have been following. Is Christ their Lord or is Satan? Are the works that are opened up the works of Christ or of Satan? These are the two books. One reveals the works of those who have followed life, the other reveals the works of those who have followed darkness. One is headed by Christ, the other by Satan.

It is so important therefore for those of us who know and love the Lord Jesus to realise that our names will be found in his book of life. We need not fear the bodily resurrection and judgment on the last day, for we have already been acquitted. We have been 'justified', declared righteous before the throne of God, because Christ has paid the penalty for our sin. As the book of life is opened for us, it will show that we are 'in Christ', and that he leads us into eternal life.

Revelation 21

Babylon, the beast and the false prophet, all who have rejected Christ, and Satan himself have been thrown into the lake of fire. Their destiny is what we have commonly called 'hell'. But pictures in our mind of Dante's 'Inferno' are not what hell is all about. True, we have seen metaphorical descriptions of hell as a fiery place of sulphur, a lake of fire, etc., but we cannot know what this place really will be like. The best description is simply to say that it is the place where Satan has been placed by God and where he and all his people are contained by God so they cannot have any further influence at all in the new heaven and new earth. There, without interruption and without sin, God's people will enjoy being in the presence of God himself. As we read through chapters 20 and 21 we discover something of the sheer wonder and beauty of what is in store for God's people as they 'go through the gates into the city' (22:14). Hell, though, is 'outside' this city of God (21:8; 27; 22:15, 19).

A New Creation

Now the scene changes again to one of the most marvellous scenes in the whole of Scripture. After all the feverish activity and terror of the final judgment that has come with the release of Satan and Christ's return and victory, we now move to a scene of great beauty and peace and quiet. Now we catch a glimpse of the full inheritance to which followers of Jesus have been looking forward for centuries. Now we see the final fulfilment of prophecies to Abraham, Isaac and the people of God down through the ages. Here Isaiah's vision of the new heavens and new earth is fulfilled. The book of Revelation reaches its great and glorious climax, because it is for this that God's suffering people in the seven churches and throughout the church age have been waiting.

1. A new heaven and a new earth

Then I saw a new heaven and a new earth, for the first heaven and the first earth had passed away, and there was no longer any sea (21:1).

In 20:11 we saw earth and sky fleeing 'for there was no place for them'. Now they **have passed away**. They were of the old order of things. Now all is **new**. Finally the great goal of creation is realised – perfect harmony and obedience to the Creator. In 4:6 we saw that a 'sea of glass' was before God's throne. This indicated God's great holiness and separated him from fallen creation and fallen creatures. Now, praise God, we find there is **no longer any sea**. Since all is holy and pure, and the only people around are righteous and justified, all the symbols of separation are gone. It is as if the Red Sea that had separated what was not holy from the Promised Land has now been removed completely. The people are in the Promised Land. As John says in verse 3, 'Now the dwelling of God is with men...'

Long ago Isaiah had prophesied of this new age and it is to those words in Isaiah 65:17-19 that John turns as he describes what he sees:[122] 'Behold, I will create new heavens and a new earth. The former things will not be remembered, nor will they come to mind. But be glad and rejoice for ever in what I will create, for I will create Jerusalem to be a delight and its people a joy. I will rejoice over Jerusalem and take delight in my people; the sound of weeping and of crying will be heard in it no more.'

2. The new Jerusalem

I saw the Holy City, the new Jerusalem, coming down out of heaven from God, prepared as a bride beautifully dressed for her husband (21:2).

Jerusalem stands as a symbol for God's people gathered as the church. This is a **Holy City** because God's people are perfected for eternity. At last **the bride** is fully prepared (see discussion of the biblical background to this picture in the comments on 19:7-9). The wedding dress is immaculate. The bride comes down **from God** (see 3:12), because it is God who has prepared and has always been preparing a people for himself. It is he who sent his own Son to die for the church and to bring her to resurrection life and to an eternity with him. It is he who is now bringing in the new heaven and the new earth. Again Isaiah (52:1-2) provides some of the background here: 'Awake, awake, O Zion, clothe yourself with strength. Put on your garments of splendour, O Jerusalem, the holy city. The uncircumcised and defiled will not enter you again. Shake off your dust; rise up, sit enthroned, O Jerusalem....'

This is the **city** that Abraham had looked forward to: 'By faith he made his home in the promised land like a stranger in a foreign country; he lived in tents, as did Isaac and Jacob, who were heirs with him of the same promise. For he was looking forward to the city with foundations, whose architect and builder is God' (Hebrews 11:9-10). In Hebrews 12:22 the city is explicitly shown to be the people of God, the church: 'You have come to Mount Zion, to the heavenly Jerusalem, the city of the living God. You have come to thousands upon thousands of angels in joyful assembly, to the church of the firstborn, whose names are written in heaven...'

3. A new world order

> And I heard a loud voice from the throne saying, 'Now the dwelling of God is with men, and he will live with them. They will be his people, and God himself will be with them and be their God. He will wipe every tear from their eyes. There will be no more death or mourning or crying or pain, for the old order of things has passed away' (21:3-4).

The Tent of Meeting, or Tabernacle, in the wilderness had been a symbol of God's presence among his people (Exodus 29:42). The Temple in the city of Jerusalem had also been that symbol (2 Chronicles 5:13-14). Now in the new order of things, however, God's home is with his people in a different way. Jesus had shown us a foretaste of what this would be like when he came to this earth as a human being (John 1:14). He had walked and talked among his people, but now he will be with all God's people for all eternity. The relationship will be one of closer intimacy than ever symbols could convey. Now it is not just Moses who is able to communicate directly with God. This is much more like the intimacy that Adam and Eve had with God when they walked and talked with him in the Garden of Eden before they sinned. As John tells us, **God himself will be with them**.

The newness of everything is again stressed with the reference back to Isaiah 65:19. What joy it will be when we realise that since death is no longer present in the new heaven and earth, so all that has been part and parcel of a world with death has also gone. The suffering that people have known, whether in illness or in persecution, the crying and pain of seeing loved ones die or simply of becoming ill or growing old and nearing death, all that is gone. **The old order of things has passed away**.

Sometimes people caricature this Christian teaching as 'pie in the sky when you die'. Provided we understand that God is concerned about us and about how we live and behave *today*, and provided the future doesn't become an excuse to opt out of the difficulties of today, then surely we should not be ashamed to proclaim clearly to our friends that indeed glory awaits us such as we have never experienced on this earth. The utopias of man's wisdom through the centuries are just dreams that never come to fruition. The new heaven and the new earth are our inheritance as Christians. This is part of the gospel message. It is a message that is full of hope and joy and encouragement for us all.

> He who was seated on the throne said, 'I am making everything new!' Then he said, 'Write this down, for these words are trustworthy and true' (21:5).

The one sitting on the throne is either God or Jesus, perhaps both. Interestingly it is he who now directly tells John that what is about to be related to him is utterly **trustworthy and true**.

We have seen this insistence on the truth of God's word before in this book. Here it is reasserted as a means of providing the suffering church with a real and genuine future to which they can look forward. This is not some dream. It may be described in symbolic language, for what else can be perceived by minds that as yet have not experienced such wonder, but it is not fantasy. This is the true word of God. More than that it is **trustworthy** in the sense that we can rest assured it will all happen. This word or promise will never be forgotten or modified or changed.

Excursus: A new creation or a renewed creation?
These opening verses speak of a **new** heaven and earth, but this is not quite the whole biblical story. There are other passages which suggest that what Christ ushers in is a re-creation and a thorough renewal of all things. For example in Romans 8:19-21 we read of the existing creation looking forward to the time when Christians come into their full inheritance because then the creation too will be freed from decay and brought into a new found freedom. 'The creation waits in eager expectation for the sons of God to be revealed. For the creation was subjected to frustration, not by its own choice, but by the will of the one who subjected it, in hope that the creation itself will be liberated from its bondage to decay and brought into the glorious freedom of the children of God.' Matthew 19:28 refers to 'the renewal of all things'; Old Testament prophets spoke of God doing something 'new' (as in Isaiah 65) as well as 'restoring' and 'changing' (for example, Isaiah 35).

There is a parallel in the type of language that is used of us when we become Christians and of when we are raised from the dead on the last day. In 2 Corinthians 5:17 we read about our conversion and regeneration: 'Therefore, if anyone is in Christ, he is a new creation; the old has gone, the new has come!' (See Galatians 6:15). And yet when Paul speaks of the death of believers and their resurrection in 1 Corinthians 15:42, he indicates that for all the newness of the resurrection body there

269

is clear continuity: 'So will it be with the resurrection of the dead. The body that is sown is perishable, it is raised imperishable…'. It always strikes me that if I were shown a seed of 'wheat' (Paul's example in 1 Corinthians 15) and then an ear of ripened wheat, and I had never seen either before, I would never link the two at all! On the other hand, because I have seen both and know that when the one is planted it will eventually grow into the other, I know there is continuity. Perhaps it is this picture that Paul uses of the seed, combined with the various different ways that the Bible uses to describe the newness of the new heaven and the new earth, that ought to make us cautious here. It seems to me that the most we can really say is that the 'new' will be so new that it will be all but unrecognisable. We will 'not remember the former things'. On the other hand, we are still the same people, and creation itself looks forward to a restoration, for we shall be living in a real and substantial new earth in which we shall serve God. Creation itself will be freed from 'the bondage to decay'. The seed will be forgotten as the new ear of wheat is revealed in all its ripened beauty!

4. The promises are inherited

i) By God's people

> He said to me: 'It is done. I am the Alpha and the Omega, the Beginning and the End. To him who is thirsty I will give to drink without cost from the spring of the water of life. He who overcomes will inherit all this, and I will be his God and he will be my son' (21:6-7).

Repeating 1:8, God declares that he is the **Alpha and Omega.** With the sentence, **It is done**, God announces that his sovereign purposes have been accomplished. The one who is there at the start and goes on for ever is totally sovereign. There is none before him and none after him. How appropriate that we should hear this great title for God both at the start of the book and at the end (here and 22:13). John has reached the stage in his vision where God, who brought creation into being, has guided it to its end. Now he fulfils his purposes for a new heaven and earth as well.

This sovereignty of God is stressed in the title he gives to himself in order to encourage God's people. They have read this whole account of John's visions, and because God is the **Beginning and the End** they can rest assured that they are safe and what has been said will indeed happen. This is reinforced by God's personal promise that he will give the **water of life** to those who thirst – and there will be no charge. This is God's wonderful grace at work. (We saw the Lamb leading his people to 'springs of living water' back in 7:17 and commented on the meaning of the water and its Old Testament background there.) God guarantees eternal life. Death has truly been vanquished. And lest anyone should forget who it is that inherits **all this**, God himself promises that it is **he who overcomes**. This was the urgent message to the seven churches, that they should 'overcome'. We have seen throughout the book how God will protect them and help them overcome by the power of his Holy Spirit. They must keep holding on to Christ and not 'share in the sins of the world' (18:4). They must continue to follow Christ, but God's word is secure and **trustworthy and true**.

In a wonderful reminder that he is always faithful to all his promises, however long ago they were made, God refers back to his covenant with David. In 2 Samuel 7:13-14 we read the promise made to King David in God's covenant with him: 'I will establish the throne of his kingdom for ever. I will be his father, and he shall be my son.' The prophet Isaiah (55:1-3) also remembers that covenant and links it, as here in Revelation 21, with 'thirsting' after God: 'Come, all you who are thirsty, … come, buy and eat! … your soul will delight in the richest of fare. … I will make an everlasting covenant with you, my faithful love promised to David.' Here God uses words that he has used before with King David and then with the prophet Isaiah. The promises to King David were first and foremost fulfilled in the first coming of Jesus. Just as he has 'overcome' and inherited what God has promised, so will his people. The Christian, the one **who is thirsty**, will receive drink – eternal life – from God and be called **my son** by God.[123]

ii) By those who have rejected God

> But the cowardly, the unbelieving, the vile, the murderers, the sexually immoral, those who practise magic arts, the idolaters and all liars – their place will be in the fiery lake of burning sulphur. This is the second death (21:8).

These last two chapters largely concern the wonders of the inheritance that belong to God's people after the last judgment. But still, from time to time, we are reminded again that those who follow Satan will have no part in these privileges. The promises God has made to them have also come to pass. A list of vices remind us who these people are. They are above all **unbelieving** and **idolaters**. The fact that cowardice starts the list and lying ends the list may indicate that God is referring here particularly to those who had been part of the church but had followed Babylon and not stood up for Christ. Such people existed in Philadelphia and are called 'liars' (3:9). Instead of coming to the great joy of resurrection to be with God for ever, they have been raised from the dead for judgment, only to find that they now face spiritual **death**. They died physically, the first death, but then they were raised from the dead to meet their Maker. Now they face the **second death**. Their destiny is the place where Satan reigns and death and Hades are found. This is the place of spiritual darkness, out of the 'City' and for ever away from God.

The Holy City

> One of the seven angels who had the seven bowls full of the seven last plagues came and said to me, 'Come, I will show you the bride, the wife of the Lamb.' And he carried me away in the Spirit to a mountain great and high, and showed me the Holy City, Jerusalem, coming down out of heaven from God. It shone with the glory of God, and its brilliance was like that of a very precious jewel, like a jasper, clear as crystal. It had a

great, high wall with twelve gates, and with twelve angels at the gates. On the gates were written the names of the twelve tribes of Israel. There were three gates on the east, three on the north, three on the south and three on the west. The wall of the city had twelve foundations, and on them were the names of the twelve apostles of the Lamb. The angel who talked with me had a measuring rod of gold to measure the city, its gates and its walls. The city was laid out like a square, as long as it was wide. He measured the city with the rod and found it to be 12,000 stadia in length, and as wide and high as it is long. He measured its wall and it was 144 cubits thick, by man's measurement, which the angel was using (21:9-17).

At the start of chapter 17 an angel 'who had seven bowls' took John and showed him the 'punishment of the great prostitute', Babylon. The angel carried him away **in the Spirit** into a desert (17:1-3). What a contrast now as an angel **who had seven bowls**, perhaps the same angel, takes John to see a very different picture! John is **carried away in the Spirit** to a great mountain. There he sees a beautiful woman, **the bride**, who is **the wife of the Lamb**.

1. The glory of the city

As he looks, he see Jerusalem coming down from heaven as we saw in verse 2. Let us remember that we have recently seen how Babylon was dressed in purple and scarlet and had a name on her forehead, 'MYSTERY, BABYLON THE GREAT, THE MOTHER OF PROSTITUTES AND OF THE ABOMINATIONS OF THE EARTH' (17:5). What a contrast here! The bride, Jerusalem, which is the church, shines **with the glory of God**, and her appearance is very special. The glory of God is a reflected glory, indicating that the church has indeed been raised up right into the presence of the Almighty. This glory will not need to be hidden as Moses had to hide his face when it reflected a little of God's glory revealed on Mount Sinai (Exodus 33; 2 Corinthians 3:13). This is the glory of the bride who has been right close to her husband. Precious jewels are then used to help describe in picture language the extraordinary beauty of this bride in all her glory. The main elements of this description are drawn once again from Ezekiel (specially 40:2; 45:1; 48:31-35).

John now goes on to describe the city. And here again we need to remember that the city is a symbol for the people of God, the resurrected church. Thus, of course, the description is also given us in symbolic and picture language. Clearly neither a 'bride' nor a group of people, the church, can actually have twelve gates! But this description helps us understand the church, the bride of Christ. The **high wall** reminds us that God protects his people. The twelve gates with the names of **the twelve tribes of Israel** reminds us of the 144,000 of 14:1. The church is the people of God, the whole of Israel. This Israel is not to be understood ethnically but spiritually. Israel is all the people in the new heaven and the new earth. It is the full church but it is continuous with all people of all ages, Jew and Gentile, who have been true believers and followers of Jesus Christ. The **twelve foundations** have the names of the **apostles** on them, for they are the ones who took the gospel out to the world and introduced the world to Jesus, the foundation of the church (1 Peter 2:4-7). If we add together the twelve tribes and the twelve apostles we probably have the twenty-four elders that we encountered in the throne room scenes earlier in the book (4:4). The fact that the elders form such a vital part of the structure of this 'city' is another indication that we are dealing with 'people', the church, and not some new city as we might imagine it.

The angel who was explaining things to John was able to **measure the city**. Again we have seen this before (see the introduction to chapter 11).[124] Measuring is an image of just how well God knows his people and protects them. None can fall away or feel unsafe, for God is fully aware. This city is perfectly measured by God and is his complete building. None has 'missed the boat'. All the elect are present and the bride is indeed perfect. This is important, as we now see a picture of a city that could never be built! This city is **laid out like a square** and yet it is described in its 'length' and 'width' and 'height'! If it were a real city of bricks and mortar, then it would be a cube. But that is not what this vision is all about. The numbers are symbolic of all of God's perfection. (Note the repetition of the figure 12 and multiples of 12 and see the comments 7:4.)

> The wall was made of jasper, and the city of pure gold, as pure as glass. The foundations of the city walls were decorated with every kind of precious stone. The first foundation was jasper, the second sapphire, the third chalcedony, the fourth emerald, the fifth sardonyx, the sixth carnelian, the seventh chrysolite, the eighth beryl, the ninth topaz, the tenth chrysoprase, the eleventh jacinth, and the twelfth amethyst. The twelve gates were twelve pearls, each gate made of a single pearl. The great street of the city was of pure gold, like transparent glass (21:18-21).

The description of the way this great city is built emphasises how precious and beautiful it is. Truly, here is the bride of Christ in all her radiant beauty. God has always regarded his people as precious to him. In Isaiah 43:4 he says, 'Since you are precious and honoured in my sight, and because I love you...'. In Exodus, a garment with twelve precious stones on it was made for the high priest, Aaron. These stones were a reminder that as he entered the presence of God he represented each tribe of Israel (Exodus 39:1-14). The same jewels are mentioned here.[125] God's precious people are now in his presence, not on the jacket of a high priest, but fully part of the city of God. No high priest's robe is needed here, for the people themselves are in the presence of their God. It is truly awe-inspiring to think that we who belong to Christ are precious to our God and will one day make up that glorious bride as part of the church.

2. No temple in the city

> I did not see a temple in the city, because the Lord God Almighty and the Lamb are its temple (21:22).

The same point is now made again even more vividly. There is no **temple** in the new heaven and earth. God had always said he would be with his people. The temple was the place where, symbolically, God showed this most clearly. But things are different now. The change began when Christ first came to this world. He is Immanuel, God with us. The temple was no longer needed as the Spirit of Christ took up residence within believers. In 2 Corinthians 6:16 Paul put it this way: 'For we are the temple of the living God. As God has said: "I will live with them and walk among them, and I will be their God, and they will be my people."' Wonderful though our experience is today of Christ's presence with us by his Spirit, it is but the firstfruits of what is in store for us when we see 'face to face'. It is this amazing experience that John is describing here. There is no physical temple building, and what we had as 'firstfruits' we will have in its fulness when we see the Lord God Almighty and the Lamb. Symbols like temples and tabernacles are not needed once the reality has come.

3. Neither sun nor moon light the city

> The city does not need the sun or the moon to shine on it, for the glory of God gives it light, and the Lamb is its lamp (21:23).

The intimacy of God's presence with his people is emphasised in yet another way. The vision pictures a scene where there is no sun or moon, because of the light that shines forth from God's **glory**. This is a glory fully shared by the Lamb, of course, and so John says **the Lamb is its lamp**. Clearly Isaiah 60:3-5 is in mind as John describes what he sees in this verse and what follows. This section precedes Isaiah's description of the new heavens and the new earth, but he looks forward to the time when God will return to his people and bring his full blessings to them. He says, 'Arise, shine, for your light has come, and the glory of the LORD rises upon you' (60:1).

4. All nations enjoy this city

> The nations will walk by its light, and the kings of the earth will bring their splendour into it. On no day will its gates ever be shut, for there will be no night there. The glory and honour of the nations will be brought into it. Nothing impure will ever enter it, nor will anyone who does what

is shameful or deceitful, but only those whose names are written in the Lamb's book of life (21:24-27).

In Isaiah 60:3 we read, 'Nations will come to your light, and kings to the brightness of your dawn;' and in John's vision that prophecy continues to be fulfilled. This is a city where there is no more fear. All who have sinned have been judged and are no longer present, as verse 27 makes clear. Those who, figuratively, 'come and go' are all the elect of all nations. Their names are in the **Lamb's book of life**. People and their leaders from all over the world are now pictured coming to this city. Mention of the **kings of the earth** stands for the way all of God's people, including their leaders, gather in the glory of the city. No one is shut out for there is no **night** (which is the time when ancient cities would close their gates). The picture is that everything that a person has of any worth at all is brought to the city. It is not literal **splendour** that they bring, but themselves. As we said above, the picture throughout is of all God's people of all races, and of all nations, being drawn together in this great city. All enjoy the presence of God and the Lamb in their midst, and all share in the wonder of God's glory. The elect, which includes people from **the nations** (Gentiles), are gathering in this city to worship God the Father and the Lamb. They are safe and they are battered no longer by the sin and suffering of the old order of things, for the new has most certainly arrived.

Revelation 22

This final chapter begins with a glorious picture of the blessings people receive as part of the city of God. Then John moves on to draw things together and repeats the message that Christ is coming soon. Christians are exhorted to take seriously what has been said in this book and to remain faithful to Christ.

5. Further blessings for residents of the city

Then the angel showed me the river of the water of life, as clear as crystal, flowing from the throne of God and of the Lamb down the middle of the great street of the city. On each side of the river stood the tree of life, bearing twelve crops of fruit, yielding its fruit every month. And the leaves of the tree are for the healing of the nations. No longer will there be any curse. The throne of God and of the Lamb will be in the city, and his servants will serve him. They will see his face, and his name will be on their foreheads. There will be no more night. They will not need the light of a lamp or the light of the sun, for the Lord God will give them light. And they will reign for ever and ever (22:1-5).

i) No more curse

The people of God, the new Jerusalem, have many blessings with God in their midst. As we read these first five verses, it is the opening words of verse 3 that contain the key to the picture before us. **No longer will there be any curse.** The 'curse' refers back to God's judgment on Adam and Eve. That judgment had a dramatic effect on all people through all generations right until the final judgment and the general resurrection. Not only did pain and death and suffering enter the world as a consequence of their sin but, most serious of all, Adam and Eve were removed from the Garden of Eden. In that Garden, the two of them had an intimate relationship with God their Creator. He talked with them and blessed them in many ways.

Leaving the Garden meant they no longer had that specially intimate relationship with God. It also meant that creation itself now struggled against them and they found life itself hard work and often unpleasant. More than that, they were now removed from **the tree of life**. This was the tree that permanently reminded them that God himself created and gave life. Part of God's judgment on them was that they would die, and so their access to the tree was removed from them. If we keep in mind this background, it helps us see the staggering beauty of the blessings of being part of the city of God. It is a restoration of Eden and even better. It is not just the expulsion from the Garden that is now 'undone', but the presence of God and of light and life is even greater and more intimate than it had been for Adam and Eve in the first place. Eden had been, in effect, a physical prophecy of the new heaven and new earth, but what it pointed forward to is even greater and more special than that original garden.

People often try to drive a wedge between prophecies describing a restoration of Eden and a building of a new Jerusalem. That such a view is misplaced is obvious in 21:19-21 where the foundations of the city are adorned with stones that Ezekiel symbolically tells us also adorned the Garden of Eden (see Ezekiel 28:13-14). In these first five verses it is again evident that two strands of prophecy come together. The bride comes to a new heaven and a new earth; the city comes down from heaven to a new earth made ready for her. Eden and Jerusalem, both the original garden and the original city, pointed beyond themselves to the new heaven and the new earth.

In a real way the paradise of Eden is now re-established, and yet what is now received is even greater than Eden ever was, for **the Lamb** is also in the Garden. Adam and Eve had talked to God, but they had not known the saving grace of God, they had not met the **Lamb**. Now God's people know him even better than Adam and Eve did, for they know him not only as Lord and King but also as Saviour and as the one who gave himself to die for his people on the cross.

ii) Pictures of life

Drawing on Ezekiel again (47:1-12), John describes a **river**. In Ezekiel it flows from the temple, but here there is no temple, because God himself is right here in the city. So the river flows directly from the **throne of God and of the Lamb**. It also reminds us of the river in the Garden of Eden (Genesis 2:8-10). The picture is one of **life**. The water is pure and clear because it comes from God, and it flows right through the centre of God's people (**down the middle of the great street**). In line with Ezekiel's prophecy, this river and its water produces an abundance of crops. It is likely that the waters that produce life and crops indicate the presence and work of the Holy Spirit (see Jesus' words in John 7:37-39). The whole of nature thus enjoys the restoration of Eden's perfection. This is the fulfilment of what the apostle Paul had said in Romans 8:21-22: 'the creation itself will be liberated from its bondage to decay and brought into the glorious freedom of the children of God. We know that the whole creation has been groaning as in the pains of childbirth right up to the present time.'

The **tree of life** is there now for people to see and to enjoy. Its **twelve crops** each year indicate its perfection in bringing life permanently to the people of God, who are no longer cut off from it. In Genesis 3:22-24 we see that eating of the tree of life results in living 'for ever'. Even the **leaves** of the tree bring **healing** to everyone. Of course, we know there is no more pain or death in the new heavens and the new earth, but this healing reminds us of the saving work of Christ on the cross that brought healing and forgiveness for sin.[126] That work of Christ is always present in the city of Jerusalem, and Christ's people are reminded constantly that Christ healed them from their sins.

iii) They will see his face

The new intimacy of God's presence with his people is vividly described: **they will see his face**. In contrast with those who have now been judged, who had the mark of the beast on them, everyone who is part of the new Jerusalem has **his name on**

their foreheads. We remember 3:12 where this was the promise Jesus gave to those who remained faithful in the church in Philadelphia. It is the promise John also holds out for us as well. The day will come when those of all ages for whom the Lamb died will have the name of God written on their foreheads, much as the high priest did in the Old Testament.[127] It is a sign of belonging and dependency, but also of close relationship.

Since the curse has now gone and God is present with his people, we are told again that God himself provides all the **light** that is needed in the new heavens and the new earth. Thus, sustained by God's gift of eternal life and his great light, his people **reign** with him **for ever and ever**.[128] They are united with Christ the King.

The Summary and Final Words of the Vision

The angel said to me, 'These words are trustworthy and true. The Lord, the God of the spirits of the prophets, sent his angel to show his servants the things that must soon take place' (22:6).

Verse 6 summarises this great vision of the new heavens and the new earth and the new Jerusalem. But in fact it goes further than this, for it also summarises the whole book of Revelation. It takes us right back to 1:1. There the book was introduced with the same words: 'The revelation of Jesus Christ, which God gave him **to show his servants** what **must soon take place**. He made it known by sending **his angel...**'

We have heard it all. In his visions John has seen and heard about what must soon take place. He has seen how the church suffers and will suffer. He has seen how it appears that Satan is the conqueror when in fact reality is altogether different. He has seen that God is sovereign even over what Satan organises and tries to effect against the people of God. He has seen the context in which Christians suffer and die, but he has also seen the glory that awaits them, both in the intermediate time after death before the general resurrection and after the general resurrection. He has had a foretaste of the glory of the new heavens and the new earth and has seen again God's people in intimate relationship with their Lord as the bride of Christ and as the heavenly city where God is in the midst. And all of this, says the angel, is **trustworthy and true**.

Little now remains to be said except for a few words of summary which we have put under different headings. The vision has been delivered. The present has been explained and the promises of the future have been seen. Salvation and judgment have been laid out clearly, but now Jesus speaks.

1. Jesus is coming soon

'Behold, I am coming soon! Blessed is he who keeps the words of the prophecy in this book' (22:7).

Jesus commends the words of this book not just to John, nor just to the seven churches, but to all who will listen and to anyone who **keeps the words of the prophecy**. This book had been called a **prophecy** back in 1:3. The word is used in the sense of being a proclamation from God not just about the future but also about the present. This is God speaking to his people throughout the ages and exhorting them to listen and to obey and above all, to 'overcome'. Those who do this, as the seven churches were urged to do, will be **blessed**. They will receive all God's covenant promises and inherit all that has been talked about through the book and especially in the last couple of chapters.

The exclamation **Behold, I am coming soon!** is a call to action. The whole contents of the book 'must soon take place', and so Christ himself must come **soon**. There is no time or place for complacency as Christians. The days are short, and the judge and Lord may return at any moment. This sense of urgency is one that recurs through the whole book but especially now in these last few verses (see verses 12 and 20). Though the imagery has often been so hard to understand, and though

Christians down the centuries have often ignored this book because they have thought it 'complicated' or 'difficult', the message is in fact clear and urgent. Christ comes soon and will return to judge and to save. Action is therefore required today if we are to be ready for that return and if he is to find us keeping the true and trustworthy words of this prophecy.

This final 'second coming' of the Lord Jesus is clearly the focus of this exclamation. But as we saw back in 2:16 and 3:3 (see the comments there), this book can also talk of Jesus' 'coming' in terms of his 'coming' to bring judgment or to help his people persevere, throughout the age of the church. As we read those seven letters and specifically these verses, we need to remember that Christ comes to his church today and we should be found serving him and keeping his word. So this exclamation is not only a call to action, it is also a great point of comfort and encouragement. For those who are suffering and even dying for the faith, Jesus' words are yet another reminder that he 'comes' now to be with them by his Spirit, and that their trials will not go on forever, for he 'will' return, **soon**.

> I, John, am the one who heard and saw these things. And when I had heard and seen them, I fell down to worship at the feet of the angel who had been showing them to me. But he said to me, 'Do not do it! I am a fellow servant with you and with your brothers the prophets and of all who keep the words of this book. Worship God!' (22:8-9)

Once again John is awestruck as he hears the words, perhaps even mistaking the angel for Christ or perhaps simply being astounded at the angel's reflection of God's glory. He has still not learned his lesson as he falls down **to worship the angel**. This is just what John had done back in 19:10. As we saw there, he is chastised and told to **worship God!** As in 19:10, there are some very important warnings here for us as well. Certainly, it is always easy to be tempted into worshipping the messenger or some greater being rather than God himself.

2. Two groups of people, two fates

> Then he told me, 'Do not seal up the words of the prophecy of this book, because the time is near. Let him who does wrong continue to do wrong; let him who is vile continue to be vile; let him who does right continue to do right; and let him who is holy continue to be holy' (22:10-11).

The book that John has been asked to write is to be read by any who will read it. It speaks of the present and the future, and it speaks of two groups of people and their relationship with the Lord God.

The first group contains those who **do wrong**. They are encouraged to **continue to do wrong**. This is very strange indeed. Surely the angel should be encouraging such people to 'do right' and turn from their **vile** behaviour. We return to this in a moment.

The second group is made up of those who do **right**. They are **holy** and are urged to **continue to do right** and **to be holy**. This latter group are obviously those who are Christians. The time is near and so they must read the book and act on it in continued righteous works and holiness of life.

As we continue to read, we shall see that these groups are further defined. In verse 14 the second group are clearly the ones who have 'washed their robes'. They are compared with those who are 'outside' (verse 15) and who have turned their faces against God. In verse 17, the second group is identified as the people who have 'heard' and 'come' to Jesus. There are others who take away words from this book or add to them (verses 18-19). They have not 'heard' 'what the Spirit says to the churches' (2:7, 11, etc.). This helps us understand the exhortation to that first group to 'continue to do wrong'. These people are being exhorted by the angel to show themselves for who they are. If they have heard what the Spirit says to the churches they have done right and should continue in it. If they stand under judgment for rejecting the word, then they should continue in that way, for it is their way and their judgment will be just.

3. Two groups, two rewards

> Behold, I am coming soon! My reward is with me, and I will give to everyone according to what he has done. I am the Alpha and the Omega, the First and the Last, the Beginning and the End (22:12-13).

Jesus now speaks. Again Jesus repeats that he will return and will bring his reward with him. Each will receive a just reward, based on which group they belong to, whether they have done what is right or what is wrong and vile. Of course, as we have seen before in the book, John is not talking of the righteous being justified by their works. The righteous are those who have been justified through faith in Jesus Christ who died for them. But for now they are assured that Jesus returns to bring justice and judgment which will reward the two groups in different ways.

Before he speaks of those rewards we are reminded of just who it is who is speaking. He did this in 21:6, when he used the title **Alpha and the Omega** and **Beginning and the End** to encourage believers that he would indeed give eternal life. The first title recalls the beginning of this book in 1:8, and also 1:17 where the title **the First and the Last** is used. The titles emphasise Jesus' eternal divinity and his sovereign power to produce what he promises. Each title serves to encourage and build up confidence in Christians.

4. The rewards

> Blessed are those who wash their robes, that they may have the right to the tree of life and may go through the gates into the city. Outside are the dogs, those who practise magic arts, the sexually immoral, the murderers, the idolaters and everyone who loves and practises falsehood (22:14-15).

The first reward is for those who are Christians. Recalling 7:14, which talks of those who 'have washed their robes and made them white in the blood of the Lamb', Jesus reminds Christians that their inheritance is dependent upon his shed blood. Their reward is access to **the tree of life** from which everyone was barred when Adam and Eve were expelled from the Garden of Eden. That tree, as we have seen in 22:1-3, is there in the city. It is the privilege of God's people, and their wonderful reward as people saved by grace, to be counted as citizens and to have direct access for ever to eternal life.

The second reward is for those who are not Christians. Their reward is to be left **outside** the city. If there is any doubt that such a move is unfair or unjust, the description of their lifestyle and behaviour reminds us that theirs was a life set against God. Here are the ones who have continued to do wrong and to be vile. They are the ones described in 21:8 who go to a 'second death' and to the 'fiery lake'. These are the ones who have been deceived by Satan's emissaries. Notice how these people **love falsehood**. It is not that they wish they were somewhere else or wish that they hadn't done what they have done. They actually have *loved* all the evil in which they have been involved.[129]

5. Come to Jesus for eternal life

> I, Jesus, have sent my angel to give you this testimony for the churches. I am the Root and the Offspring of David, and the bright Morning Star (22:16).

A more direct translation of the first part of this verse can help us see its meaning more clearly: 'I, Jesus, sent my angel to testify to you (plural) these things concerning the churches.' Jesus is thus recalling the purpose of the whole book. The testimony is for 'you' (the seven churches) concerning their position before God now and in the future. More than that, the angel has 'testified' in the sense that one might testify in a law court. What he has said has, as it were, been under oath. What he has said is true and it will be the basis on which judgment will take place. This becomes clear in verses 18-19, where any addition to this angel's declaration or any reduction of it will result in judgment.

Jesus further identifies himself, using a title previously seen in 5:5 (see comments there). That he is **the Root and the Offspring of David** reminds us of Jesus' pre-existence. In an extraordinary combination of titles we are reminded that David himself had his existence because of Jesus, and yet Jesus, the King, comes to us from the kingly line of David.

> The Spirit and the bride say, 'Come!' And let him who hears say, 'Come!' Whoever is thirsty, let him come; and whoever wishes, let him take the free gift of the water of life (22:17).

The Spirit, as we have seen in the seven letters and throughout this book, has spoken. He has challenged and has revealed much of what is to come. The Spirit has consistently pointed us to Christ and his coming. The true people of God are the ones who have 'heard' this message (2:7 etc). Therefore, the church, **the bride**, who has understood these things, longs for the wedding and repeats the Spirit's own cry of '**Come!**' But to whom is this cry addressed? Are the Spirit and the church calling for Christ to come as in verse 20 below? Or is this a call to Christians to persevere? Or is this the call of the gospel, that all should come to Christ for eternal life so they can join in the inheritance of the saints?

In view of the way that the seven churches were being urged to keep up their mission to the Gentiles even when persecuted, and in view of the second half of this verse, it seems likely that this cry of **Come!** refers to the proclamation of the gospel. This is the work of the Spirit and the church in this age. The church proclaims the truth of life in Christ and of the **free gift of the water of life**,[130] and the Spirit draws people to Christ. This is the gospel we have to proclaim. The words of Revelation have given us so much more understanding of the urgent need for this proclamation that it is surely right the book should come to its conclusion urging us to get on with the gospel task while there is still time. We too are to call out, 'Come!'

6. This is God's Word

I warn everyone who hears the words of the prophecy of this book: If anyone adds anything to them, God will add to him the plagues described in this book. And if anyone takes words away from this book of prophecy, God will take away from him his share in the tree of life and in the holy city, which are described in this book (22:18-19).

This is a final warning to all who read the **prophecy** (see on 1:3) of this book. It is a warning to those in the church who will receive this prophecy but not 'hear' it. Remember we have seen that this is a trustworthy legal document under which God will hold the churches accountable. There are some in every church who sit week by week hearing the word of God and yet not actually *listening* to it. They do not allow that word to have any effect either in their thinking or on their actions or on their approach to daily life. Such people, in their actions, are involved in both *adding* to and *taking away from* God's word. We do not need to write more or to delete passages from the book to achieve what is being talked about here. If we fail to take to heart the challenges, for example, to avoid idolatry and compromise, then we have subtracted from God's word. If we demand of people actions or works that are not required in Scripture (a problem faced by Paul in Galatians), then we are 'adding' to Scripture. We all know how easy it is to do this and so we must pray that God will keep us as he has promised. We also must pray against those false teachers in the church who would try to undermine the testimony of this book and other Scriptures, claiming that we cannot trust it as the Word of God, or that it may be partly God's Word but much of it isn't. This is the way of much teaching today.

Rather we must rejoice in our faith and that he has 'marked' us for his own, and we must set about treating this Word of God for what it is, *his* Word. Our view of the Word of Scripture is thus considered here, as elsewhere, to be a real indication of our holiness and our commitment to him. How dreadful it would be to know about the **tree of life** and **the holy city** and yet not to **share in** them. The **plagues** remind us again of what we have read in so much of this book. But they also remind us of what happened to the Egyptians who had heard and seen so much of the true God at work and yet continued to rebel against him, believing they knew best.

7. Come, Lord Jesus

> He who testifies to these things says, 'Yes, I am coming soon.' Amen. Come, Lord Jesus. The grace of the Lord Jesus be with God's people. Amen (22:20-21).

It is interesting that, as the book concludes, we return to the idea that Jesus himself is the one who **testifies to these things.** John has testified (1:2), the martyrs have testified (6:9; 17:6; 20:4); the church has testified (12:17), the angel has testified (22:16), the Spirit has testified (see the end of each of the seven letters), and so, above all, has Jesus. He is the 'Faithful and True witness' (see 1:5; 3:14; 19:11). His word is utterly to be trusted and he is the one who now promises his suffering and often persecuted people, **Yes, I am coming soon**. What a wonderful final word of comfort from the Lord of glory! Jesus comes to us through his Holy Spirit throughout our time on this earth, but he will come soon to usher in the new heaven and the new earth. How the church of all God's people through the ages has longed for that day. So it is that John responds on behalf of us all: **Amen. Come, Lord Jesus.**

The word **Amen** is not easily translated and so it has come over into English from the Hebrew. Here it signifies a commitment to the faithful word of God and indicates a trust in this promise that Christ makes to his people.

And so John concludes by invoking **the grace of the Lord Jesus** on all **God's people**. In Scripture we find that **grace** is needed if we are ever to come to faith in the first place but, more than that, we also find that remaining *in* the people of God is to be entirely of grace as well. The Christians in the seven churches and all Christians through the ages have been urged to 'overcome'. They will need to stand for the Lord Jesus and the truth of his testimony in the midst of all the trials and sufferings of this world. Again and again, this book has shown that they will have to depend on God if they are to do this. They will need to trust him completely. For it will be by his **grace** alone that any will survive the judgments that are coming and will come. How appropriate that the very last words of the book remind us, therefore, not of what we should do, not of how we should act, not of the works God looks for in us, but rather of the grace that undergirds everything we are and do as God's people. Let us affirm our commitment and submission to the **grace of the Lord Jesus** as we say with John, **Amen!**

Concluding Comments

For me this book is one of the most marvellous and inspiring of Scripture. It is hugely practical and faces up to the realities of trying to live for Christ in a fallen and sinful world. It speaks of the temptations and sin that could so easily draw the church of God away from her Master. It urges repentance and missionary zeal. Yet it faces up to the questions we ask, such as, 'How long will this suffering or persecution go on?' As I write, I have just finished reading a booklet outlining the horrific events going on in Indonesia as thousands of Christians are killed and many are forced to convert to Islam, undergoing the most horrible torture of forcible circumcision. When some of you read this commentary that persecution will likely be forgotten as further persecutions will have come to the fore. This book of Revelation faces up to these issues squarely. Yet it points us to a sovereign God who is working out his purposes. It reminds us that martyrdom for the faith is but one of the great 'witnesses' to the truth of all that Christ has done for us in his death and resurrection.

Here in Revelation we find once more the God who so loves his people that he has them measured and protected for all eternity. Here Jesus insists that we can have genuine assurance of faith in spite of what we see going on around us. Here is the sovereign Lord Jesus who will one day return to judge the living and the dead and to usher in the new heaven and the new earth in which there will be no more curse. Here we find that God will, at last, fully and completely be among his people in all his light and glory. What more could we want to hear as Christians step gingerly into the first couple of decades of the twenty-first century?

We do not know what is in store for us personally, but we look forward to his grace being seen in our lives. We look forward to more and more people coming to faith as we carry out the mandate to speak for Christ to our pagan world, and we look forward to his protection even if we should be persecuted and put to death for our faith. We commit ourselves to trust his Word in Scripture as we move forward confident in the promises of God. Finally, as the Creed says, 'We look for the resurrection of the dead and life everlasting.'

NOTES

1. The Greek word here gives us the word 'apocalypse' which means 'disclosure'. No doubt, it also refers to the genre of literature in which we receive this disclosure from God. See more on this in the Introduction.

2. See 2:7, 11, 17, 29; 3:6, 13, 22. See also 13:9.

3. 2 Corinthians 5:17-21.

4. See also 3:14. These three titles probably have their origin in Psalm 89:27 and 37. In that messianic Psalm which points forward to Christ's coming, the king that will come in David's line is called 'firstborn' and 'the faithful witness'. This makes the third assignation ('the ruler of the kings of the earth') quite obvious because Psalm 89 refers to this Davidic king who will be exalted above other kings (see verse 27).

5. 'from the dead' might better be translated 'from among the dead'. Jesus is thus the one who in his resurrection inaugurates the new creation (Beale, p.191). In Colossians 1:18 we see a similar idea: 'he [Jesus] is the beginning and the firstborn from among the dead, so that in everything he might have the supremacy.'

6. That the church fulfils Israel's role and carries it forward is clear in many places in the New Testament (e.g. 1 Peter 2:4-10), but note particularly in Revelation what is said in 2:9 and 3:9. As G. B. Caird says: 'This is the first of many instances in which John applies to the church Old Testament descriptions of Israel' (p. 17).

7. Throughout this book we discover that, in fact, Jesus' 'coming' happens throughout history as he brings blessing and judgment to his people. So, for example, in 2:5 and 16 Jesus says he will *come* to the churches of Ephesus and Pergamum. Any such 'coming' with blessing or judgment is a pointer towards the final second coming of Christ, but reminds us that Jesus is always present to bless or to judge and does not have to wait until that final day.

8. See Matthew 16:27; Mark 8:38, etc. Also John 1:14.

9. Mark 9:1-8; 2 Peter 1:17.

10. See also 15:3; 16:7, 14; 19:6, 15; 21:22.

11. We may remember Paul's terror on the road to Damascus (Acts 9:3-4). But note also Isaiah's reaction in Isaiah 6:5, or Ezekiel's in Ezekiel 1:28. However, it may be Daniel's description in 10:9-11 that again best explains what is happening. See also Daniel 8:17.

12. It is strange that the NIV translates one Greek word in two different ways. The 'patient endurance' of 1:9; 3:10; 13:10 and 14:12 is the 'perseverance' of 2:2, 3, 19.

13. The suggestion here is not, as some have suggested, that the people in the church no longer love each other as they should, or worship Jesus as they should. Rather, as we see above, it is that their loss of 'first love' for Jesus has led specifically to the lamp of witness not shining properly. Notice that the 'two witnesses' of 11:3-4 are also called 'lampstands'.

14. In 21:7 we read, 'He who **overcomes** will inherit all this, and I will be his God and he will be my son.'

15. For detail on this ancient city and on the background of the six other cities mentioned in Revelation 2–3, see Hemer, *Letters*.

16. Same Greek word as 'afflictions' in 2:9.

17. The word 'martyr' in English comes from the Greek word for 'witness'.

18. Hemer, p. 116.

19. See comments on 1:4.

20. It is possible that 'what remains' may refer to the 'few people' who have not 'soiled their clothes' (verse 4). In which case the priority is to look to these people as the ones who can, by their example, lead the church out of its crisis.

21. In Revelation 13:8; 17:8; 20:12, 15; 21:27.

22. Hemer, chapter 8.

23. See also Acts 14:27; Colossians 4:3.

24. Caird, p. 53.

25. For discussion of the Jewish attitude here and **the synagogue of Satan**, see comments on 2:9.

26. See a similar idea in Philippians 2:10-11.

27. Sweet, p. 102.

28. In John 17:15 Jesus prays, 'My prayer is not that you take them out of the world but that you protect them from the evil one.'

29. What follows is mostly described by Hemer, pp. 178-209.

30. See comments on 1:10.

31. Note that the reference to **six wings** draws on Isaiah's description of the same angelic creatures in Isaiah 6:2 where this prophet also has a vision of the Lord Almighty on his throne.

32. In verse 2 the NIV has altered the Greek order of this question. The Greek reads, 'Who is worthy to open the scroll and to break its seals?' The original has caused some problems because it implies that the book can be opened before the seals are broken. However, we are in the world here of imagery, so we should not press these points too far. On the other hand, as we read on, it appears that the seals were progressively broken and that as each is broken more is revealed. This might help explain John's order in verse 2, as the scroll (or book) would be opened (see 5:5), and then one seal after another is broken (see 6:1-12) as each reveals more of God's redemptive plan.

33. Hughes, p. 79.

34. 'as if it had been' can be a misleading translation. More accurately: 'a Lamb standing as slain'.

35. 2 Chronicles 16:9 points in the same direction of God's sovereignty, 'For the eyes of the LORD range throughout the earth to strengthen those whose hearts are fully committed to him.'

36. In Daniel 7:9-14 there is a courtroom scene with the Ancient of Days taking his seat upon the throne. Thousands stand before him in worship. The 'books' are opened. The beast is slain, and then 'one like a son of man', a messianic figure, approaches the throne and is given 'authority, glory and sovereign power; all peoples, nations and men of every language worshipped him.' What John sees is the fulfilment of this prophecy of Daniel with Christ at the centre.

37. So Mounce, p. 147.

38. The Greek may in fact be a present tense, 'they reign'.

39. Also see comments on 2:26 and 3:21.

40. See particularly 1 Corinthians 16:22; Revelation 22:17, 20.

41. In Matthew 10:34 Christ speaks of the suffering that will come upon real believers and says: 'Do not suppose that I have come to bring peace to the earth. I did not come to bring peace, but a sword.'

42. More accurately this should be 'pale green horse'.

43. See also Psalms 6:3; 13:1,2; 35:17; 74:10; 82:2; 94:3; 119:84; Daniel 8:13;12:6

44. See comments on 3:4, 5 and note verse 18. But also look ahead to 7:13-14.

45. For example Ezekiel 32:6-8 and Isaiah 13:10-13.

46. For a further and more detailed explanation of this, see Beale, pp. 388-89.

47. See also Daniel 7:2-3.

48. G. B. Caird, p. 94.

49. In the forthcoming chapters we read more of this ongoing release of judgment into this world. The description of the plagues listed with the trumpets and 'bowls' are taken from the plagues of Egypt. This helps us see why the sealing is modelled on the Passover sealing for the protection of God's people. (See also Ezekiel 9 which provides another picture as the faithful are sealed from judgment that comes upon the unfaithful.)

50. See also 22:3-4.

51. See also 3:9.

52. Note the use of multiples of twelve for this purpose in 21:12, 14, 16; 22:2.

53. In one sense we have already seen how many shall stand. It is 144,000. But this is a symbol for God's perfect number, those whose names are written in the Lamb's book of life. From our point of view, the question still needs to be answered, will this be many or

just a few? The answer is that God's complete people is a great multitude.

54. In these last verses of Romans 8 Paul shows how he relies personally upon the truth of what John sees in his vision, and calls upon all Christians to do the same. Note that he specifically says that not even **angels or demons** 'will be able to separate us from the love of God that is in Christ Jesus our Lord.' This is surely exactly what John is teaching us through his vision here!

55. See for example Genesis 48:15; 49:24; Psalm 23; Isaiah 40:11; Jeremiah 31:10, etc.

56. See also Isaiah 65:19.

57. In a number of places in the Old Testament we read of nations and even God's people being *silenced* under God's judgment (e.g. Jeremiah 51:55; Amos 8:3), but this not the same as we see in Revelation 8. Here the silence is *in heaven* and no mention is made of any silence upon earth.

58. See also Ezekiel 7:14.

59. See also 1 Corinthians 15:51-52: 'We will not all sleep, but we will all be changed – in a flash, in the twinkling of an eye, at the last trumpet. For the trumpet will sound, the dead will be raised imperishable, and we will be changed.'

60. See 14:8; 16:19; 17:5; 18:2, 10, 21.

61. See (in Authorised Version) Deuteronomy 29:17-18; Jeremiah 23:15; Amos 5:7 etc.

62. See Beale, pp. 478-79, for more detail.

63. The same word is translated here 'vultures' as is translated 'eagle' in Revelation 8. The RSV translates both as 'eagle'.

64. See comments above on the 'fallen star' and Luke 10:18. Also note how God kept his people safe in the wilderness from snakes and *scorpions* (Deuteronomy 8:15).

65. In Ephesians 6:12 Paul speaks of 'the powers of this dark world' and 'the spiritual forces of evil'. These are what John describes here.

66. See also Psalm 78:49 which talks of *destroying angels* having brought the damage to Egypt.

67. The **horns** of the altar were at the corners, see Exodus 27:2.

68. Also see Deuteronomy 32:16-17.

69. Caird, p. 113.

70. See 10:6: 'There will be no more delay!'

71. The same word is used in Greek for 'earth' (verse 2) and 'land' (verse 5).

72. See Romans 1:2 where Paul uses a similar for of the same verb and there the NIV translates it as 'the gospel he promised beforehand through his prophets in the Holy Scriptures'.

73. Ultimately the reason the whole people of God can be referred to as God's temple is because they are 'in Christ' or represented by Christ (Ephesians 2:19-22). For it is Christ who is the true temple (see John 2:19; Revelation 21:22). In 1 Peter 2:4-5 Christians are also like *living stones* (as Christ is 'the living stone'), and 'are being built into a spiritual house to be a holy priesthood'. This last passage especially demonstrates how Old Testament cultic imagery is fulfilled in Christ. He is both the temple and the high priest, but, in Christ, what is true of him is true of his people, and so here we see that they are both being built into a temple but are also the priests in that temple!

74. See above on the length of time and its meaning.

75. In view of verse 5 some think the 'witnesses' refer to a reappearance of Moses and Elijah right before the end. Others have suggested they refer to the Law and the Prophets, or to the Prophets and Apostles. Others have said that they refer specifically to the martyrs of the church.

76. It is a sign of the last days, commencing on the day of Pentecost, that God *will pour out* his *Spirit* on all his people … and they *will prophesy* (Joel 2:28).

77. Given the repeated mention of three and a half years, it is interesting to note that this was the time during which the drought under Elijah lasted. It was, of course, a time during which Elijah

was protected by God from what was going on around, and a time during which he made some of his most damning prophecies (1 Kings 17).

78. The same word is used here in Greek as in 10:7. See there for a comment on the word 'accomplished' as it relates to God's plan.

79. Caird, p. 137.

80. See comments on 6:10.

81. The figure of 7,000 is quite obscure. It may represent around one tenth of the population of the city of Jerusalem in John's day or be a symbolic figure for the number of God's choice. But the important point is that the number is limited.

82. See the discussion of the trumpets with the comments on 8:6.

83. See also Isaiah 9:6-7; 26:17-18; Micah 5:2-3.

84. See Daniel 8:8-10.

85. So Beale, p. 668. So Authorised Version.

86. The fact that the ark of the covenant remains central to this protection of the Israelites may be a further reason for thinking that John has this in mind as he describes his vision.

87. This link between the beast and the kings of earth is made explicit in 19:19 where the beast and kings unite before their final overthrow by God.

88. See also Deuteronomy 33:29; Psalm 35:10; 89:6, 8, etc.

89. See Psalm 69:28 for the exclusion of many from the 'book of life'. See also comments on 17:8.

90. See for example 2 Corinthians 11:13-15; 2 Thessalonians 2:9; 2 Peter 2:1

91. See Psalm 2:6-11. 'I have installed my King on Zion, my holy hill...'

92. See 5:9 for comments on 'the new song'.

93. Literally 'for they are virgins' (as Authorised Version).

94. Some have taken this literally as a reference to a group of celibate men. Yet nowhere in Scripture are sexual relations seen as evil in

themselves. Others have suggested that there is a picture here of holy warfare. Israelite soldiers used to have to keep ceremonial purity prior to war (Deuteronomy 23:9-11), and so perhaps the picture here speaks of those Christians who have fought the spiritual fight and overcome. However, later in Revelation 19:7 and 21:2 the whole church of all God's people is referred to as a 'bride' prepared for her husband. This bridal imagery again suggests the picture of virginity for all God's people who have not gone after other women (gods) but held themselves 'pure' and ready ('virgins') for their Lord and Saviour.

95. It is referred to again in 16:19; 17:5 and three times in chapter 18.

96. 'Babylon was a gold cup in the LORD's hand; she made the whole earth drunk. The nations drank her wine; therefore they have now gone mad. Babylon will suddenly fall and be broken' (Jeremiah 51:7-8).

97. See comments on 5:9 and 14:3 where the 'new song' is mentioned.

98. Elsewhere in this book 'smoke' is used as a description of judgment (e.g. 14:11; 18:9). The only other instance of 'smoke' is the incense that is offered in 8:4.

99. Beale, p. 810.

100. See comments on 13:2.

101. See Isaiah 11:15-16; Jeremiah 50:35-40.

102. See comments on 8:10-11 and 14:8-10.

103. See comments on 8:13.

104. See further on the saints fighting with Christ, in comments on 19:14.

105. See comments on 2:9.

106. Morris, p. 191.

107. For example, Psalms 111:1; 112:1.

108. See comments on 11:17.

109. The Greek uses a past tense: 'has reigned' or, better, 'has begun to reign'.

110. See the whole book, particularly 2:20.

111. Genesis 3:15, God said to the serpent, Satan, that one day the offspring of woman would 'crush' his 'head'.

112. This picture is drawn from Ezekiel 39:17-22.

113. See the discussion about him in the comments on 13:11-15.

114. Although chapter 20 most clearly shows the differences between these three positions, different interpretations of this chapter will affect the understanding of symbolism and teaching in the whole book.

115. For further explanation from a pre-millennialist view point of the purpose of Christ's 1000-year rule prior to the final judgment, see Johnson, p. 581.

116. For example, Matthew 6:32; 10:5; Romans 9:24, etc.

117. In 2 Thessalonians 2:5-12 we read a summary of just what we have seen here in Revelation 20. Satan, the *lawless one* is now 'held back', but will be 'revealed', at which time he will be overthrown and destroyed 'with the breath of [the Lord Jesus'] mouth'.

118. 2:7, 11, 17, 26; 3:5, 12, 21.

119. Gog and Magog look back to Ezekiel 38–39. There we read that Gog, of the land of Magog, is determined to fight against the Israelites. God speaks against Gog (38:18), 'When Gog attacks the land of Israel, my hot anger will be aroused, declares the Sovereign LORD.' Thus, for John, Gog and Magog become a picture of forces arranged against God's people. Gog in fact prefigured in history the final day when all like Gog amass to fight the people of God.

120. E.g. Deuteronomy 23:14.

121. This teaching is affirmed in a number of places in Scripture. For example, see John 5:28-29; 6:39-40; Acts 24:15.

122. Also Isaiah 66:22.

123. While we might say 'sons and daughters' rather than just 'son', it is specially interesting to remember that in biblical times and specially Old Testament times, only the son inherited the blessings

of his father. By insisting here that we shall all be God's 'sons', as the apostle Paul does on a number of occasions, God is saying to women as well as men, and to slaves as well as to free, that all inherit his covenant blessings because he regards all as his 'sons'. What a privilege to be regarded in this way by the Almighty God!

124. The angel measuring the temple in Ezekiel 47–48 probably lies behind this image.

125. Although the names of some stones vary in English between the translation of Exodus and Revelation, most scholars assume that the same stones are in fact intended.

126. For 'healing' of sin, see Hosea 14:4 and Malachi 4:2.

127. In Exodus 28:36-38 the high priest was told to wear a gold plate on his forehead and attached to his turban which was engraved with the words: 'Holy to the LORD.'

128. See comments on 5:10 and on 20:4-6.

129. 'Dogs' are generally nasty and hated creatures in Scripture. They run around in packs and eat carrion. When Israel's leaders are condemned for their spiritual blindness in Isaiah 56:10-11 the prophet says: 'Israel's watchmen are blind, … they are all mute dogs.... They are dogs with mighty appetites; they never have enough.' In other words, dogs always look out for their own appetites.

130. See 21:6.

A Select Bibliography

Beale, G. K., *The Book of Revelation* in *The New International Greek Testament Commentary* (Carlisle: Paternoster, 1999).

Caird, G. B., *The Revelation of St. John the Divine* (London: A. and C. Black, 1984, second edition).

Hemer, C. J., *The Letters to the Seven Churches of Asia in their Local Setting* (Sheffield: JSOT Press, 1986).

Hughes, P. E., *The Book of Revelation. A Commentary* (Leicester: IVP, 1990).

Johnson, A. F., *Revelation* in *The Expositor's Bible Commentary* (Grand Rapids: Zondervan, 1981).

Morris, L., *The Revelation of St. John* in *The Tyndale New Testament Commentaries* (Leicester: IVP, 1969).

Mounce, R. H., *The Book of Revelation* in *The New International Commentary* (Grand Rapids: Eerdmans, 1977).

Sweet, J., *Revelation* in *SCM Pelican Commentaries* (London: SCM Press, 1979).

Subject Index

Focus on the Bible Commentaries

Below are listed the commentaries currently available in the series.
When finished, the series will cover the entire Bible.

Deuteronomy	Alan Harman
Joshua	Ralph Davies
Judges	Ralph Davies
Judges/Ruth	Stephen Dray
1 Samuel	Ralph Davies
2 Samuel	Ralph Davies
Job	William Cotton
Proverbs	Eric Lane
Song of Solomon	Richard Brooks
Daniel	Robert Fyall
Hosea	Michael Eaton
Jonah–Zephaniah	John L Mackay
Haggai–Malachi	John L Mackay
Matthew	Charles Price
Mark	Geoffrey Grogan
Romans	Paul Barnett
1 Corinthians	Paul Barnett
2 Corinthians	Geoffrey Grogan
Thessalonians	Richard Mayhue
Pastoral Epistles	Douglas Milne
James	Derek Prime
1 Peter	Derek Cleave
2 Peter and Jude	Paul Gardner
Revelation	Paul Gardner

Mentor Commentaries

1 and 2 Chronicles – Richard Pratt
(hardback, 512 pages)

The author is professor of Old Testament at Reformed Theological Seminary, Orlando, USA. In this commentary he gives attention to the structure of Chronicles as well as the Chronicler's reasons for his different emphases from that of 1 and 2 Kings.

Psalms – Alan Harman
(hardback, 456 pages)

The author, now retired from his position as a professor of Old Testament, lives in Australia. His commentary includes a comprehensive introduction to the psalms as well as a commentary on each psalm.

Amos – Gary Smith

Gary Smith, a professor of Old Testament in Midwestern Baptist Seminary, Kansas City, USA, exegetes the text of Amos by considering issues of textual criticism, structure, historical and literary background, and the theological significance of the book.

Mentor Commentaries

Exodus – John L Mackay
(hardback, 624 pages)

Professor Mackay has produced a strong commentary on the Book
of Exodus. It is filled with excellent material for the pastor and
the serious-minded Bible student. I especially appreciate the work
on application that is normally so difficult to draw out of historical
literature. I recommend this work highly. It is a valuable tool for
the study of this most important period in Israel's history.

John D. Currid,
Professor of Old Testament,
Reformed Theological Seminary, USA

A *tour de force* of conservative evangelical exposition. Massively
researched, painstakingly explained, theologically nuanced,
reliably expounded, simply expressed and sensitively applied; this
volume will be of considerable value to all preachers and Bible
students. For accessible and scholarly comment Mackay's work
should quickly become the standard evangelical work on the Book
of Exodus.

Stephen Dray
Lecturer in Old Testament Studies and Christian Spirituality,
Moorlands College, Christchurch, England.

Christian Focus Publications publishes biblically-accurate books for adults and children. The books in the adult range are published in three imprints.

Christian Heritage contains classic writings from the past.

Christian Focus contains popular works including biographies, commentaries, doctrine, and Christian living.

Mentor focuses on books written at a level suitable for Bible College and seminary students, pastors, and others; the imprint includes commentaries, doctrinal studies, examination of current issues, and church history.

For a free catalogue of all our titles, please write to
Christian Focus Publications,
Geanies House, Fearn,
Ross-shire, IV20 1TW, Great Britain

For details of our titles visit us on our web site
http://www.christianfocus.com

Rev. Dr. Paul Gardner is a minister and Rural Dean in the Church of England. He and his wife Sharon, a teacher, now live in Hartford, Cheshire, and have three children, Jonathan, David and Hannah. Formerly Dr. Gardner was a lecturer in New Testament at Oak Hill Theological College in London. For Christian Focus, Dr. Gardner has also written a commentary on 2 Peter and Jude.